THE COMICS OF R. CRUMB

CRITICAL APPROACHES TO
COMICS ARTISTS

David Ball, Series Editor

THE COMICS OF
R. CRUMB

Underground in the Art Museum

Edited by Daniel Worden

University Press of Mississippi / Jackson

The University Press of Mississippi is the scholarly publishing agency of
the Mississippi Institutions of Higher Learning: Alcorn State University,
Delta State University, Jackson State University, Mississippi State University,
Mississippi University for Women, Mississippi Valley State University,
University of Mississippi, and University of Southern Mississippi.

www.upress.state.ms.us

Designed by Peter D. Halverson

The University Press of Mississippi is a member of
the Association of University Presses.

First printing 2021

∞

Library of Congress Control Number: 2021934625
Hardback ISBN 978-1-4968-3375-4
Trade paperback ISBN 978-1-4968-3376-1
Epub single ISBN 978-1-4968-3377-8
Epub institutional ISBN 978-1-4968-3378-5
PDF single ISBN 978-1-4968-3379-2
PDF institutional ISBN 978-1-4968-3380-8

British Library Cataloging-in-Publication Data available

CONTENTS

III. Cartoons of Scripture, Self, and Society

IV. The Fine Art of Comics

ACKNOWLEDGMENTS

Many thanks to the contributors to this volume, all of whom brought unique perspectives to one of the landmark artists in comics history. Special thanks, as well, to Robert Crumb, for his support of this book.

I owe thanks to the School of Individualized Study, the Department of English, and the College of Liberal Arts at the Rochester Institute of Technology for supporting my work on this book. I also wish to thank the David Zwirner Gallery for their assistance, and Lora Fountain for her astute help. David Ball, Katie Keene, and Vijay Shah were invaluably supportive editors at the Critical Approaches to Comics Artist series and the University Press of Mississippi. Frederick Luis Aldama, Frances Andreu, Bart Beaty, Alex Beringer, Caitlin Cass, Dave Chisholm, Hillary Chute, Stephen Cooper, Clayton Cowles, Jackie Davis, Shawn Dunwoody, Tom Galambos, Stephen Galbraith, Jared Gardner, Nicholas Gurewitch, Charles Hatfield, Susan Kirtley, Adam Kubert, Martha Kuhlman, Susan Liberator, Don Lombardo, Caitlin McGurk, Nancy Pedri, Andrew Perry, Ed Piskor, John Porcellino, Barbara Postema, Jenny Robb, Joe Sacco, Tate Shaw, R. Sikoryak, Nancy Silberkleit, Nick Sousanis, Marc Tomko, Brittany Tullis, Carol Tyler, Noah Van Sciver, Rebekah Walker, Franzie Weldgen, Qiana Whitted, Kriota Willberg, and Caitlin Yarsky have all helped me to think about Crumb and comics more generally, and I thank them for being a part of my comics studies world. Students in my art comics courses at RIT have provided invaluable thoughts and reflections on Crumb and his legacy for contemporary artists and fans, and my work on this book has been informed by their insights.

Finally, and most importantly, thanks to Catherine Zuromskis and Clementine.

THE COMICS OF R. CRUMB

INTRODUCTION

R. Crumb in Comics History

Robert Crumb makes comics about himself. How Crumb appears in his comics has varied over his long career. In his earliest comics, many written and drawn collaboratively with his brother Charles Crumb, Crumb's childhood desires and preoccupations are filtered through the cartoon styles of Carl Barks and Walt Kelly. In his celebrated underground comics of the 1960s, those funny animals and cartoony icons morph into characters like Fritz the Cat, a ne'er-do-well, sexually rapacious feline, and Mr. Natural, a sage looking for his next paycheck, both of whom prey upon the drug and hippie countercultures of the late 1960s for their own benefit. As he notes in *The R. Crumb Coffee Table Art Book*: "[M]y approach to comics has always been somewhat spontaneous. I'm usually only a few panels ahead—I don't like to plan it out too much. . . . I use the old-time comic stereotypes to reveal myself to myself. I'm both Mr. Natural and Flakey Foont. I'm also Mr. Snoid" (Crumb and Poplaski 1998, 247). Through the conventions of classic funny animal and humor comics, including the racism and sexism endemic to those forms' histories, Crumb explores an inner world on the comics page.[1] Indeed, Crumb's drawing of "the little guy that lives inside my brain" from 1986 depicts his unconscious desires as electricity (fig. 0.1). This image's central figure and electrical motif refer to the cover of *Zap Comix* #0, where a similar-looking figure "plugs in" to an electrical socket (fig. 0.2). The unconscious energy that Crumb channels into his "somewhat spontaneous" comics "plug you in," as a reader and a viewer, to the artist and, by extension, the history of comics and cartooning through which he channels his desires and thoughts.

Characters like Fritz the Cat and Mr. Natural express the levels of attachment and critical detachment from the counterculture that have defined Crumb's role as an artist closely identified with San Francisco's Haight-Ashbury in the 1960s, and as someone who has openly expressed his alienation

Fig. 0.2. R. Crumb, *Zap Comix* #0 cover, Copyright © Robert Crumb, 1967. All right reserved.

from the music and mysticism rampant during that period. In the 1970s and beyond, Crumb would increasingly draw himself as a centerpiece in his comics, and sometimes fantastical, sometimes mundane stories of daily life would structure his collaborative work with his wife, Aline Kominsky-Crumb, and *American Splendor* creator Harvey Pekar. Even when Crumb takes on someone else's story, as in his later works *Kafka* and *The Book of Genesis*, shades of Crumb's themes inevitably appear, as the sexual anxieties of Kafka or the patriarchal cruelty of the biblical world resonate with his more overtly autobiographical work.

Perhaps more than with any other comics artist, it is difficult, maybe even impossible, to separate Crumb's persona and biography from his work. While many modern and postmodern schools of art and literary criticism have built themselves around the idea of examining the artwork itself rather than the conditions of its production or the idiosyncrasies of its creator—from William K. Wimsatt and Monroe C. Beardsley's "Intentional Fallacy" and Roland Barthes's "Death of the Author" to Michael Fried's distinction between "Absorption and Theatricality"—the exclusion of context, production, or personality is difficult to do with an artist like Crumb, whose persona and personal history are so well documented in his works and in other media. Crumb's work evokes the artist not just as a craftsman or creator of meaning but as a person who renders in crosshatched detail anxieties, desires, pleasures, and politics.

For instance, Crumb's single-page comic "Definitely a Case of Derangement" introduces his early underground work. It appears on the inside front cover of *Zap Comix* #1, and as the first comic in *R. Crumb's Head Comix*, a book published in 1968 by the Viking Press collecting his now iconic work from venues like the *East Village Other*, *Yarrowstalks*, and *Zap*. With an opening sentence that sets the scene—"My wife cringes in the corner while I stalk the house, a raving lunatic!"—the comic depicts an enraged Crumb, exclaiming in the foreground, while a nude female (presumably Dana Morgan, Crumb's first wife) covers her face in the corner, next to toppled furniture. As the page continues, Crumb addresses the reader directly though the text, and his illustrated character looks directly out of each panel. He claims to be "one of the world's last great medieval thinkers," whose master plans have all been successful, including "this comic book ... but you've read too much already ... I have you right where I want you ... so, kitchee-koo, you bastards!" The comic's direct address positions the reader as both a confidante and a victim of the artist, and Crumb represents himself as a mad scientist, bent on both changing our society as a whole and entangling himself in intimate relations with his readers by inviting them into his house and tickling them.

Fig. 0.3. R. Crumb, "Definitely a Case of Derangement," Copyright © Robert Crumb, 1967. All rights reserved.

At turns aggressive and confessional, "Definitely a Case of Derangement" presents the artist through his artwork and binds the reader in an explicitly confrontational relation to the deranged, lunatic figure on the page, a figure who is also, by extension, the artist who is drawing the page.

Crumb's assertion of personality and desire draws the reader into a relation of uncomfortable proximity. This foregrounding of the expressivity possible within the comics medium is, indeed, one of the accomplishments of Crumb's work. Not produced as work for hire or under the supervision of a managing editor, like most comic books throughout the medium's modern history, Crumb's comics express the aggression, anxiety, and thematic concentrations that we associate with modern art. This expressive mode is balanced by Crumb's interest in the medium of cartooning. As he has claimed in numerous interviews, he views the print versions of his comics as the finished work, not the original pages that now command high prices on the art market. Engaging fine arts expressivity in a commercial and historically lowbrow medium, Crumb's work asks both to be viewed as artistic expression, and to be read and viewed as a pop culture artifact that is nonetheless a product of a singular artistic vision.

CRUMB AS ICON

Crumb has a unique position in comics studies and in culture more broadly. On the one hand, Crumb has been one of the artists routinely invoked and celebrated as breaking new ground in the comics medium. As Jared Gardner notes, Crumb and his fellow underground comics artists helped to shape the intensely personal and autobiographical focus that has come to define independent comics in a way that pushed against the status of comics in midcentury America: "Reclaiming comics as 'comix,' now distributed not on newsstands but in head shops and record stores free from the Comics Code Authority (although not, of course, from antipornography raids from local police), the underground comix movement sought to take the comic form as far as it could go in exploring and representing everything Congress and the doctor [Fredric Wertham] did not want them to see" (Gardner 2012, 120).[2] In this sense, Crumb's "focus on personal liberation through expressing in comix what was explicitly taboo" was a way of opening the medium up to mature and reflective stories, transforming American comics into a potentially artistic and literary medium (125).

On the other hand, his work has often been critiqued for its indulgence in sexual fantasy and stereotype. As Trina Robbins notes in her memoir *Last Girl Standing*, after 1967 and his first wave of success, "Crumb's very sweet retro comics took on a darker look, and he started drawing women being humiliated and raped, men having sex with little girls. The guys (and some of their girlfriends) continued to think Crumb was hilarious, but, suddenly, I didn't get it. Rape and humiliation—and later, torturing and murdering women—didn't seem funny to me" (Robbins 2017, 110–11). Crumb's use of African and African American caricatures is also problematic, as Charles

Johnson notes in a discussion of how many cartoonists of the 1960s were moving beyond stereotypical caricature: "Thus, I cannot believe that Robert Crumb's grotesque and pornographic character 'Angelfood McSpade' in the underground comics of the 1960s is avant-garde or provocative in any positive way" (Johnson 2002, 13).[3] To reconcile these two dominant approaches to the artist—Crumb as comics pioneer, and Crumb as comics controversy—his formative role in postwar comics culture should be complemented by, as Corey Creekmur argues, an understanding of "his significant historical function as a cartoonist who inherits, reworks, and maintains rather than invents certain American comics and visual traditions" (Creekmur 2015, 26).

This book is designed to provide new perspectives on Crumb and his comics, not to celebrate or defend the artist but to offer an archival and context-based assessment of Crumb's work. Understanding how his comics operate as aesthetic, political, rhetorical, and social objects does not mean that a critic must defend all of Crumb's work, nor that a critic needs to necessarily decide what should or shouldn't be read or put on display. Instead, the purpose of this volume is to bring the interdisciplinary tools of comics studies to bear on one of comics history's most controversial and notable artists. Crumb is unique, in part because of the narratives that swirl around him. As Laura Kipnis notes in her account of Terry Zwigoff's 1995 *Crumb* documentary, the film's framing of Crumb fits into a familiar set of tropes often used to characterize groundbreaking artists:

> Watch Crumb being hurtled up from the low-rent cultural precincts of underground comics into the lofty environs of Art, with Zwigoff crosscutting between Robert's tragically crazy brothers and his cartoons, coasting on the familiar Romantic trope linking artistic inspiration to neurotic and psychosexual origins. Of course, this hasn't exactly hurt Crumb's ascent from Comic-Con to the museum walls. (Kipnis 2012)

Indeed, the psychological approach to Crumb is one that the documentary encourages through its return to family melodrama and domestic settings, and it is also present in the earlier *Confessions of Robert Crumb* documentary, which begins with Robert Crumb and Aline Kominsky-Crumb playing mandolin and guitar in front of their California home. The camera zooms in for the opening dialogue, spoken directly to the viewer:

Robert: Hello, my name is Robert Crumb, and this is my wife Aline. We're underground cartoonists.

Aline: On the surface, our life appears to be really quaint and
  charming.
Robert: Yes, doesn't it. But underneath, it's a steaming cauldron of
  sexual perversion, drugs, and twisted neurosis. (Dickerson 2001)

This emphasis on the "quaint and charming" domestic appearance of the
Crumbs is reinforced in both Crumb documentaries by the artist's nostalgic
mode of dress—Crumb wears a suit and tie and often a hat, looking like one
of the workaday commercial artists with whom he mingled at American
Greetings—and his collection of old toys and records (the Zwigoff documentary opens with a montage of handmade objects and antique toys in
Crumb's studio, and in both films Crumb talks about and plays from his
collection of old records).

These tropes have constituted Crumb's iconic status in comics history and,
more generally, in art and cultural history. He is at once a tortured artist,
exploring his childhood and neurotic relationship to sex and society, and a
nostalgic artist, channeling his expression through the history of cartooning.
As Bart Beaty has argued, this framework has led to Crumb's incorporation
into the art museum, as well. As he notes, "in Crumb, art museums have
chosen to honour all of those aspects of comics that they traditional dis-
dained," thus finding especially in Crumb's comics about race and sex both a
postmodern engagement with the history of cartooning and a psychosexual
confession from the artist (Beaty 2012, 209).

Along with his presence in art and culture more broadly, Crumb has of
course been central to many narratives about the history of comics in the
United States. The underground comix moment that he is so closely identified with is routinely thought to have breathed new life into the comics
medium, after the implementation of the restrictive Comics Code in the
1950s. Underground comix, so the story goes, opened comics in the United
States to adult and mature themes, and they ushered in a mode of DIY publishing and distribution that severed the decades-old connection between
comic books and the newsstand. Charles Hatfield chronicles this moment
in alternative comics: "[I]n the formative *Zap* period, comix constituted a
genuinely romantic, highly individualistic movement that sought to liberate
the comic book as a vehicle for personal expression, while yet wallowing
in the medium's reputation for lurid, rough-hewn, populist entertainment"
(Hatfield 2005, 18). Indeed, one of the most iconic Crumb stories centers on
the artist as a romantic figure, distributing the first issue of *Zap* in public: "In
February 1968, Robert Crumb, a 24-year-old ex-greeting-card artist, and his
wife Dana ambled through a fair on San Francisco's Haight Street selling a

Fig. 0.4. R. Crumb, "Haight-Ashbury, Early '68," Copyright © Robert Crumb, 1992. All rights reserved.

comic book of Robert's creation from a baby carriage" (Levin 2015, 7). This moment is a recurring feature of the Crumb biography, often invoked as something like an origin story for the grassroots emergence of the autonomous comics artist, striking out on his own. Indeed, in Crumb's own sketch of this moment, he draws a halo around his head, presenting this scene as a nativity, his wife Dana as a pregnant Mary and the baby carriage full of *Zap* #1 as the Christ child (fig. 0.4).

No longer bound by the Comics Code and no longer produced in a factory-like setting, so the story goes, comics could be about anything after the underground moment, and Crumb in particular would become an emblem of how a cartoonist could become a cultural icon. His "Keep on Truckin'" comic, originally published in *Zap* #1, was and still is widely reproduced on T-shirts, stickers, and hats. Crumb's lawyer, Albert Morse, filed copyright infringement lawsuits against companies using Crumb's illustration in the 1970s, which resulted in the work being placed for a time in the public domain. In 2005, though, Crumb sued Amazon.com, which was using a large-footed illustration similar to the figures in "Keep on Truckin'" to signal a failed search. Amazon withdrew the image (Levin 2013).

Along with his iconic work from the late 1960s, published in places like *Yarrowstalks*, *Zap*, the *East Village Other*, and other underground and countercultural periodicals, Crumb's interest in traditional music is part of his public image, from his three records from the 1970s with the group R. Crumb and His Cheap Suit Serenaders to his recent collaborations with Eden and John's East River String Band. His personal life and work has been chronicled in two widely available documentaries, the BBC production *The Confessions of Robert Crumb* (1987) and Terry Zwigoff's award-winning film *Crumb* (1995). As the founder and editor of *Weirdo* magazine, Crumb also published a younger generation of cartoonists, including Phoebe Gloeckner and Joe Sacco among many others, thus contributing alongside Françoise Mouly and Art Spiegelman's *RAW* magazine to the increasing artistic and literary legitimacy of the comics medium in the 1980s. As Frederik Byrn Køhlert has argued, Crumb and other artists like Justin Green and Art Spiegelman contributed to a tradition of autobiographical comics that has proven to be artistically and culturally vibrant, as the comics medium provides for a representation of the "autobiographical self as a site of ideological struggle" and thus a kind of nexus for thinking about art and the self's contentious relationship with social norms (Køhlert 2019, 4). In recent years, Crumb's work has migrated into art galleries and museums and into modes of publication like exhibition catalogs and coffee table art books, which might seem like an unlikely phenomenon for an artist so avowedly committed to the comic book and sketchbook as formats. As Hillary Chute notes in a discussion of Crumb and artist Philip Guston, comics are uniquely figurative when placed alongside the abstract expressionism that dominated midcentury American painting: "[C]omics is an aesthetic practice in [the underground] period in which figurative drawing, however experimental the frame, is legible" (Chute 105). Crumb's presence in the art gallery and museum, then, is one example of how comics as a medium, and how narrative material more generally, has expanded the category of art after modernism.

From his comics work to his persona, Crumb has influenced independent and alternative comics art. His use of traditional art materials, his affection for the history of cartooning and illustration, and his self-styled identity as a man out of time have informed the comics art and artistic personas of figures like Alison Bechdel, Ed Piskor, Seth, Noah Van Sciver, Carol Tyler, and Chris Ware. In many ways, Crumb fashioned the tropes that have become associated with the modern art cartoonist.

LIFE AND WORKS

Robert Crumb was born on August 30, 1943, in Philadelphia. His childhood has been the frequent subject of his comics and is discussed extensively in interviews as well as in Zwigoff's *Crumb* documentary. With his siblings, Crumb began making comics at a very young age, and some of these early comics are collected in the first volume of *The Complete Crumb Comics*. After graduating from high school in 1961, Crumb got a job at the American Greetings Corporation in Cleveland, where he worked initially on color separations and later as a greeting card artist. Some of Crumb's early work appeared in Harvey Kurtzman's *Help!* magazine, which led Crumb to move briefly to New York City, where he found a job with the Topps Trading Card Company before returning to Cleveland and American Greetings. In 1965, Crumb and his wife Dana began experimenting with LSD, which in Crumb's own words "definitely altered my work drastically. . . . [T]hat's when I thought up all those characters that dominated my comics from that period: Mr. Natural, Shuman the Human, the Snoids, Flakey Foont. . . . It was a state of grace in a way" (Groth 2015, 24). Traveling with some friends, Crumb left Cleveland for San Francisco in 1967, where he would publish *Zap Comix*. Published in 1968, the first issue of *Zap* contained work only by Crumb, and another issue featuring only Crumb work would appear later in 1968 as *Zap #0*, after those comics, initially thought lost, were later recovered. Starting with *Zap #2*, Crumb's work appeared alongside the work of other artists in the underground comix scene. By the time the final issue of *Zap* was published in 2014, eight artists including Crumb had contributed to the series over its sixteen issues.

From 1968 onward, Crumb's work would appear consistently in underground comics publications, and even after the "collapse" of underground comics, Crumb would publish work in his own titles, such as *Best Buy Comics* in 1979 and *Hup*, which ran for four issues between 1987 and 1992. Along with these comic-book publications, Crumb's work would be collected in a number of book-length collections, and while long-form works are rare in his corpus—most Crumb comics are a few pages long—his *Book of Genesis Illustrated by R. Crumb* was published in 2009 by mainstream publisher W. W. Norton. Crumb collaborates in his work frequently, from his childhood fanzines and his participation in the exclusive *Zap* group of artists, to his coauthored and coillustrated comics with his wife since 1978 Aline Kominsky-Crumb and his daughter, born in 1981, Sophie Crumb. In 1991, the Crumb family left California and moved to a small village in southern France. In recent years, with the exception of *The Book of Genesis*, much of Crumb's artistic attention has been focused on sketches and portraits rather than comics, as in his *Art and Beauty Magazine*, the last issue of which appeared in 2016. Like his sketchbooks, which have been collected and published in art book editions by Taschen, *Art and Beauty Magazine* features illustrations, many of female figures, alongside handwritten notes and quotations.

While Crumb's style in the 1960s tended to feature bold lines and characters who looked like classic comic strip figures, his later work is more heavily crosshatched and naturalistic, emphasizing the hand of the artist. As in *Hup* #3, Crumb self-consciously invokes and describes his linework. The character Stan-the-Man Shnooter, a parody composite of Marvel Comics editors Stan Lee and Jim Shooter, apologizes to the reader that Crumb has taken so long to get this issue out: "As I'm speaking to you R. is back there slaving away on th' last page of this book. . . . He's gotta fill in every last millimeter with little lines—teensy little noodlings an' chicken scratches" (Crumb, "Stan-the-Man"). Stan then says that Crumb could draw in a simpler style, to produce more comics and more profits: "I keep tellin' 'im, R., look, this is an industry—this comic thing—we got people waiting—distributors, retail outlets—lighten up! Give 'em what they want—all this fussy little crosshatching—ten people in th' world really care; other artists . . . but what do they ever buy? Some art supplies an' a new pair a' sandals every ten years!" In the page's last panels, Crumb draws Stan in a more cartoonish, less naturalistic style, thus demonstrating both his virtuosic variability and his commitment to intricate detail. Stan acknowledges the change in linework: "Hey! So, a new simpler style, huh, R.? I like it, but it's a little late to start streamlining, bubby . . ." While Crumb often comments on the spontaneity of his comics and describes them as outpourings of his unconscious mind, he also emphasizes here the labor of making comics. As he comments in an interview with Fantagraphics publisher Gary Groth: "[D]rawing good comics is really a lot of work, really a lot of work. It's not only thinking up interesting characters;

it's storyline, plot, and all that. Then, you have to lay out the panels, do the balloons, letter, you have to develop some sort of facility for drawing the same characters over and over again, while making them enjoyable to look at and make sense. It's hard. Not many people can pull it off" (Groth 2015, 41). When Groth follows up by asking, "[W]here does most of the labor come in?" Crumb responds, "Inking. Most of the labor's inking, but it's also very enjoyable" (41). This emphasis on both the work and enjoyability of making comics signals a key element of Crumb's aesthetic, a populist assertion of craft as both labor and pleasure.

Crumb is, then, an artist who bridges the different understandings of the artist in the 1960s and 1980s, as Alison Gerber has distilled them: "In the 1960s and 1970s, artists imagined themselves as primarily producers of objects: they argued that their labor was worthy of renumeration because they had *made things*. But beginning in the 1980s artists began to think of themselves in a new way, and today they are much more likely to say that their labor is worthy of remuneration because they have *done things*" (Gerber 2017, 12). This vocational shift maps onto Crumb. His interest in making and publishing comics coincides with his focus on his own lived experience. The painstaking experience of doing the work of making comics meshes with the reflexive content of many of his comics, which comment on the artist's life. Making comics as objects and experiencing the life of a comics artist dovetail in Crumb's art.

The coextension of life and work in the comics of Robert Crumb means, as I asserted earlier, that Crumb's comics are ultimately about the artist himself. They are expressive, maybe to an unprecedented degree for comics in the 1960s. Yet, that expression is also necessarily limited by the positionality of an artist who views himself as a perpetual outsider. Indeed, Crumb's comics are balanced by, on the one hand, a repeated emphasis on the artist's marginal status in mainstream America and, on the other, an assertion of fame and fantasy as a way of getting comeuppance against those who would deny the artist privilege and sexual favors. In *Hup* #3, for example, a comic titled "Point the Finger" begins with Crumb addressing the reader. He explains: "In this issue of *Hup* we're going to point that merciless finger at one of the more visible of the big-time predators who feed on this society. . . . He didn't ask to make an appearance in *Hup* but we've brought him here anyway as a special surprise to you, our readers. . . . So, let's get him out here! Ladies and Gentlemen, one of the most evil men alive, real estate tycoon Donald Trump!" Trump is brought in by two "tough ladies," and the men proceed to yell at each other. The comic has two endings. In the first ending, Trump charms the two females and invites them to a fancy banquet, leaving a humiliated Crumb to be arrested by the police. In the second ending, Crumb wins. Trump is humiliated, and in the comic's final panel, Crumb mounts the face of one of his female assistants, a typical sexual pose for his comics. In both endings, a male figure asserts dominance over both another male and the two female figures in the narrative. The difference between the Trump ending and the Crumb ending is, then, negligible in terms of patriarchal imagination, even as Crumb projects himself as a countercultural, outsider hero who does not conform to traditional standards of masculinity. As Edward Shannon has remarked about Crumb's autobiographical comics, "Crumb positions himself as a lone (and often impotent) defender of the oppressed—a victim of the fascists he just as often wishes to emulate" (Shannon 2012, 646). The two endings track as an articulation of what Anastasia Salter and Bridget Blodgett have theorized as "geek masculinity," wherein "the relationships between men and women within geek media are defined according to deeply gendered beliefs despite existing as a response to traditional masculinity" (Salter and Blodgett 2017, 37). In this framework, Crumb's comic relies on regressive gender norms to envision a livable fantasy life for nontraditional masculinity, a masculinity that indeed looks more traditional than the comic wishes it were.

This curious impasse—comics that imagine themselves as countercultural, when in fact they trade in traditional gender and racial hierarchies—marks the intellectual and political difficulty of Crumb's comics for our time. Yet I believe there is some value to art that exposes its own limitations so consistently and clearly. Crumb's comics are stuck within their own historical set of references, their own resistance to the conservatism of 1950s America, their own commitment to unleashing the unconscious onto the page through virtuosic displays of comics craft. This artistic commitment is valuable, perhaps because it makes clear its limitations just as much as it presents a worldview that is distinctly of a time.

CRITICAL APPROACHES TO THE COMICS OF R. CRUMB

This book is divided into four sections, each of which focus on central elements of Crumb's comics and their circulation. In keeping with the sheer amount of Crumb's work over the years, some essays deal with singular texts, such as *The Book of Genesis*, while others approach Crumb through thematic lenses that bring together work from different periods and periodicals. A selected bibliography of collected editions of Crumb's works follows the book's four main sections, for readers who wish to track down readily available texts that collect Crumb's work from across the years.

Section I, "Aesthetics of the Underground," presents Crumb in the context with which he is most often associated, the underground comix movement of the 1960s and 1970s and the interest in satire, taboo, and social critique emblematic of that era. Beginning with some recent debates about Crumb's legacy at contemporary comics festivals, Jason Polley develops a reading of the boundaries between satire and hostility in Crumb's comics. Opening with a different anecdote of an art festival controversy involving Crumb, Paul Sheehan explicates the blend of anarchism, nihilism, and utopianism that structures Crumb's comics about society. Finally, in this section, I approach Crumb through the lens of *Zap Comix* and detail how that iconic underground series imagined an audience in ways that are linked to but drastically different from the audiences imagined by contemporary comics artists.

Section II, "Political Imaginaries," focuses on how Crumb's works have engaged with a range of political issues. José Alaniz explores Crumb's most overtly political theme, environmentalism, by analyzing his work about pollution and consumerism. Turning to one of Crumb's earliest published works, "Bulgaria: A Sketchbook Report," Stiliana Milkova and Liliana Milkova investigate Crumb's foray into Cold War rhetoric during one of his early assignments for *Help!* magazine. In a comics contribution to this volume, Julian Lawrence blends memoir with theory to explore how Crumb's comics work as signifying acts that push beyond the boundaries of taste.

Section III, "Cartoons of Scripture, Self, and Society," addresses how Crumb has approached representation and adaptation. Zanne Domoney-Lyttle offers a nuanced reading of Crumb's *Book of Genesis* and its roots in scriptural interpretation, finding in Crumb's adaptation a feminist viewpoint steeped in theology. Focusing on a persistent theme in Crumb's comics, Ian Blechschmidt analyzes the different modes of masculinity that circulate within many iconic works from the 1960s. Turning to Crumb's collaboration with David Zane Mairowitz about Franz Kafka, Lynn Marie Kutch finds in Crumb's representations of the writer shades of Crumb himself and the vision of the artist we have come to associate with both figures.

Section IV, "The Fine Art of Comics," dwells on Crumb's role in the art world. David Huxley offers an account of how Crumb has negotiated the discourse of fine art, and alternately, how art discourse has incorporated his work. Kim A. Munson surveys the ways that Crumb's work has been exhibited in art galleries and museums, pinpointing tactics and frameworks that have made his work available to art discourses and influential on contemporary artists working across media. Focusing on a particularly vibrant adaptation of Crumb into fine art, Clarence Burton Sheffield Jr. charts how the artist Öyvind Fahlström found inspiration for his installation *Meatball Curtain (for R. Crumb)* through his exposure to Crumb's underground comics. In the final essay in this volume, Paul Fisher Davies explicates Crumb's relationship to one of the most important concepts in modern art, abstraction.

Through this multidisciplinary set of essays, I hope that this book will provide new approaches to the comics of R. Crumb. Much of the discourse around Crumb today is either celebratory or defensive, spinning out of various controversies around his work. I think it is the role of comics studies to figure out why Crumb is such a divisive figure, and to come up with ways of thinking about his work as a part of comics history. Neither to celebrate nor denigrate, but to understand in context is what we have tried to accomplish. I hope this book will help to open up new ways of thinking about the history of the comics medium and its continuous controversies.

NOTES

1. For a detailed account of Crumb as an autobiographical, confessional artist that links him to the confessional poets John Berryman and Sylvia Plath, see Shannon 2012.

2. For a history of the underground comix movement, see Rosenkranz 2002.

3. This quotation came to my attention because of its citation in both Corey Creekmur (2015) and Leonard Rifas (2004), both thorough accounts of racist caricature in Crumb's work and underground comics more generally.

WORKS CITED

Beaty, Bart. 2012. *Comics versus Art*. Toronto: University of Toronto Press.

Chute, Hillary. 2016. *Disaster Drawn: Visual Witness, Comics, and Documentary Form*. Cambridge, MA: Harvard University Press.

Creekmur, Corey. 2015. "Multiculturalism Meets the Counterculture: Representing Racial Difference in Robert Crumb's Underground Comix." In *Representing Multiculturalism in Comics and Graphic Novels*, edited by Carolene Ayaka and Ian Hague, 19–33. New York: Routledge.

Crumb, Robert, and Peter Poplaski. 1998. *The R. Crumb Coffee Table Art Book*. New York: Back Bay.

Dickerson, Mary, dir. 2001. *The Confessions of Robert Crumb*. Home Vision Entertainment, DVD. First released, BBC, *Arena*, 1987.

Gardner, Jared. 2012. *Projections: Comics and the History of Twenty-First-Century Storytelling*. Stanford, CA: Stanford University Press.

Gerber, Alison. 2017. *The Work of Art: Value in Creative Careers*. Stanford, CA: Stanford University Press.

Groth, Gary. 2015. "A Marathon Interview with Legendary Underground Cartoonist Robert Crumb." *Zap: The Interviews*. Comics Journal Library, vol. 9, edited by Michael Dean, 11–45. Seattle: Fantagraphics.

Hatfield, Charles. 2005. *Alternative Comics: An Emerging Literature*. Jackson: University Press of Mississippi.

Johnson, Charles. 2002. Foreword to *Black Images in the Comics: A Visual History*, by Fredrik Strömberg, 5–19. Seattle: Fantagraphics.

Kipnis, Laura. 2012. "Papa Paparazzo: A Gilt-Edged Tribute to the Godfather of Celebrity Photography." *Bookforum*, June–August. https://www.bookforum.com/print/1902/a-gilt-edged-tribute-to-the-godfather-of-celebrity-photography-9469, accessed May 31, 2019.

Køhlert, Frederik Byrn. 2019. *Serial Selves: Identity and Representation in Autobiographical Comics*. New Brunswick, NJ: Rutgers University Press.

Levin, Bob. 2013. "Albert and Robert Excerpt." *Comics Journal*, no. 302 (February 13). http://www.tcj.com/the-comics-journal-302-albert-and-robert-excerpt/, accessed May 30, 2019.

Levin, Bob. 2015. "Draw, Write, Talk." *Zap: The Interviews*. Comics Journal Library, vol. 9, edited by Michael Dean, 7–9. Seattle: Fantagraphics.

Rifas, Leonard. 2004. "Racial Imagery, Racism, Individualism, and Underground Comix." *ImageTexT* 1, no. 1 (Spring). http://imagetext.english.ufl.edu/archives/v1_1/rifas/.

Robbins, Trina. 2017. *Last Girl Standing*. Seattle: Fantagraphics.

Rosenkranz, Patrick. 2002. *Rebel Visions: The Underground Comics Revolution, 1963–1975*. Seattle: Fantagraphics.

Salter, Anastasia, and Bridget Blodgett. 2017. *Toxic Geek Masculinity in Media: Sexism, Trolling, and Identity Policing*. New York: Palgrave Macmillan.

Shannon, Edward. 2012. "Shameful, Impure Art: Robert Crumb's Autobiographical Comics and the Confessional Poets." *Biography* 35, no. 4 (Fall): 627–49.

Zwigoff, Terry, dir. 2010. *Crumb*. Criterion Collection, Blu-ray. First released Sony Pictures, 1995.

Part I

AESTHETICS OF THE UNDERGROUND

Chapter 1

TOWARD A RECONCILIATION OF SATIRE AND HOSTILITY IN CRUMB

JASON S. POLLEY

In 2018, the Massachusetts Independent Comics Expo (MICE) announced that it would be "retiring the name of the Crumb Room," an honorary title of one of the expo's exhibition halls (Dan Mazur, ComixScholars Listserv 2018). Notwithstanding the "great value of Crumb's radical and inventive freedom of expression," Dan Mazur explained, Crumb is "seriously problematic because of the pain and harm caused by perpetuating images of racial stereotypes and sexual violence. The simple appellation, 'Crumb Room,' without context or opportunity for dialogue, can function more as an insult to those we want to feel welcome and respected, than as a fitting homage to an artist." Three minutes after this announcement was posted on the ComixScholars Listserv, comics artist and longtime Crumb critic Trina Robbins responded, "This is amazing! Times have truly at last changed, and I am grateful." The thread about the Crumb Room generated over fifty more posts in ten hours, debating MICE's decision and Crumb's larger role in comics culture today.

The vibrant ComixScholars thread made it apparent that closing the door on Crumb without complex qualifications proves impossible. MICE's decision to rename the Crumb Room created, in the digital space of the listserv, the "context" and "dialogue" that MICE entreated in its announcement. Soliciting the same exchange of ideas, the editor of this book, Daniel Worden, circulated the MICE Crumb news in hopes of petitioning volume contributors "to move beyond either celebrating or condemning Crumb, and instead [. . .] bring ne[w] ways of appreciating, understanding, and critiquing Crumb's work." In the MICE thread, Aidan Diamond dismissed concerns over "a form of erasure" (Charles Hatfield) perpetrated by "retiring the name of the Crumb

Room" (Mazur): "In no way does this suggest that Crumb's work will be erased from future expos, but rather that it will be contextualized, analyzed, and engaged with critically, as one would expect at a comics event." As the thread veered more overtly toward questions of history and censorship, Kate Polak wondered whether there was "a reason some [listserv contributors] are equating removing a wholehearted celebration with censorship? The next thing you'll tell me is that taking down statues of traitorous slavers is erasing history." Christopher Pizzino, who "work[s] at a flagship university in the U.S. south," provided a "thought about names, monuments, etc.," all of which offer "a vexed question because they serve two clashing purposes." He clarified how "one is to narrate history; the other is to commemorate greatness. The slippage between the two has become a flashpoint for public debate, obviously. Where some see, or claim to see, a privileging of a certain ideology, others see, or claim to see, useful educational history-telling."

In telling the history of, or providing the critical context for, Crumb—an appellation that metonymically evokes the man, his work, his public persona, and the academic and vernacular treatment and vilification of these—"flashpoint[s] for public [and/or critical] debate" continue to occupy center stage, as my cobbled-together gloss of the MICE listserv regarding the Crumb Room aims to introduce. I have elected to provide such an introduction to my chapter about the sometimes indistinct space between satire and hostility in Crumb as an example of the complex discourse that circulates around Crumb in comics studies and in comics culture more broadly. Crumb's so-called uncompromising art—which, again, includes his arguably affected public persona, the one we encounter in Terry Zwigoff's documentary *Crumb*—fosters serious caution and self-qualification. In the mode of the autobiographical and self-reflexive Crumb comics I discuss in what follows, the very sentence before this very one, complete with its several circumventions, illustrates the notorious difficulty of discussing Aline Kominsky-Crumb's "infamous husband, cartoonist Robert Crumb," a designation that acknowledges the shifting reputations of the two cartoonists today (Precup 2011, 546). Mihaela Precup notes that "R Crumb is notoriously difficult to discuss, especially because it is impossible not to agree that someone like Trina Robbins may have been somewhat right in her sacred rage; however, one cannot afford to admit it without being immediately steeped in ridicule for too simplistically slapping on the wrist one of underground comics' founding fathers" (546).

Allow me to again reflexively refer to the sentence immediately preceding the current one: even in my ostensibly candid admission to hedging when it comes to thoughtful "Crumb" criticism, I hedged. I deflected the issue about the difficulty of discussing Crumb by turning to a review by a woman of an analysis by a woman of a book that includes a consideration of Crumb's cartoonist wife and three other contemporary female comics artists. Yet, so I posit in this chapter, this deflecting and connecting is an important facet, if not *the* vital characteristic, of the "Crumb criticism problematic" that I trace in this chapter. My endeavor to provide supplementary context and dialogue to Crumb criticism, a field I presently address vis-à-vis intimacy, satire, reflexivity, and ire, begins with a look at some Crumb collaborations with Aline Kominsky-Crumb. Although these revealing, hyperreflexive collaborations from the 1970s were published before the couple's 1978 marriage, I use the name Kominsky-Crumb for the sake of clarity, as they have been republished in book editions under that name in recent years. Next, I look at Terry Zwigoff's 1995 documentary *Crumb*, which complicates the Crumb corpus because its intimacy invites viewers to examine their own senses of social accountability. In *Crumb*, reflexivity extends outward. Discomfited audience members are asked to question their own complicity in "the playground brutality" of America. Finally, I examine Crumb's rejected *New Yorker* cover from 2009 in order to approach audience responsibility, this time in terms of how the representation of a readership's own prejudices may limit authorial agency or freedom. My study of the intimacy of comics throughout this chapter illustrates how even the works of a comics artist like Crumb can be determined by the market-saturated expectations of their publishers and audiences. From his collaborative comics in the 1970s to the recent MICE controversy, Crumb at once connotes and invokes contradictory critical perspectives.

COLLABORATION

The metonym "Crumb" historically registers critical complication just as it currently triggers personal indignation. Hillary Chute's book chapter "Scratching the Surface: 'Ugly' Excess in Aline Kominsky-Crumb" addresses a key aspect of the "Crumb criticism problematic" with a close look at the "new textual modes" "that place pressure on notions of what a 'correct' feminist sexual politics should look like" (Chute 2010, 29). Kominsky-Crumb's "life stories," Chute asserts, "refuse to ignore the complex terrain of lived sexuality that includes both disgust and titillation" (29). By including "a range of sexual activity, from the traumatizing to the pleasurable, to the everyday" (29), by "mix[ing] degradation and pleasure" (51), "Kominsky-Crumb does the crucial and compelling work of both de-mystifying sex, and sexualizing the everyday" (54). Chute labels Kominsky-Crumb "the 'godmother' or at least the central pioneer of women's comics autobiography" (34). Seeing her as a "pioneering—if underrecognized—figure in the broad world of feminist visual culture" (30), Chute understands "Kominsky-Crumb's style [a]s a specifically feminist response to an idealized and culturally male methodology" (60). Kominsky-Crumb, in sum, "visualize[s] how sexuality, even when disruptive, does not have to be turned over to the gaze of the other" (30).

R. Crumb—one of "the men [who] were responsible for interesting her in comics in the first place, for helping her get published, and for encouraging her work" (Chute 2010, 37)—similarly speaks to his wife's uncompromising style and the historically male visual culture it disregards. Addressing her (and her work) directly, Crumb says, "You remain amazingly impervious to the pernicious influence of all cartoon stylistic tricks . . . which is mainly why so many devotees of the comic medium are put off by your stuff" (qtd. in Chute 2010, 32). In light of compromise and its categorical cousin, censorship, Chute lauds both Crumb and Kominsky-Crumb for their "share[d] commitment to the comics page as an uncensored autobiographical space" (38). The couple's unrestricted—and reflexive—comics art is, for instance, evident in their piece "Turnabout's Fair Play" (1974).

The one-page comic is bookmarked by two reflexive panels, the opening one distinguished by white openness and the closing one by dark confession. In each of these paratexts, or narratives about the primary narrative, the authors reveal something about themselves and their collaborative story, a short story evincing what Jacques Lacan might have seen as emblematic of the Mirror Stage, of how the Self is (first) defined in terms of the Other, or the Ideal externalized image of Self. But the couple complicates any formulaic interpretive archetype by ironically combining humor, insult, honesty, and inanity as they by turn caricature one another and the social norms that should delimit their gendered desires and behaviors. In the final frame, not unlike the opening one, each returns to drawing themselves, as the brief performance—or Victorian-modeled "little hour"—is replaced by sympathetic-seeming agreeability. Here, faces and hands literally reach beyond the black frame as though intimately offering viewers a final, candid look at the "Real" relationship beyond the injunctions of comics form.

"Turnabout's Fair Play" addresses gender performance while acting as a reflexive coda to the couple's coauthored and -drawn thirty-page-plus "Aline 'n' Bob's Funtime Funnies" (1974), a road fiction registering class and subculture around America in the early 1970s. This dark bildungsroman likewise has a foreword, "Let's Have a Little Talk" (1974). Mirroring the one-page coda, this single-page foreword begins with Aline admitting that she's "afraid my drawing looks too crude and ugly next to yours." The piece ends, however,

Fig. 1.1. Aline Kominsky-Crumb and R. Crumb, "Turnabout's Fair Play,"
Copyright © Robert Crumb and Aline Kominsky-Crumb, 1974. All rights reserved.

Fig. 1.2. Aline Kominsky-Crumb and R. Crumb, "Let's Have a Little Talk,"
Copyright © Robert Crumb and Aline Kominsky-Crumb, 1974. All rights reserved.

with Kominsky-Crumb asserting her agency by manipulating Crumb, by countering him, by directly inviting male readers to write to her, and by reflexively concluding the work on her terms, to wit, "Ha ha no more room." Like Crumb's own hand, hanging as defeated emblem of his stymied voice, Kominsky-Crumb's final five words lie beyond the frame, as though stepping outside the confines of mere representation. In the preceding panel, Kominsky-Crumb admits to being "proud of being gross" insofar as she herself "thought up the most depraved panel where [Crumb] pushes my head in the vomit," which is an unsettling sex scene frame near the midpoint of "Aline 'n' Bob's Funtime Funnies" (25).

No doubt taking into account the generally open, though often shocking and ironic, sexuality of Crumb and Kominsky-Crumb's combined and separate work, acclaimed comics artist Alison Bechdel views the couple as "very much an inspiration in terms of trying to be as honest as I can, especially about sexual stuff" (qtd. in Chute 2010, 30). This is not to say, however, that endorsements like Bechdel's about Crumb and Kominsky-Crumb's uncompromising and inspiring influence remain unproblematic. As Chute emphasizes: "[T]he community of feminist underground cartoonists" did not "embrace" or "widely publish" Kominsky-Crumb due to her "supposedly underdeveloped feminist politics—a move that [Kominsky-Crumb] interprets as punishment for failing to idealize women in her narratives" (37). The godmother of comics autobiography furthermore felt that the "gender proprieties generated by Robbins and her cohort were too stark, [. . .] and too invested in a sense of victimization" (37).

This impression of a putatively overdetermined investment in victimization returns us to the "Crumb Room" discussion that opens this chapter. On the ComixScholars Listserv, Brittany Tullis accentuated the palpability and immediacy of the #MeToo movement's visceral resentment. In *Graphic Women*, where the Kominsky-Crumb chapter appears, Chute speaks to the "intimacy of comics" on account of the "centrality of the cartoonist's hand": "What feels so intimate about comics is that *it looks like what it is*" (Chute 2010, 11). Comics, then, counteract the lost aura Walter Benjamin attributes to "mechanical reproduction" (Benjamin 1969, 1). An audience/viewer's remove from an original work results in a loss of that artifact's originary aura. (Consider, for instance, the distantiation between a handwritten penciled manuscript and a Perpetua-typefaced paperback, or that between Rodin's *The Thinker* and the bronze sculpture's photographic reproduction on a postcard.) Although comics are certainly mechanically and/or digitally reproduced and circulated, we could argue that aura or at least proximity to the artist is preserved by the very uniqueness of each cartoonist's hand, in terms of the "languages" of both images and words. Even in the prefatory handwritten paratexts of longer works, such as *Bob and Harv's Comics* (1996) and *The Book of Genesis Illustrated by R. Crumb* (2009), readers encounter Crumb's own block lettering. The author-reader encounter is therefore personalized not only because the author discusses his own drawings but also because the author does so in his own hand.

In a 2014 talk titled "What the %$#! Happened to Comics?," Art Spiegelman "suggest[ed] that the 'mongrel' hybridity of word and image, of legitimacy and vulgarity present in comics has found acceptance thanks to the contemporary pervasiveness of polyvocality, of 'using two different languages'" (qtd. in King 2015, 139). Spiegelman, "who has spent most of his creative life seditiously tweaking the arbitrary boundaries held to separate the worlds of highbrow and lowbrow art" (Callahan 2004, 10), linked the image to vulgarity, thus recalling the debates that until around thirty years ago—with the respective publications of Dave Gibbons and Alan Moore's 1986 Hugo Award–winning *Watchmen* and Spiegelman's 1992 Pulitzer Prize–winning *Maus*—kept comics typically absent from university syllabi, if not actually unconnected to campus life. But it is this "vulgarity"—whether we understand vulgar to mean unrefined, crude, indecent, common, or vernacular—that lends comics its very immediacy. The propinquity between author and reader that Spiegelman's formulation about "acceptance" concerns might return us to the continued ironic poignancy of the words Crumb uses to close his 1969 comic book *Despair*: "And remember: it's only lines drawn on paper, folks!" (qtd. in King 2015, 140). As a Crumb comic, *Despair* offers readers the immediacy of Crumb's own intimate hand. As one of Crumb's comix, meaning an underground comic not compromised or tempered by the Comics Code Authority, a reader who is acutely affected by *Despair*'s preceding panels might feel all the more discomfited by the last line's deceitful frivolity. Aura, here, functions definitively—and paradoxically. Potentially rendered even more embodied by the usage of "folks," at once a *Mad*-influenced parody of *Looney Tunes* and until more recently a marker of the "backslapping" and "neighborly" "narrow circle" of the "familiar, and even the familial" (Schillinger 2014), Crumb intimately tells readers not to be troubled by what continues to touch them. Complicated crossroad or not, the avuncular Crumb makes a haunting virtue of readerly investment.

COMPLICITY

Crumb's artistic and public persona might be read as delighting in these moments of honesty and connection. Read otherwise, however, Crumb's troubling honesty, seemingly enacted so effortlessly in Zwigoff's *Crumb*, may not be of the enfant terrible variety. Rather than intentionally eliciting shock, or the initial "revulsion" felt by Kominsky-Crumb readers, which Chute attributes to the nefarious normalization of the male gaze, we might in turn ask ourselves if it is (at least in part) honesty *tout court* that proves so discomfiting about Crumb. As more than one of my female students in Hong Kong has put it, "He's just too honest about himself." Reading this honesty as distinctly socially expressive, Steve Burgess appraises Crumb's "'commitment to brutal honesty,' both about his society and about himself," as "the most consistently admirable aspect of [Crumb's] work" (qtd. in Shannon 2012, 639). Edward Shannon equates Crumb's honesty to "a flood from a burst dam, detailing what is not right with his [own] mind in excruciating detail—and overtly political terms" (628). What Crumb is actively doing with his "underground comix," Shannon, Burgess, and my students would agree, is "violat[ing] taboos" (629). Whereas my students seem to attribute this honest violation as distressingly *and* uncalculatingly vulnerable, Shannon and Burgess read Crumb's openness as an "excoria[tion of] the kind of commodification of the self demanded by and celebrated in hit films and commercial autobiographies" (630).

In the documentary *Crumb*, Crumb (or "Crumb" to those who read his insouciance as judiciously staged) appears seriously disaffected by the product placement that defines corporatized America in the late twentieth century. Crumb sees an America of "Colonized Minds," consisting predominantly of "bought, sold, [and] market-researched everything." This critique of commercialization might retrospectively remind audiences of Crumb's paean to the work of Harvey Pekar. In his "A Mercifully Short Preface" to the collection *Bob and Harv's Comics*, Crumb applauds the fact that in lieu of "chase scenes," "punch lines," "rage," "murder 'n' mayhem," and conventional usages of a deus ex machina, "all you get from Pekar is . . . real life":

> There's no money in telling the truth. People want *Escape*. They want *Myths*. This slice-of-life stuff with no spices added, no glamour, no heroes, it's only going to reach a small, select audience, no matter how eloquent or "poetic" it's done. And just who are they, this small, select audience? We don't know. They can't be nailed down. They can't be market-researched or "targeted." . . . It's an odd scattering of individuals.

As close as possible to home, Crumb, or the "Crumb" of *Crumb*, appears genuinely horrified that his "market-researched or 'targeted'" daughter, Sophie, who's about ten, craves an emblazoned, puffy "49ers' jacket" (Zwigoff 1995).

Crumb/"Crumb" is also horrorstruck by the coarseness of his flock of new neighbors, whom Kominsky-Crumb brazenly refers to—in spite Crumb's self-conscious pleas for her to speak more quietly—as "rich rednecks with their dream homes at the top of every hill" (Zwigoff 1995). At least partly due to the "air-conditioned nightmare houses" colonizing the open hills around their longtime home, with an extensive record collection Crumb had "never imagined" moving, they are relocating to a chateau in a hamlet in the south of France. *Crumb* the documentary is, then, a critique through the artist's perspective of "the playground brutality" of America (Feaster 1995–1996, 46), a place where, so critic Robert Hughes reminds viewers, the dystopian masquerades as the puritanical (Zwigoff 1995). According to Felicia Feaster, "*Crumb* is an all-encompassing, overwhelmingly bitter rejection of the shiny lies and sordid promises of our culture via, in John Powers' words, Crumb's roles as a 'nerd Messiah'" (46). Most relevant to my overall concern with intimacy and its affects, no enmity or neurosis or quirk remains unmentioned in *Crumb*—a disquieting closeness that applies to Crumb himself, to his eccentric (but not carnivalized) brothers Maxon and Charles, to his aging mother, and to their combined and individual memories of the deceased, "overbearing tyrant" patriarch of their "project in Philadelphia" 1940s suburban home.

Feaster sees the unsettling intimacies of *Crumb* as an indelible manifestation of the artist and his work, an oeuvre I evaluate as interrogating readerly responsiveness and responsibility. We could describe Crumb's interrogations as unrepressive. The qualifier conjures the spirit of the Beat Manifesto reverberating in the work of confessional poets and authors in the 1950s. In his evocatively titled essay "Shameful, Impure Art: Robert Crumb's Autobiographical Comics and the Confessional Poets," Edward Shannon reminds us that "Crumb's confessions urge the reader to consider the artist as a survivor not just of his personal demons but of a culture crippled by its own materialism, racism, bigotry, and neuroses" (2012, 628). Crumb transformed the comics medium in order to build upon the partly Renaissance-inspired project of his "disaffected and anti-bourgeois" Beat forbears, who "participated in the protest against Impersonality as a poetic value by reinstating an insistently autobiographical first-person engaged in resistance to the pressure to conform" (628). The Beats worked to counter the orthodoxy and oppression of the 1950s. Crumb extends this personal, cultural critique to the medium of comics in the 1960s and 1970s. Harvey Pekar's characterization of Crumb's early autobiographical mission speaks not to calling out co-optation but to signaling social reversion. "From 1967 to 1974," Pekar clarified, "people talked about the California-based Crumb's work because it was considered an important element of the counterculture" (Pekar 1996). Pekar continued by stressing the contemporary disenfranchisement of marginal figures, the very figures that both he and Crumb often speak to *and* speak for: "Nonwhites, the chronically poor and uneducated, bohemians, and other nonconformists from the late 1970s to the present have gone back to the position they occupied during the Eisenhower administration" (Pekar 1996).

Returning more explicitly to the documentary context of Zwigoff's *Crumb*, Feaster notes that on account of his "[h]aving risen to prominence in the anti-authoritarian Berkeley of the 1960s and reevaluated by the often dictatorial phenomenon of political correctness, Robert Crumb becomes a theoretical barometer who tests our ideas of artistic responsibility and license" (45). The documentary *Crumb*, Feaster continues, "is steeped in a rich subtext that expands its mission from simple biography to include every one of us" (45). Director Zwigoff, in other words, "establishes a rare intimacy with his intelligent, introspective subjects" (47), one that "invites [our] collusion with [brothers] Charles' or Maxon's perspective[s]" (47). In being made complicit, *Crumb* viewers and critics, particularly those who still "believ[e] in documentary as unvarnished truth," are "exploited" (47).

Feaster closes her review by gesturing toward a central tenet of documentary studies: "[T]he brilliance of Zwigoff's film lies in its challenge to and contestation of our notions of what documentary is capable of revealing" (47). Recognizing the artifice (the cuts and edits) that realism requires, Zwigoff himself essentially dismisses the classical objectivity of direct cinema and cinema verité as "bullshit" (47). He knows the "weight" of his choices (47), choices that also interpellate his film's viewership. As Jane Chapman says in *Issues in Contemporary Documentary*: "The role of the documentarist as an active producer of discourse as well as a witness and participant emerges as distinctly different to the role of a neutral narrator or knowledgeable reporter" (2009, 97). In *Watching the World: Screen Documentary and Audiences*, Thomas Austin includes audience agency and obligation in the production of cinematic discourse: "[T]he power of documentary enlarge[s] viewers' capacity [not only] for 'generous imaginings' of others, but also for confronting, re-imagining, and grappling with a new, less complacent sense of self" (2007, 181). Here, then, we've come full circle. The discomfiting intimacy of Crumb (or "Crumb"), and by extension Zwigoff's *Crumb*, appears to result from immediacy or embodiment, which includes a reader/viewer's sense of personal accountability. The uncompromising Crumb, no matter how you read his (non)performativity, reflexively interpellates his readers into the texts they are reading.

RESPONSIBILITY

Notwithstanding all appearances to the contrary, Crumb recently claimed *not* to be categorically inflexible vis-à-vis the personal limits of artistic freedom, expression, and honesty. For *American Splendor* author Harvey Pekar (the unofficial "poet laureate of Cleveland," an everyman who got his start in 1972 when Crumb illustrated and published his basic stick figures), "Crumb came across [...] as likable and uncompromising, but so many people badmouthed him" (1996, n.p.). Apropos to the contemporary Crumb context, Pekar unemotionally addresses Crumb hate, an animosity or odium Pekar attributes to Crumb's "lack of sentimentality" (1996, n.p.). Disgruntled Crumb audiences, Pekar reminds us, are the historical norm, not just a signature of the present. In keeping with Crumb reception, Jared Gardner explains how "pioneering work" by Crumb "hijacked the comic book form," which until the early 1970s was "associated with juvenile entertainment," by making the medium "speak unspeakable (and often deeply disturbing) new fantasies" (2008, 6). Gardner later appraises "the drive in the earliest autobiographical comix" as "more about shock value than about exposing the self" (8). Echoing the (creepy) sense of embodiment in Crumb comix, as propounded by Chute and Patrick Jagoda in terms of an "*empathetic*" or intimate "interaction" between author and reader (Chute and Jagoda 2014, 3), and by Zwigoff and Feaster in terms of audience obligation, Gardner points out in "Autography's Biography, 1972–2007," that "[i]t is a truism of autobiography studies (and of narratology more generally) that the narrator and subject are not one and the same; but in no form is this more graphically clear than in graphic memoir" (2008, 10). Crumb's reflexive "collapse of the distance between autobiography and autobiographical subject," to borrow Gardner's apt phrasing, makes Crumb and Kominsky-Crumb's unsentimental approach to comics and their readers all the more discomfiting (12).

We could argue that what makes Crumb so moving is the paradoxical conjunction of the refined and the crude in his work—and in his persona. Perhaps it's this very complex reconciliation—one embroiled in serious tensions revolving around questions of sexism, racism, realism, representation, refinement, and vulgarity from the 1960s to today—that makes the autobiographical work of the self-conscious Crumb so deeply affecting. Some of these tensions are best embodied in the tempered close of Françoise Mouly's May 2012 "Talk on *Blown Covers*." The subtitle of her book *Blown Covers* makes the playful title clear: "*New Yorker*" *Covers You Were Never Meant to See*. Mouly's talk includes the comments of respondents Daniel Clowes, Chris Ware, and R. Crumb, the latter of whom is the most vocal. Most important

Fig. 1.3. R. Crumb, rejected *New Yorker* cover, Copyright © Robert Crumb, 2009. All rights reserved.

to our purposes is Crumb's rejected 2009 *New Yorker* cover submission. In Mouly's words, *New Yorker* editor David Remnick vetoed her recommended Crumb cover after it "sat and sat and sat," because "he was uncomfortable with Robert's portrayal of gays and he felt that, oh, it's out of date with the times" (Mouly 2014, 193). Mouly continues: "It's true that a lot of the fight for gay marriage is one for normalization—today's gay advocates are not presenting themselves as freaks" (193). At that time in her seventeenth year as the *New Yorker*'s artistic director, Mouly's opinion rested on the concept of "an artist." She briefly explained this industry idea: "You can override a correction" by a copy editor or fact checker "by saying that's the intent of the artist" (193). In this instance specifically, and for better or worse, Mouly had argued that a Crumb submission is a Crumb submission. So *New Yorker* readers ought to be entitled to see it.

Mouly ultimately deferred to Remnick for the clear reason that he's "always backed up everything he has published" (193). She eventually "agreed that 'Well, it's an R. Crumb' was a weak argument" (193). Crumb candidly concedes that without any "explanations," such as "it was too lurid or whatever," the *New Yorker* rejection left him feeling "a little bit insulted" (193). Crumb then describes how he, based on personal experiences, understands the *New Yorker*'s audience. Letters that Mouly shared with him illustrate that both "schoolteachers in Iowa" and "lawyers who lived in midtown Manhattan" "were [incredibly] offended" by his 1994 Eustace Tilley cover (194). Crumb carefully (and haltingly) describes how this readership is "on the liberal side generally, but they just . . . so when you work for the *New Yorker* you kind of have that audience in mind to some degree" (194–95). Consequently, he resumes, "[y]ou have to kind of bend whatever lurid qualities your work might have to fit that sort of lite, L-I-T-E, it's lite" (195). Although at once an admirer of what's on "the covers. And in the magazine" (195), it's this "bending" that Crumb bemoans. He explains that his customary audience of "about twenty thousand" "will accept pretty much anything" (195). Yet the readership of the *New Yorker*, which lies somewhere between "a million-two or a million-three" (195), does not grant him that same permission.

As a result, Crumb comprehends the compromising nature of *New Yorker* work. Retaining his signature social criticism, sincerity, and shock, he describes the inherent compromise of appealing to a readership such as *The New Yorker*'s:

> That's like the Faustian deal, again, the allure of the bigger audience. You're going to reach 1 million people and you get paid well. Okay, I'll pull back a little bit. I know you can't push this lurid grotesqueness too much. It is not going to be acceptable to those schoolteachers in Iowa and those lawyers in the skyscrapers. So, all right, I'll compromise a little bit. Oh, they loved it. Okay. Great. I'll do another one. Oh, that one is not acceptable. Oh, gee, I went too far that time. Okay, I'll pull back again. Eventually you just might as well go get your dick cut off. (Mouly 2014, 197)

Crumb's peroration resonates as distinctly belonging to Crumb. With illustrative figures and examples, he plainly delivers consequentialist logic about how artistic compromise can ultimately foster the unintended consequence of silencing social critique, which he imagines here as castration. Crumb's personal analogy for arresting artistic agency, of course, proves crude. If we revisit his rejected *New Yorker* cover (fig. 1.3), we might reevaluate the piece not as Crumb painting an unflattering portrait of queer communities, but rather as a variation on his typical gender and sexual tropes. Crumb's heteronormativized "husband" is a feminized figure. He is less traditionally manly, most obviously, because he's besotted, as his suppressed smile shows. He is smitten by the "wife" he is about to marry. This "wife," who is not only large, muscled, tattooed, and symbolically controlling him by means of gently gripping his wrist, is likewise a person of color. This couple—a slight masculine figure, and a powerful feminine one—reproduces the way Crumb represents himself and his feminine objects of desire. The older, white male clerk examines the applicants in much the same way as a general viewer/voyeur. And perhaps it's their mutual attachment, that is, "his" coy submissiveness and "her" gentle control, that complexly surprises—or is it scares?—this establishment figure, one already economically disempowered or silenced by virtue of his job as a clerk. "Ordinary life," so Paul Giamatti as Harvey Pekar in the film *American Splendor* avers, "is pretty complex stuff" (Pulcini and Berman 2003).

In the early Kominsky-Crumb and Crumb collaborations specifically (figs. 1.1 and 1.2), and throughout Crumb's oeuvre generally, classical gender roles are parodied, and often reversed. If anything, Crumb fetishizes women as loud, pushy, and often physically overpowering—a move we might interpret at once as self-emasculating and as female affirming. Not unlike the masculine "wife" in the rejected *New Yorker* cover, the Aline we see in Crumb's work, whether it's Crumb or Kominsky-Crumb who produces her, is at once physically imposing, sexually attractive, and psychologically independent. Crumb, in other words, sees Kominsky-Crumb in the same way the "husband" in the rejected *New Yorker* cover sees his intended—as beguiling and beautiful, notwithstanding "her" deviations from historical modes of gender performance. Certainly, the exposure of racist, sexist, and homophobic marginalization risks being confused for or conflated with the simple expression of racism, sexism, and homophobia—this most especially in the satirical work of a privileged, white male. As Deirdre English comments in the Zwigoff film, Crumb appears to "get off" on stepping "over the line of satire" and "just producing pornography" (Zwigoff 1995). According to Trina Robbins, who also appears in *Crumb*, Crumb stopped doing "good work" and became "incredibly hostile to women" (Zwigoff 1995). Edward Shannon, however, reminds us that "what to Robbins is a simple rape fantasy" has been interpreted by comics critic Liz Wilson as "resistance to and subversion of

Fig. 1.4. Aline Kominsky-Crumb and R. Crumb, from "Aline 'n' Bob's Funtime Funnies,"

male control—result[ing] in ironic reversals" (Shannon 2012, 642). Crumb, whom Robert Hughes likens to Pieter Bruegel and whom art dealer Martin Muller likens to Honoré Daumier (Zwigoff 1995), makes a career of toeing the line between satire and hostility. Although Crumb professes not to "work in terms of conscious messages," his work often features his own engagement with society and politics. We understand as much via his insult at being rejected by the *New Yorker*. Consequently, Crumb and, by extension, his work, are not "completely uncompromising," which he in fact confesses in the Mouly talk following his declamation on the Faustian bargain of commercial illustration (Mouly 2014, 197). Crumb's art exists within and exploits tensions between self and society, between expression and expectation.

To close, I return to "Aline 'n' Bob's Funtime Funnies." As noted earlier, Crumb and Kominsky-Crumb often use metatextual devices to comment on the representational status of their comics within the comics themselves. In other words, the two comics artists often suspend the suspension of disbelief; they thus remind readers that they (the readers) are investing in a representational construction, and that they (the authors) are directing and monopolizing this investment in a representational construction. In the first panel, Crumb informs Kominsky-Crumb that her seriousness is uncalled for, as their collaborative piece, so its title portends, concerns laughs. Rather than check this form of control or authoritarianism, Crumb exaggerates it in the next frame, further infantilizing and oppressing Kominsky-Crumb and her "neurotic hang-ups" to the point that the panel's background turns black, and his hands constrict her voice and face. In the subsequent panel, Crumb transforms into a carnival barker, ironically intoning (as he slips on a banana peel) empty platitudes about "Show Biz," "Patter," "Punch Lines," and "Slapstick." In the final panel, Kominsky-Crumb morphs into an elastic, malleable figure, and Crumb violently slaps her, complete with accompanying stars of discombobulation. The ironic message of this comic is reflexive. For Crumb and Kominsky-Crumb, "funnies," or comics, are not always "fun." When Crumb insists on conforming to audience expectations, the inherent violence of patriarchal privilege and traditional slapstick takes over, thus silencing his collaborator. Crumb's work reflexively occupies a precarious or disputed contentious space, one between satire and hostility, between expressing and exposing, between art and anger. The closing of MICE's Crumb Room is, if anything, an invitation to the arbiters of culture to continue to interrogate why and how we accept what we accept and dismiss what we dismiss. Who legitimates the putatively legitimate? Who determines what no longer deserves critical enquiry? Crumb's collaborations with Kominsky-Crumb and others, alongside his struggles with commodification, publicity, and reader response, all speak to keeping open the doors of reception—so that we remain aware of the contradictions in comics art, at both their moments of production and reception.

WORKS CITED

Austin, Thomas. 2007. *Watching the World: Screen Documentary and Audiences.* Manchester: Manchester University Press.

Benjamin, Walter. 1969. "The Work of Art in the Age of Mechanical Reproduction." In *Illuminations,* edited by Hannah Arendt, translated by Harry Zohn, 1–26. New York: Schocken Books.

Callahan, Bob. 2004. "Introduction: No More Yielding But a Dream." In *The New Smithsonian Book of Comic-Book Stories from Crumb to Clowes*, edited by Bob Callahan, 1–17. San Francisco: New College Press.

Chapman, Jane. 2009. *Issues in Contemporary Documentary*. Cambridge: Polity Press.

Chute, Hillary. 2010. *Graphic Women: Life Narrative and Contemporary Comics*. New York: Columbia University Press.

Chute, Hillary, and Patrick Jagoda. 2014. "Special Issue: Comics and Media." *Critical Inquiry* 40, no. 3 (Spring): 1–10.

ComixScholars Listserv. 2018. "Re-naming the Crumb Room." Noah Berlatsky, Aidan Diamond, Charles Hatfield, Christopher Pizzino, Kate Polak, Dan Mazur, Trina Robbins, Brittany Tullis, and Meg Worley, March 26.

Crumb, R. 1996. "A Mercifully Short Preface." In *American Splendor Presents Bob and Harv's Comics*, by Harvey Pekar and R. Crumb, n.p. New York: Four Walls Eight Windows.

Crumb, R. 2009. *The Book of Genesis Illustrated by R. Crumb*. New York: W. W. Norton.

Crumb, R., and Aline Kominsky. 1997a. "Aline 'n' Bob's Funtime Funnies." In *The Complete Crumb Comics*. Vol. 10, *Crumb Advocates Violent Overthrow*, edited by Mark Thompson with Gary Groth, 12–44. Seattle: Fantagraphics.

Crumb, R., and Aline Kominsky. 1997b. "Let's Have a Little Talk." In *The Complete Crumb Comics*. Vol. 10, *Crumb Advocates Violent Overthrow*, edited by Mark Thompson with Gary Groth, 11. Seattle: Fantagraphics.

Crumb, R., and Aline Kominsky. 1997c. "Turnabout's Fair Play." In *The Complete Crumb Comics*. Vol. 10, *Crumb Advocates Violent Overthrow*, edited by Mark Thompson with Gary Groth, 45. Seattle: Fantagraphics.

Feaster, Felicia. 1995–1996. "Crumb." *Film Quarterly* 49, no. 2 (Winter): 45–47.

Gardner, Jared. 2008. "Autography's Biography, 1972–2007." *Biography* 31, no. 1 (Winter): 1–26.

King, Zachary. 2015. "Comics and Media." *Twentieth-Century Literature* 61, no. 1 (March): 138–45.

Mouly, Françoise. 2014. "Talk on *Blown Covers*." *Critical Inquiry* 40, no. 3 (Spring): 187–97.

Pahls, Marty. 1987. "Introduction: Right Up to the Edge." In *The Complete Crumb Comics*. Vol. 1, *The Early Years of Bitter Struggle*, edited by Gary Groth with Robert Fiore, vii–xii. Seattle: Fantagraphics.

Pekar, Harvey. 1996. "Crumb." In *American Splendor Presents Bob and Harv's Comics*, by Harvey Pekar and R. Crumb, n.p. New York: Four Walls Eight Windows.

Precup, Mihaela. 2011. Review of *Graphic Women: Life Narrative and Contemporary Comics*, by Hillary Chute. *Biography* 34, no. 3 (Summer): 545–48.

Pulcini, Robert, and Shari Springer Berman, dirs. 2003. *American Splendor*. HBO Films.

Schillinger, Liesl. 2014. "Hi, Folks." *Matter*, October 17. https://medium.com/matter/how-a -once-friendly-neighborly-word-folks-became-a-quiet-sort-of-insult-c54e05b6a069.

Shannon, Edward. 2012. "Shameful, Impure Art: Robert Crumb's Autobiographical Comics and the Confessional Poets." *Biography* 35, no. 4 (Fall): 627–49.

Zwigoff, Terry, dir. 1995. *Crumb*. Sony Pictures.

Chapter 2

CRUMB AGONISTES

The Passion of a Disenchanted Utopian Scatologist

PAUL SHEEHAN

In August 2011, Robert Crumb was scheduled to appear at the Graphic Festival, a weekend of comics, animation, and music held annually in Sydney, Australia. Three weeks before the festival opened, Crumb gave a characteristically frank and open interview in the *Sydney Morning Herald*, admitting that he was still a "butt man" and a "weird pervert" (Purcell 2011). Although hardly major revelations given Crumb's history ("I'm probably one of the few, maybe the *only* human on this planet with no secrets" [Holm 2005, 140]), his comments caught the attention of a right-wing tabloid newspaper, which used them to discredit both the artist (a "self-confessed sex pervert") and the festival organizers—even going so far as to solicit shocked responses from a sexual assault crisis group (Groth 2011). In the face of right-wing hostility and potential aggression, and mindful of the concerns of his wife and daughter, Crumb made the decision to cancel his appearance at the festival.

Almost twenty years earlier, Crumb's work was embraced by the right—not the soft, moral majority strand, though, but the far right, which advocated white supremacy and "race war." In 1994, two strips that Crumb had originally published in his comics anthology *Weirdo*, "When the Niggers Take Over America" and "When the Goddamn Jews Take Over America," were reprinted without the artist's permission in the neo-Nazi magazine *Race and Reality*—a publication based in Massachusetts but with an international circulation (Armstrong 1994). Relocated to this new context, Crumb's virulent, ironic attacks on middle-American prejudice were presented as literal-minded calls to arms, for the country to protect itself from its enemies within.

On the left, Crumb has been similarly polarizing. Although considered in some quarters to be a scourge of the establishment and supporter of essential freedoms, both individual and communal, to others his work merely increases the quantum of racist, sexist, and misogynist images and stories in the world. As far as the latter group is concerned, Crumb's extreme imagery reveals more about his own repressed bigotry than it does about America's racial or gender politics. The feminist writer and cartoonist Trina Robbins spoke for this group when she said, in 1988: "It's weird to me how willing people are to overlook the hideous darkness in Crumb's work. . . . [W]hat the hell is funny about rape and murder?" (1988, 93).

As I will show in this chapter, Crumb's politics are clear-cut in that he knows what he stands for and has been fairly consistent in this across more than a half century of interviews, despite appropriations and characterizations of his work by the political right and left. It is also the case, though, that many of the works that Crumb has produced in the same period are overburdened with political meanings—some of them contradictory, a few indefensible, but adumbrating a political temper that is at least strong and searching, even if its means of expression does not always favor coherence. What I will be doing in this chapter, then, is using the more reflective Crumb, the interviewee and public confessor, as a point of approach to his scatological, id-saturated work. In so doing, I will articulate the critical rationale that underpins Crumb's comics about American culture.

CRUMB'S AGON WITH AUTHORITY

To begin with, let us note that Crumb is not an ideologue, in that he does not espouse support for any *systematic* political creed or doctrine. His beliefs do, however, more or less align him with anarchism.[1] In 1970, when Crumb was still enjoying his initial wave of underground celebrity and notoriety, one of the most important books on the subject appeared: Robert Paul Wolff's *In Defense of Anarchism*. For a political philosopher such as Wolff, anarchism arises from the fundamental clash between *authority* and *autonomy*. Authority is bound up with the right to rule—to command, and to be obeyed—exercised by the state (Wolff defines the latter as a group of persons that has supreme authority either within a given territory or over a certain population). In contradistinction, the autonomous subject—or, to use Wolff's term, the "responsible man"—arrives at his own moral decisions through the advice of others, and through his own reflection. And so, writes Wolff, "we may say that he gives laws to himself, or is self-legislating. . . . [I]nsofar as he is autonomous, [he] is not subject to the will of another" (1998, 14). The anarchist does not see the state's commands as legitimate, which is to say, possessing a binding moral force. Because of this, anarchism stands as the "only political doctrine consistent with the doctrine of autonomy" (18).

Crumb's agon with authority—his struggle to escape being "subject to the will of another"—has by now assumed the status of myth, albeit one that has its roots in biography. It begins at home with his father, Charles Crumb Sr., a master sergeant in the US Marine Corps, whom Robert recalls as being a "very intimidating man. Deep booming voice. A hot temper. If he got angry he might strike you" (Arnold 2005). Crumb has further recounted how his father did not just "strike" him when he was six years old but also broke his collarbone (Zwigoff 1995). Crumb's artistic response is to lampoon patriarchal rule by coupling it with incest, sexual mania, or repressed rage, in comics such as "Whiteman," "Joe Blow," and "The Family That Lays Together Stays Together." In all these instances, the upright fifties father figure surrenders to "impure" physical urges, his authority propped up—or overtaken by—by the power of libido.

But Crumb's disdain for authoritarian practices does not stop with the family. It is also brought to bear on social, political, and cultural institutions and conventions, most notably the following: government intrusion in people's lives, and the state's attempts to shape or regulate aberrant behavior; censorship in all its various forms, as mandated by bodies both religious and secular; the corporatization of modern American life, exacerbated by the ubiquitous pressure of capital; the different varieties of "hero worship" promulgated by the media, whether directed at sports champions, musical idols, or Hollywood celebrities; and the culture of romance and seduction, especially insofar as it underpins the masculinist domination of women.[2]

With such a broad list of grievances, Crumb's anarchist sensibility might seem to shade over into misanthropy, in which it is not so much authoritarian impulses that are being derided as humankind itself. Crumb even admits, in a screed entitled "The Litany of Hate" (2005), that "humanity in general fills me with contempt and despair. . . . For me, to be human is, for the most part, to hate what I am" (Crumb and Poplaski 2005, 386–87). The key site for this unyielding distaste is Crumb's sexual politics, through which anger and hatred are directed equally at *both* sexes. Men are targeted for the sexual assertiveness and aggression that he, Crumb, does not possess and so cannot abide; and women are seen as equally culpable for allowing this "alpha male" forcefulness to thrive, thus perpetuating the cycle of exclusion that embittered Crumb as a young man.

Many writers have, of course, explored the psychodynamics of failure and frustration, from J. D. Salinger to J. M. Coetzee. Yet Crumb's response is severe in the extreme: his male characters brutalize women in ways that are at once sadistic and seemingly gratuitous. On the one hand, this shows both the violent underside of male assertiveness and the female willingness to affirm this assertiveness, even if it is now being used to demean and degrade. On the other hand, though, and more immediately, it is Crumb carrying out his own fevered examination of the pent-up rage that he still feels from the years of rejection, overlaid with a resentful awareness that fame has now made him worthy of female attention. However, as I will argue, misanthropy—or the politics of sexual privation and disappointment—does not fully elucidate Crumb's conflict with authority, nor the amplitude and integrity of his critical sensibility.

Insofar as anarchy can, according to Gerard Casey, "signify the absence or non-recognition of authority and order in any sphere whatsoever, for example, in morals or religion and not only in society at large" (2012, 61), then it may also do so in the sphere of art and culture. And so Crumb's anarchistic animosity is not just aimed at authority figures and institutions but at anything that limits his freedom as an artist. In the first instance, Crumb's anti-authoritarian stance pits him against much that comes under the umbrella of the "modern," insofar as it shapes subjectivity in the affluent, capitalist West. And second, as a visual artist working in a medium histori-cally regarded (at least in America) as lowbrow and populist, Crumb is wary of "intellectualist" posturing and impatient with pretension and cant. These two interrelated topics provide the basis for his brand of artistic anarchism.

MODERNITY ON TRIAL: CRUMB AND THE OLD TIMES

Given Crumb's antagonistic relationship with his father, the ur-authoritarian in his life, it would be natural to regard his artistic response as an oedipal reaction that gave him both a subject (middle-class hypocrisy) and a method (scatological mockery). The oedipal dynamic is generally seen as a catalyst for artistic modernism in the first half of the twentieth century. According to this ethos, at least in the Anglo-American cultural sphere, one's forefathers (i.e., the Victorians) must be censured for their earnest, rigid, moralistic ways and swept aside to facilitate the birth of the new (see Childs 2000, 18–19). In Robert Crumb's case, however, this logic does not hold. Reluctant to let go of the past (including the recent past), he openly embraces certain folk-oriented aspects of the American tradition, insofar as it can "keep cul-ture on an authentic human level, the homespun as opposed to the mass produced" (Crumb and Poplaski 2005, 180). In accordance with this belief, he evinces suspicion and distrust of the "new." While this does not define

Crumb categorically as an "antimodernist," it nevertheless complicates how we might understand what I am calling his agon with authority.

"The America that I missed died in about 1935": Crumb is referring here to the new audiovisual media ecology ushered in first by the radio in the mid-1930s and then by television in the 1950s, to the detriment of live musical performances made by and for the "common people" (Hyzagi 2015). Over the years, Crumb has issued similar jeremiads against everything from modern architecture (Crumb and Poplaski 2005, 49) to modern art supplies (Widmer 2010, 25–26). "Old things seemed to have more life, more substance, more humanity to them" (Crumb and Poplaski 2005, 23), he says, where "old" is equated with authenticity and legitimacy. The world that Crumb misses is a premodern, analogue, acoustic one, the polar opposite of what he calls "industrial commodity culture" (56). Living in a "medieval hamlet" in the south of France, as Crumb and his family have done since 1991, protects him from the day-to-day afflictions of this culture, even if (as a professional artist) he cannot afford to ignore it altogether. And yet, unlike other postwar American nostalgists such as Woody Allen or, more recently, Michael Chabon, Crumb has taken full advantage of certain modern mores, such as the permissiveness that allows his work to be produced and made publicly available—something that a performer such as Lenny Bruce, a touchstone for Crumb's uncompromising disposition, never enjoyed (Crumb and Poplaski 2005, 164).

Crumb's attitude to modernity thus seems clear-cut and oppositional (notwithstanding his gleeful embrace of its more relaxed censorship laws). However, his attitude to modern*ism*—itself a multifaceted response to modernity (see Friedman 2015, x)—is more complicated. He writes: "I like the social realists, surrealists, and expressionists of the 1920s and 1930s, but you lose me with postwar abstract expressionism" (Crumb and Poplaski 2005, 298). In accordance with this dictum, Crumb singles out for praise the postexpressionist, *Neue Sachlichkeit* artists of the 1920s: George Grosz, Otto Dix, and Christian Schad (Hyzagi 2015). Indeed, in "R. Crumb's Universe of Art," an illustrated list that divides the universe into "Cartoonists & Illustrators" and "Fine Art!," Grosz and Dix, along with those obdurate masters van Gogh, Picasso, and Dali, are the only modern fine artists present (Crumb and Poplaski 2005, 432).

That Crumb might see Grosz in particular as a kindred spirit is instructive. A modernist who also exemplified the virtues of German realism in the 1920s, Grosz anticipates the nuanced simplicity that is Crumb's stylistic signature. Insofar as there is eroticism in Grosz's pictures, for example, it serves a critical function. As Beth Lewis notes, he attacks the moral hypocrisy

Fig. 2.1. R. Crumb, "R. Crumb's Universe of Art," Copyright © Robert Crumb, 2005. All rights reserved.

of the bourgeoisie by depicting it "as a degraded class wallowing in copulation and coition" (1971, 166). Grosz's work thus indicates potential points of contact between Crumb and this brand of 1920s modernism: realist, yet still amenable to caricature; and satirical, without being moralistic. Perhaps most importantly, it is grounded in a politics of protest that is socially engaged (antinationalist, antimilitarist, and anticlerical), as opposed to the more rarefied "immanent politics" of autonomous form associated with high-modernist aesthetics—a credo that finally played itself out in the postwar abstract expressionism that Crumb abjures.

Crumb, in other words, may be drawn to the anarchist desire for "autonomy," in the lengths that he has gone to unshackle himself from the will of others. But he does not grant that same quality of separation and dissension to art itself. This makes sense in the context of, say, "Art for Art's Sake" but is more questionable when applied to modernist autonomy. The latter, after all, exerts its own kind of resistance against Crumb's bête noire, "industrial commodity culture." Why should he be so scornful of a critical agenda that has similar objectives to his own, and that extends it to the academy? The answer, I suggest, lies in Crumb's attitude to "intellectualist" formations and modes of expression.

The sustained influence of Crumb's work across generations of comic-book writers and artists of different stripes, from Harvey Pekar and Daniel Clowes to Chris Ware and Alison Bechdel, is part of post-1960s comic-book lore. But perhaps the most unlikely of these scions—who is also a quasi-contemporary—is Art Spiegelman. For although he and Crumb shared certain underground publishing venues in the early to mid-1970s—*Funny Aminals* [sic], *Gothic Blimp Works*, *Bijou Funnies*, *Bizarre Sex*, *Arcade*—Spiegelman's subsequent journey through the comics medium contrasts starkly with Crumb's. The divergent paths that their careers have followed are bound up, to a large extent, with the fate of American underground publishing.

As early as 1974, Mark Estren noted that legal and other problems had forced a number of underground cartoonists out of the comics medium altogether, and that the fluidity and volatility of the field meant that the most prominent names were changing all the time (1974, 264). Exacerbating this chronic instability was the nature of the comix distribution network itself: mainly "head shops" specializing in cannabis-related paraphernalia, deemed to be illegal in many places from the mid-1970s on. At the same time, the hippie ideals that underpinned the underground comix mindset had run aground, overtaken by history and by the dispersion of countercultural protest into various semipolitical subcultures (such as punk, which was explicitly "anti-hippie" in its orientation [see Sabin 1996, 126]). As "alternative comics" took shape in the deterritorialized spaces of the underground, those comix creators who had survived the latter were forced to adapt to the new, more businesslike economies of the medium.

Françoise Mouly, a French *émigré* involved in various publishing projects in New York City, took a pragmatic approach to the postunderground scene. She purchased a printing press, enrolled in courses on how to use it, and became a publisher (Kartalopoulos 2005). Working alongside Spiegelman, Mouly decided to put together a large-size magazine made up of work that was "very urban, personal, with an edge" from artists who had their own "individual stylistic voice[s]" (Spiegelman and Mouly 1987, 7). The result was *RAW* magazine, Spiegelman and Mouly's attempt to conjugate the taboo-breaking spirit of the undergrounds with the formal adventurism of the avant-garde—a move that meant looking not just to America but also to Europe. The anthology's aspiration was announced in the slogan, the first of many, that adorned the debut issue in July 1980: "The Graphix Magazine of Postponed Suicides." Keeping a safe distance from the nomenclature of the industry, the term "graphix magazine" encompassed a broader visual-arts base than just comics narratives. Moreover, the word "graphix" recapitulated the undergrounds' spelling of "comix," with its implicit detachment from mainstream convention and its promulgation of "X-rated" material. And to cap if off, there was a nod to the Romanian anti-natalist philosopher, E. M. Cioran, and his cryptic aphorism: "A book is a postponed suicide" (Cioran 2012, 99). *RAW* was, in sum, a singular attempt to force the comics medium to take the modernist turn, not least because it presupposed a new kind of comics readership, one that did not yet quite exist.[3]

Crumb contributed one strip, "Jelly Roll Morton's Voodoo Curse," to *RAW* in 1985. This anomaly aside, his way of negotiating the 1980s comics landscape was to stay on the "low" road and keep the underground flame alive, via his comics anthology *Weirdo* (1981–1993). In a recent interview, Crumb recalled comics in the mid-1950s as being "somewhat disreputable; they were the lowest of the low in those days" (Widmer 2010, 33). Unlike Spiegelman and Mouly, then, who were trying to advance the form through stylistic innovation, Crumb sought to return it to its "disreputable" origins, with material that was outrageous and deliberately squalid.

Calling itself "the Magazine for Modern Misfits," *Weirdo* featured fake ads and strip cartoons in addition to the usual six- or eight-page stories. Staying true to his "low" inclinations, Crumb also included *fumetti* or photo-comics in the first eight issues of the magazine. Without the charm of his "bigfoot" illustrations, however, the often inane stories or situations on which these photo-and-word-balloon strips were based gave the anthology a tawdry, disposable look. Spiegelman, who made a minor contribution to *Weirdo* toward the end of its run—a one-page collaboration with *RAW* stalwart Charles Burns—was, not surprisingly, dismissive of Crumb's new periodical.[4]

Visceral rather than cerebral, *Weirdo* was Crumb's way of reaffirming his own roots, even in the business-oriented 1980s. As he notes:

> I love the old, cheap comic-book format so much because the format itself is a statement. It keeps you from becoming too pretentious. . . . Keep it cheap and low-grade, keep it accessible, and then you're not required to be overly artistic or have a deep, profound meaning. All that stuff that can make you very self-conscious. (Widmer 2010, 54–55)

It is not philistinism that underlies this "anti-intellectual" statement; nor is it populism, with its implicit goal of expanding the demographic by talking down to one's audience. "Becoming too pretentious" is what Crumb is afraid of, and to him, that is the pitfall of experimental or avant-garde art. I suggest, too, that a claim such as this is not unconnected to Crumb's political outlook. Anarchist movements, writes David Goodway, "have been exceptionally hostile not only to the middle classes in general, but also bourgeois intellectuals." If hostility arises, it is because anarchism, unlike Marxism or reformist socialism, "does not fetishise theory or cleverness or intellectual ability. Its appeal has been as much, if not more, emotional than rational" (Goodway 2012, 197). In evading authority, then, Crumb is committed also to evading "theory" and the persnickety refinements of "bourgeois intellectuals."

Beyond the era-defining *Weirdo* and *RAW* divergency, Spiegelman's "intellectualist" bent has brought him into conflict with Crumb's stance. A minor, yet telling, instance of this concerns a one-page strip that Crumb published in 1969, "Drawing Cartoons Is Fun!" Although the parodic form and cheerful, exuberant tone of the strip might imply Crumbian irony, the views expressed—that self-declared artists and "decadent, ivory-tower critics" are racketeers; that the notion of "inborn talent" is fraudulent—represent Crumb's own. The sign-off line, too, is one of his most quoted: "And remember: It's only lines on paper, folks!!" At a comics forum in 2012, Spiegelman took issue with that last remark, calling it the "most pernicious thing I've ever heard" (Mitchell and Spiegelman 2014, 27). The visual language of cartooning can be used for innocent, whimsical ends, or it can be used to reinforce dangerous, pseudo-scientific beliefs. Because the distinction is not always clear-cut, it is a "dangerous thing" to shrug off the entire practice with an "only" (27).

Fig. 2.2. R. Crumb, "Drawing Cartoons Is Fun!," Copyright © Robert Crumb, 1969. All rights reserved.

Yet Spiegelman's rebuff does not quite go far enough. Is Crumb really only saying that no one can be harmed by cartooning—unlike, say, by physical violence and torture, or by persecution and discrimination? A further implication of "it's just lines on paper, folks" is that it is, therefore, a safe enough medium for Crumb to project his fantasies, tics, perversions, and even his prejudices. If Crumb is merely "discharging his unconscious"—something that he and others like to claim about his work—that does not make the resulting representations agenda-free, as if his unconscious were simply baseness itself, without any political attestation. To the contrary, more than a century of Freudian colloquy has made us aware that the unconscious is *precisely* where all manner of chauvinism and bigotry is first of all stored, then scrambled, split, recoded, and sent back through the body—manifesting as symptoms, nervous disorders, and other indicators of "somatization" (or, as Freud terms it in his study of hysteria, "somatic compliance" [2013, 33–34]). Crumb's violent, sexually and racially charged drawings almost certainly mean more than they (or their creator) can say.

This last point was, in a sense, proven when *Race and Reality* appropriated Crumb's two "When the Niggers / Goddamn Jews Take Over America" strips for its own malodorous purposes. Once again, it was Spiegelman who spoke up most vehemently about the incident. "For me, all he was doing was recapitulating the stereotypes without stretching the boundaries," said Spiegelman. "Crumb failed as a satirist in this case. If he did his job right, it wouldn't fit, it couldn't fit" (Armstrong 1994). This last, categorical remark begs an important question: is there such a thing as a maximum-degree satire, such that it can only be taken one way, namely nonliterally? Failing to "stretch . . . the boundaries" also suggests that Crumb did not go far enough, that he did not reach the optimum degree of satirical distortion. Yet his anti-Semitic satire concludes with a medieval crusader citing the Holy Book and advocating suicide through nuclear annihilation. It is hard to imagine how this might be pushed further, without switching from horror to hyperbole.

In their sociological study of comic-book "greatness," Bart Beaty and Benjamin Woo note the relative scholarly neglect of Crumb's work in literary studies, compared with the surfeit of attention given to Spiegelman and his major work, *Maus* (Beaty and Woo 2016, 7). They proffer two reasons for this lack of engagement: the difficulty of teaching a range of short strips and stories rather than a self-contained graphic novel; and the controversial nature of much of the material, in regard to its racial and sexual politics (30). In light of my argument above, I suggest a third reason: it is work that resists, even rejects, academic "respectability." Yet Crumb's reaction to the "intellectualist" milieu of experimental art, scholarly inquiry, and theoretical analysis—all of which are embodied by Spiegelman as a spokesperson for the comics medium—should not be taken as one-sided and obtuse. His actions, for one, often belie statements that he has made in interviews and through his art.[5] It is the insider authority wielded by proponents of an avant-garde mindset, finally, that raises Crumb's hackles and leads back to his "old times" defense of unpretentious American culture.

PLAYING WITH POISON: COUNTERCULTURAL EXPERIMENTS AND REMAINDERS

In this final section, let us return to the primal scene, so to speak, of Crumb's artistic birth—the 1960s countercultural movement that turned Robert Dennis Crumb of Milford, Delaware, into "R. Crumb," cultural anarchist, sexual deviant, and confessional cartoonist. Crumb's relationship to the counterculture is much less straightforward than the cover of *The Complete Crumb Comics*, vol. 4—the artist as the trippy, phantasmagorical "Mr. Sixties"—might suggest. For although Crumb produced some of the era's most striking and iconic images ("Stoned Again," "Keep on Truckin'," the cover art for Big Brother and the Holding Company's *Cheap Thrills*), he was never entirely comfortable with what the counterculture stood for, nor with the place inside it that he was, and still is, assumed to occupy.

The politics of the counterculture is at once vague and very goal oriented. During this period, anarchism was folded into pacifism and social activism, along with the championing of free speech and civil rights and the pursuit of alternative lifestyles based on anticapitalist, neo-bohemian principles. There was also a strong environmentalist ethic, taking practical shape as back-to-the-land experiments in communal self-sufficiency (see Miller 2002, 328–29). Crumb's attitude to the "old times" puts him in step with this desire to escape from urban-industrial ways of living. Moreover, his LSD experiences from 1965 onward—which, by his own admission, expanded his artistic horizons and "broke me out of my social programming" (Crumb and Poplaski 2005, 132)—make him an early advocate of psychoactive drug usage.[6]

In its more idealist forms, the counterculture dreamed of toppling the established order and changing the system as the prelude to building a new society. To that end, it sought to emphasize the "interconnection of the political, the cultural, and the social" (Bloom 2001, 8). Beyond this point, however, countercultural objectives become less clearly defined—reshaping human consciousness, for example, in order to achieve a quasi-shamanistic relationship to existence. This more rarefied aspiration was often the spur behind the archetypal social formation of the commune. "Dropping out," then, meant not just out of college but out of mainstream society and consumerist culture *tout court*, in order to get beyond or outside of the power bases of the political. Crumb has made negative overtures toward this kind of utopian, apolitical space. In a 1991 interview, he expressed his "horror" at fixed gender roles in the late 1960s, and his disappointment that hippie idealism had not produced genuine liberation. As he noted, "It certainly didn't bring down the citadel of capitalism or the corporate-state. Another one of the many waves that splashed against that in almost total futility" (Groth 1991, 88). A comment such as this suggests that Crumb had more invested in the values of the counterculture than he would like to admit, that he is another disenchanted sixties utopian who quickly learned to channel his despondency—and his critical energies—into aggressive, confrontational imagery and discomfiting scenarios.

Countercultural politics would also seem to have fostered Crumb's anti-authoritarian disposition. At least three of his targets outlined above—the state, the corporations, and censorship bodies—were also castigated by the communards and became trademark features of hippie rhetoric. By contrast, Crumb's other two bugbears, the glorification of celebrity and the culture of romance, can arguably be found, in altered form, in the counterculture itself. As regards celebrity, for example, Crumb has made pointed remarks about Bob Dylan—also a strong contender for the title of "Mr. Sixties" and also not really fitting the profile. Crumb grudgingly concedes that there might be some merit in Dylan's lyrics but scorns his reverential fans: "It used to irritate me in the mid-sixties when he was worshipped like a god. I thought that was really annoying. I thought his schtick with the whiney voice was really irritating" (Wood 2011). Crumb is referring here to the most celebrated yet also the most abbreviated period in Dylan's career circa 1965–1966, yet he does show awareness that this is not the sum total of his artistic legacy. "Someone told me he was an aficionado of old 20s, old time music, and that he listens to the same kind of stuff I like," says Crumb (Wood 2011). Indeed, there are strong commonalities between the two artists, as Ian Buruma has noted:

Like Bob Dylan . . . [Crumb] transformed the style of a bygone era into something rather different and personal. Both artists reworked popular, even proletarian arts. . . . [L]ike Dylan, [Crumb] used a popular idiom to express feelings and ideas normally reserved for more sophisticated forms, such as poetry or the novel. (Buruma 2006)

Yet despite these affiliations, Crumb cannot see beyond the reactionary stereotype of Dylan as the cowboy dandy who electrified folk music, thereby in Crumb's reckoning inflicting permanent damage on a perfectly good vernacular form. He also seems to be unaware of *The Basement Tapes*, the lo-fi set of recordings that Dylan and his band (later to become The Band) made when Crumb was beginning his run as "America's Best Loved Underground Cartoonist" (Crumb and Poplaski 2005, 142). Insofar as these recordings provide a sound-map or sonic topography for the "old, weird America,"[7] they inhabit the same imaginary space that we would now characterize as "Crumbland"—the quasi-utopian, pre-1935 agrarian America of folklore, filled with railroads, homespun artifacts, and backwoods settings and peopled with various colorful, marginal characters.

There is, however, a higher "authority" that attaches itself to a musical artist such as Dylan and that prevents Crumb from seriously engaging with his work: good taste. Liking Dylan was considered to be de rigueur for countercultural credibility, a sure sign that you were not only against the establishment but also had a taste for poetic-intellectual phraseology. Crumb's courting of taboo subjects was a way not only of keeping a safe distance from the mainstream media—a "big hungry beast" and a "cold, merciless mechanism" (Crumb and Poplaski 2005, 180)—but also of combating the self-satisfied hauteur that is the mark of "good taste."[8] And so Crumb's admiration for van Gogh and Picasso does not rest on their status as modern masters. It comes instead from the provocations that they initially caused and the scandals that ensued. But Crumb's assault on the "tyranny of good taste," I suggest, can better be understood via an early strip from the *Weirdo* years entitled "I Remember the Sixties" (1982).

Although the strip goes under the banner of "Nostalgia Dept.," Crumb is recalling events from only twelve or fifteen years earlier. Further, there is self-irony in Crumb's portrayal of himself as a pipe-smoking bourgeois, looking back on his wild years; and self-chastisement, as he voices ambivalence about every aspect of the counterculture. The drugs that "awakened" Crumb are the same drugs that caused a decade-long come-down. "I was a 'burn-out' case for years," he says. "All the LSD . . . All the dope . . . The craziness . . . My mind was shot. . . . I'm not so sure I ever totally recovered" (Crumb 2013, 66). Yet despite this grim self-reckoning, a strain of idealism tempers Crumb's reverie. At the height of the Summer of Love in 1967, Crumb "believed that we were creating a new world. People would love one another and be kind and we'd all have loose sex forever" (Crumb 2013, 64). By 1969, however, paranoia was rife, and hard drugs, guns, and commercialization had quelled all the inflated optimism. The strip ends with a dream of centaurs in an Edenic

paradise inhabited by innocent, gamboling "flower children," who regard Crumb as quaint and baffling. Is Crumb chiding them for entertaining such foolish hopes ("Stoopit horse-asses!" he says, as he exits the dream)? Or is he berating himself, for once thinking that he belonged with them? Either way, it is a piquant reminder that, try as he might, Crumb cannot quite abandon his own utopian imaginings.

Although Crumb immersed himself in the counterculture, there was (as "I Remember the Sixties" underscores) always a deep-seated conservatism underlying his cultural preferences. At the same time, however, it is a *radical* conservatism, in that Crumb openly admits to having tendencies and compulsions that no self-respecting hippie activist would countenance—yet nonetheless simmer just below the surface of the "peace and love" generation. One such admission was made explicit when *Race and Reality* appropriated Crumb's two satirical strips, and the artist provided a kind of rationale for his approach. As Crumb told the *San Francisco Examiner*, he wanted to purge himself of any lingering racist toxins: "I release all the stuff inside myself: taboo words, taboo ideas. It pours out of me as sick as possible" (Armstrong 1994). Such a strategy, which could be described as "using racism to combat racism," puts the onus on context and artistic intent to prevent misunderstanding or misappropriation. The philosophical name for this elimination-through-contamination process—although Crumb would never avow as much—is *pharmakon*.

Inspiring arguments that stretch from Plato (*Protagoras*, *Philebus*) to Jacques Derrida ("Plato's Pharmacy"), *pharmakon* turns on the double meaning of the word, which encompasses both "poison" and "remedy."[9] There are also real-world applications of the term, such as practices of homeopathy (based on the principle that *like cures like*) and vaccination (priming the immune system with an antigen). Just as it is necessary to *taste* the poison (drawing on racist stereotypes or, for that matter, violent and/or misogynistic images) in order to *defeat* the poison (the artist purging himself of his prejudices), disagreeable subject matter must be depicted in order to be confronted. The outcome, in other words, is that there are more offensive images in the world, even if their purpose is to ensure that there might (eventually) be fewer. This "playing with poison" does, then, raise the pressure on works of art to be politically responsible, to ensure that the object of attack is properly castigated.

Problematic though it might be, Crumb's stance is hardly unique. In fact, a version of it made world headlines in January 2015. Just over two years earlier, *Charlie Hebdo*, the French satirical magazine, had published a series of cartoons satirizing the Prophet Muhammad—the most outrageous of which depicted the Prophet naked, in a pose (and with matching dialogue) that parodied Brigitte Bardot in Jean-Luc Godard's *Le Mépris*. So it was that on January 7, two Al Qaeda–trained gunmen broke into the *Charlie Hebdo* offices in Paris, and shot and killed twelve people, including seven of the magazine's cartoonists. In the immediate aftermath of the shooting, Crumb was one of the many artists solicited for a response. *Libération*, a center-left French newspaper known for its funny and caustic cartoons, published the typically irreverent result: a depiction of "The Hairy Ass of Mohamid!" This was not a reference to the Prophet Muhammad, however, but to Crumb's "friend Mohamid Bakhsh, a movie producer who lives in Los Angeles, California!" Entitled "A Cowardly Cartoonist," the illustration has Crumb mocking himself for not taking a stronger stance, even as he stands in solidarity with his "martyred comrads [*sic*]" (Crumb 2015). From a reader's perspective, initial disbelief gives way to relief and, perhaps, to beguilement.

Yet Crumb's cartoon was "cowardly" in a quite different way, in that it ignored the wider issues stirred up by the shooting. Irreverence aside, it overlooked the knee-jerk response of the mainstream press, eager to vilify Islam for failing to see the joke of the caricatures, or for misunderstanding the satiric tradition. As Crumb said to the *New York Observer*: "[*Charlie Hebdo*] insulted everybody. The Pope, the President of the country . . . You know, they didn't let anybody off the hook, which was good" (Farber 2015). Like many others in the mainstream media, Crumb would seem to hold the view that, if their nets are cast widely enough, satirical cartoons can somehow be ideology-free and nondiscriminatory.

This was not the view of Joe Sacco, a cartoonist influenced by Crumb and a *Weirdo* contributor,[10] who published a pensive, reflective strip in the *Guardian* entitled "On Satire." What Crumb signs off with is, in a sense, where Sacco's one-page, ten-panel piece begins: with an expression of sadness that a number of cartoonists had been killed ("my tribe"). He then questions

the uses—and the limits—of satire, implicitly putting in question Crumb's dictum: "[L]ines on paper are a weapon, and satire is meant to cut to the bone" (Sacco 2015). Cartoons can *hurt*. Their power to satirize is bound up with their power to offend, in equal measure. Referring to the notorious image from Abu Ghraib prison in Iraq of the "Hooded Man" being tortured, Sacco asks us to consider "what it is about Muslims in this time and place that makes them unable to laugh off a mere image." If Crumb's "cowardly cartoonist" statement seems evasive, then, that is because it disregards the racial politics of the issue—which is to say, the *context* on which the strategy of "using racism to fight racism" depends. Even if it were true that *Charlie Hebdo* "insulted everybody,"[11] Muslims in France, unlike the pope or the president, have little or no political representation, effectively making them one of the country's most vulnerable and assailable ethnic groups.[12]

Crumb's veiled approval of *Charlie Hebdo*'s "equal opportunity" satire does, however, make good historical sense, for reasons that go all the way back to the dawn of the underground. As Jeet Heer points out, "Crumb's work was almost immediately translated into French in the late 1960s and had a profound influence on cartoonists at *Charlie Hebdo* and many other publications" (Heer 2015). One of Crumb's "legacies," then, almost a half century on, might be that giving offense is not just an unavoidable side-effect of cartooning but a kind of professional duty. To fall short of this standard is to fail as an artist.

Sacco's remark about how difficult it is for some "to laugh off a mere image" could be seen as an echo of Trina Robbins's earlier plaint about Crumb's more extreme work ("[W]hat the hell is funny about rape and murder?"). Both these tendencies can be traced back to Crumb's agon with authority. As he said in a 1991 interview:

> There's a little Trina in all of our brains that's always judging and saying, "No, no, that's bad, that's wrong," some little nun or school teacher or authority figure that always wants us to be correct and good and polite, and do the things that are most acceptable to everyone—always, at all times. (Groth 1991)

To be socially "acceptable" is, then, tantamount to submitting to the "will of another"—to surrendering one's autonomy. And just as having taste is a passport to bourgeois acceptability, there are various formulas for social conformity that impose themselves across the classes. The cartooning tradition that Crumb inaugurated—the residue of his countercultural protest—pushes back against these formulas, claiming the artist's freedom to contest, to mock, to vilify, and to offend. Spiegelman, as we have seen, questions the ethical adequacy of this attitude, principally by denouncing Crumb's use of "anti-racist racism" as an artistic strategy. "If I could remake Crumb in my own image," he said in 1995, "I'd probably cut out some of that shit" (Groth 1995, 138). Yet this is to miss the point, because without "that shit," Crumb would not be Crumb. As a disenchanted sixties provocateur, Crumb's confrontational style—the assaults on good taste and political propriety, the confessional openness, the bourgeois baiting—is as much a part of his artistic temper as his pre–World War II "old times" fixation.

I have characterized Crumb in the foregoing argument as a "utopian scatologist" (albeit a disenchanted one) rather than an "anarchist," because his relationship with anarchism is instinctive and intuitive rather than ideological; which is to say, there is nothing programmatic or methodical about it. Yet at the same time, it is consistently driven by the belief that social normativity operates as a subtle lever for the instruments of authority. Against this dominance, Crumb pits the agencies of desire: the spontaneously violent and obscene behavior of his characters, on the one hand; and Crumb's artistic compulsion to express his most antisocial urges ("It has to come out"), on the other. The utopian foundation of his work—the only positive constituent in his political makeup—is, then, transmuted into the negative mode of implicit critique. Yet protest that is driven by reflex or impulse eventually becomes routinized and attenuated, even doctrinaire. Although this is not quite the case with Crumb, his aversion to ideology has undoubtedly encouraged his blind spots and critical shortcomings, even as it has enabled him to maintain his agon. The "hideous darkness" that Robbins sees in the work could therefore be seen as a reluctance, a studied refusal, to let the redemptive light shine.

NOTES

1. Frederik Byrn Køhlert and Ole Birk Laursen suggest that the comics form itself is inherently anarchic, or at least that it attracts and emboldens anti-authoritarian creative sensibilities. They note "the form's multimodal combination of various visual and verbal codes, which combine to create meaning that is always unstable and in danger of becoming unfixed from authoritative models of interpretation" (2017, 8). Crumb's work would seem to fit this schema, not least for the different political uses to which it has been put.

2. A significant part of Crumb's corpus implicitly pushes against the constraints of censorship. As for the other four areas, examples of Crumb's attitudes can be found, respectively, in "Four More Years" (1972); "Trash" (1982); "Academy Awards" (1991); and "My Troubles with Women Part 2" (1987).

3. The film critic Colin MacCabe, in his biographical study of Jean-Luc Godard, argues that "it is possible to understand [Godard's] career . . . as an attempt to find an audience on his own terms, and this, in fact, might serve as the very definition of modernism" (2003, 157). In some ways, MacCabe is echoing a remark that the painter-writer Wyndham Lewis made in 1950, looking back on his modernist past: "It was, after all, a new civilisation that I—and a few other people—was making the blueprints for. . . . A rough design for a way of seeing for men *who as yet were not there*. . . . [O]ne was manufacturing fresh eyes for people" (Lewis 1984, 135; emphasis added). Mouly and Spiegelman might have been less programmatic than Lewis, but they were nonetheless trying to establish a comix (or graphix) nexus

that would break out of the ghettoizing "specialty" shops and find a readership already interested in, say, arthouse cinema or experimental fiction.

4. It may have been the "photo-funnies," more than any other feature, that prompted Spiegelman to call it "a piece of shit" (qtd. in Holm 2005, 84).

5. For example, Crumb was an active participant in the Comics: Philosophy and Practice conference at the University of Chicago in 2012—archived in the Spring 2014 *Critical Inquiry* issue from which I have quoted above (Mitchell and Spiegelman 2014). In addition, Crumb's perspicuous take on same-sex marriage, drawn for (and rejected by) the *New Yorker*, also graces the cover of the same issue.

6. The former political activist and musician Barry Melton describes LSD usage as the "article of faith and rite of passage of a new movement" (2001, 147).

7. The "old, weird America" is Greil Marcus's term, coined in *Invisible Republic: Bob Dylan's Basement Tapes* (1997), later to become the revised title in a subsequent edition of the book.

8. Not just to have taste but to be *seen* as having it is, of course, a bourgeois affectation. As Pierre Bourdieu (1984) has argued, it is what gives this class *distinction*.

9. A third meaning of *pharmakon* is "scapegoat," or political sacrifice. Derrida focuses on the first two significations, *remedy* and *poison*, but (unlike Plato) resists treating them as an oppositional pair. He argues, instead, that *pharmakon* is ambivalent and irreducible, and "cannot simply be assigned a site within what it situates, cannot be subsumed under concepts whose contours it draws" (1981, 103).

10. Crumb's influence is not so evident in the comics journalism that Sacco has been producing for more than twenty years—about his on-the-ground experiences in Gaza, Sarajevo, and Goražde—as it is in his earlier work in *Yahoo*, collected in the volume *Notes from a Defeatist* (2003), and his more recent political satire *Bumf* (2014).

11. Sacco points out, in a terse aside, that the *Charlie Hebdo* editors allegedly fired a cartoonist for writing an anti-Semitic column. By contrast, as Adam Shatz noted in 2015, *Charlie Hebdo* had "in recent years ... come to lean heavily on jokes about Muslims" (Shatz 2015).

12. In a probing discussion of *Charlie Hebdo* and its political agendas, Matt Jones poses the kind of question that Crumb does not ask, namely: "Can a comic still be considered anarchic when it lashes out against marginalized communities, effectively defending normative power relations?" (2017, 72).

WORKS CITED

Armstrong, David. 1994. "Is Crumb a Neo-Nazi Bigot? He Says Racist Magazine Didn't Get Satire; Others Say He Should Have Known Better." *San Francisco Examiner*, September 28.

Arnold, Andrew D. 2005. "R. Crumb Speaks." *Time*, April 29. http://content.time.com/time/arts/article/0,8599,1055105,00.html.

Beaty, Bart, and Benjamin Woo. 2016. *The Greatest Comic Book of All Time: Symbolic Capital and the Field of American Comic Books*. New York: Palgrave Macmillan.

Bloom, Alexander. 2001. "Introduction: Why Read about the 1960s at the Turn of the Twenty-First Century?" In *Long Time Gone: Sixties America Then and Now*, edited by Alexander Bloom, 3–9. Oxford: Oxford University Press.

Bourdieu, Pierre. 1984. *Distinction: A Social Critique of the Judgement of Taste*. Translated by Richard Nice. Cambridge, MA: Harvard University Press.

Breuer, Josef, and Sigmund Freud. 1991. *The Penguin Freud Library*. Vol. 3, *Studies on Hysteria*. Harmondsworth, Midd., England: Penguin.

Buruma, Ian. 2006. "Mr. Natural." *New York Review of Books*, April 6. https://www.nybooks .com/articles/2006/04/06/mr-natural/.

Casey, Gerard. 2012. *Libertarian Anarchy: Against the State*. London: Continuum.

Childs, Peter. 2000. *Modernism*. London: Routledge.

Cioran, E. M. 2012. *The Trouble with Being Born*. Translated by Richard Howard. New York: Arcade.

Crumb, R. 1989. *The Complete Crumb Comics*. Vol. 4, *Mr. Sixties!* Seattle: Fantagraphics.

Crumb, R. 2013. *The "Weirdo" Years: 1981–'93*. London: Knockabout.

Crumb, R. 2015. "A Cowardly Cartoonist" ("Dessins: 'Charlie' traits pour traits"). *Libération*, January 12.

Crumb, R., and Peter Poplaski. 2005. *The R. Crumb Handbook*. London: MQ Publications.

Derrida, Jacques. 1981. "Plato's Pharmacy." In *Dissemination*, translated by Barbara Johnson, 61–172. London: Athlone Press.

Estren, Mark James. 1974. *A History of Underground Comics*. San Francisco: Straight Arrow.

Farber, Celia. 2015. "Legendary Cartoonist Robert Crumb on the Massacre in Paris." *Observer*, January 10. https://observer.com/2015/01/legendary-cartoonist-robert-crumb -on-the-massacre-in-paris/.

Freud, Sigmund. 2013. *A Case of Hysteria (Dora)*. Oxford: Oxford University Press.

Friedman, Susan Stanford. 2015. *Planetary Modernisms: Provocations on Modernity across Time*. New York: Columbia University Press.

Goodway, David. 2012. "Literature and Anarchism." In *The Continuum Companion to Anarchism*, edited by Ruth Kinna, 192–211. London: Continuum.

Groth, Gary. 1991. "A Couple of White Guys Sitting Around Talking." *Comics Journal*, no. 143 (July): 77–92.

Groth, Gary. 1995. "Art Spiegelman, Part II." *Comics Journal*, no. 181 (October): 97–139.

Groth, Gary. 2011. "Robert Crumb, Live Online: The Interview That Didn't Happen." *Comics Journal*, October 31. http://www.tcj.com/crumb-and-groth-live-online/.

Heer, Jeet. 2015. "The Aesthetic Failure of 'Charlie Hebdo.'" *New Republic*, May 8. https://new republic.com/article/121748/arrested-development-and-aesthetic-failure-charlie-hebdo.

Holm, D. K. 2005. *Robert Crumb*. Harpenden, Herts., England: Pocket Essentials.

Hyzagi, Jacques. 2015. "Robert Crumb Hates You." *Observer*, October 14. https://observer .com/2015/10/robert-crumb-hates-you/.

Jones, Matt. 2017. "Vomiting on New Friends: *Charlie Hebdo* and the Legacy of Anarchic Black Humor in French Comics." *SubStance* 46, no. 2 (issue 143): 71–94.

Kartalopoulos, Bill. 2005. "A RAW History, Part One." *Indy Magazine*, Winter. https://web .archive.org/web/20080210081618/http://64.23.98.142/indy/winter_2005/raw_01/index .html.

Køhlert, Frederik Byrn, and Ole Birk Laursen. 2017. "Introduction: Comics and the Anarchist Imagination." *SubStance* 46, no. 2 (issue 143): 3–10.

Lewis, Beth Irwin. 1971. *George Grosz: Art and Politics in the Weimar Republic*. Madison: University of Wisconsin Press.

Lewis, Wyndham. 1984. *Rude Assignment: An Intellectual Autobiography*. Edited by Toby Foshay. Berkeley, CA: Gingko Press.

MacCabe, Colin. 2003. *Godard: A Portrait of the Artist at Seventy*. New York: Farrar, Straus and Giroux.

Marcus, Greil. 1997. *Invisible Republic: Bob Dylan's Basement Tapes*. New York: Henry Holt.

Melton, Barry. 2001. "Everything Seemed Beautiful: A Life in the Counterculture." In *Long Time Gone: Sixties America Then and Now*, edited by Alexander Bloom, 145–57. Oxford: Oxford University Press.

Miller, Timothy. 2002. "The Sixties-Era Communes." In *Imagine Nation: The American Counterculture of the 1960s and '70s*, edited by Peter Braunstein and Michael William Doyle, 327–51. New York: Routledge.

Mitchell, W. J. T., and Art Spiegelman. 2014. "Public Conversation: What the %$&# Happened to Comics?" *Critical Inquiry* 40, no. 3 (Spring): 20–35.

Purcell, Charles. 2011. "I'm a Very Eccentric, Oddball Character." *Sydney Morning Herald*, July 30. https://www.smh.com.au/entertainment/art-and-design/im-a-very-eccentric -oddball-character-20110728-1ior3.html.

Robbins, Trina. 1988. "Comments on Crumb." *Blab!*, no. 3 (Fall): 92–94.

Sabin, Roger. 1996. *Comics, Comix and Graphic Novels: A History of Comic Art*. London: Phaidon.

Sacco, Joe. 2003. *Notes from a Defeatist*. Seattle: Fantagraphics.

Sacco, Joe. 2014. *Bumf*. London: Jonathan Cape.

Sacco, Joe. 2015. "On Satire: A Response to the Charlie Hebdo Attacks." *Guardian*, January 10. https://www.theguardian.com/world/ng-interactive/2015/jan/09/joe-sacco-on-satire -a-response-to-the-attacks.

Shatz, Adam. 2015. "Moral Clarity." *London Review of Books, LRB Blog*, January 9. https:// www.lrb.co.uk/blog/.

Spiegelman, Art, and Françoise Mouly. 1987. "Raw Nerves." In *Read Yourself Raw*, edited by Art Spiegelman and Françoise Mouly, 6–8. New York: Pantheon.

Widmer, Ted. 2010. "R. Crumb, the Art of Comics No. 1." *Paris Review*, no. 193 (Summer): 19–57.

Wolff, Robert Paul. 1998. *In Defense of Anarchism*. Berkeley: University of California Press.

Wood, Alex, ed. 2011. "Crumb on Others, Part One." The Official Crumb Site, May. https:// www.crumbproducts.com/Crumb-On-Others-Part-1_ep_57.html, accessed May 24, 2019.

Zwigoff, Terry, dir. 1995. *Crumb*. Sony Pictures.

Chapter 3

READING, LOOKING, FEELING

Comix after Legitimacy

DANIEL WORDEN

Comics do not fit easily into traditional academic categories, even though the field of comics studies has grown tremendously since the turn of the twenty-first century.[1] Comics belong neither to the domain of literary studies, because they are inherently visual, nor to art history, due to their mass culture roots and reliance on long-form narrative. These qualities make them both suitable and not suitable to the methods of either discipline. Indeed, in the burgeoning field of comics studies, hybrid methodologies are emerging that fuse together tools from art history, communications, digital humanities, literary studies, periodical studies, and visual culture to better grasp the unique qualities of comics. As Marc Singer has noted, interdisciplinarity is necessary for the development of comics studies so that the field does not get caught "forever reinventing the wheel, caught up in endless arguments over naming and definition instead of expanding its field of knowledge" (Singer 2019, 30). Comics studies has developed alongside the growth of comics archives in universities, making comics available to researchers outside of the collectibles market, which values comic books for their pristine condition and thus discourages the handling and reading of print artifacts.[2]

In its early years, comics studies scholars tended to focus on book-length works—Art Spiegelman's *Maus* inaugurated the mainstream study of comics in academia—and those book-length works do not look like most comics.[3] *Maus* is published by Pantheon, an imprint of Penguin Random House, so its predominant method of distribution has been bookstores, not the comic-book stores through which most print comics have been sold since the 1970s through a unique distribution system.[4] It makes sense that literary studies scholars would have found *Maus* attractive—it circulated more like a book than a comic book. Yet, comic books are by and large a lot less like books than they are like other periodicals. Published serially, often featuring multiple contributors, and sold either on newsstands or at comic-book stores that restock new titles every week, comic books are rooted in the material and temporal conditions of periodicals. Like dime novels, pulp magazines, and popular glossy magazines, comic books have not been traditionally valued as archivally worthwhile objects for research libraries. Archiving comics poses unique challenges, especially when it comes to accessibility and searchability. Many comics contain multiple stories by multiple contributors, and these contributors are sometimes uncredited. Searchable catalogs of comic books have long been the domain of fan cultures rather than libraries and archives. Indeed, the most comprehensive compendia of comics history are digital resources like the Grand Comics Database and the Digital Comics Museum, and print resources like *The Photo-History of Comic Books* and the annual *Overstreet Comic Book Price Guide*. As scholars increasingly turn to periodical comics themselves to understand comics history rather than the more anomalous book-length publications that have led to the medium's increasing legitimacy in art and literary cultures, we must think of comics as print artifacts and as objects that circulate among varied readerships from their moment of publication to their possible afterlives with fans, collectors, archivists, and scholars. In this chapter, I explore how one unique comics series, *Zap Comix*, can be read through this framework, and what it might reveal about the comics medium's unique role in print culture.

R. CRUMB IN CONTEMPORARY COMICS CULTURE

As Jason S. Polley noted earlier in this volume, the Massachusetts Independent Comics Expo (MICE) announced in March 2018 that it would no longer name one of its exhibitor spaces after Robert Crumb. MICE posted the announcement on their website:

> Since 2010, MICE has featured exhibitor spaces with the names Bechdel Room, Crumb Room, Doucet Hall, and Eisner Level. The purpose of these room names is to pay tribute in a fun and fitting way to some of the most influential creators in the history of independent comics and graphic novels.
>
> As of this year, we will be retiring the name of the Crumb Room.
>
> This was a decision that we did not come to easily. It reflects a difficult and complicated set of issues facing the world of independent comics and the arts in general.

We are very sensitive to, and opposed to, any form of censorship. We do not want this re-naming of the Crumb Room to be seen as an attempt to erase Robert Crumb from the history or current reality of independent comics. We recognize Crumb's singular importance to the development of independent and alternative comics, the influence that he has had on many of our most respected cartoonists, and the quality and brilliance of much of his work.

However we also recognize the negative impact carried by some of the imagery and narratives that Crumb has produced, impact felt most acutely by those whose voices have not been historically respected or accommodated during the period in which Crumb has so effectively challenged and shattered many cultural taboos. The great value of Crumb's radical and inventive freedom of expression is, we acknowledge, seriously problematic because of the pain and harm caused by perpetuating images of racial stereotypes and sexual violence. The simple appellation, "Crumb Room," without context or opportunity for dialogue, can function more as an insult to those we want to feel welcome and respected, than as a fitting homage to an artist. (MICE 2018)

Following MICE's announcement in March, Crumb's legacy became the subject of debate again, at the September 2018 Small Press Expo (SPX), another independent comics festival. At SPX, comics artist Ben Passmore delivered an opening address in which he remarked on the political progress of the independent comics community, noting in particular that "it was a little while ago that someone like R. Crumb would be 'outstanding.'" After Passmore mentioned Crumb's name, members of the audience "booed," and Passmore responded: "That's right. A little while ago, there would be no 'boos.'"[5] For both Passmore and MICE, Crumb represents a tradition of independent comics that has become irrelevant, and even harmful, by contemporary standards. It is in this moment that the meaning of the work of an artist like R. Crumb can be rethought. While Crumb's reputation has been contested for decades—in Terry Zwigoff's 1995 documentary film *Crumb*, for example, *Mother Jones* editor Deirdre English and comics artist Trina Robbins both critique Crumb for his misogynist and sexually violent work—our contemporary moment has seen an institutional shift away from Crumb as a symbolic figurehead for subversive, independent comics, as independent comics festivals like MICE and SPX acknowledge his complicated politics by removing his name from celebratory invocation. As comics have become more legitimate as an artistic and literary medium, and as a more nuanced relationship to comics as an art medium becomes possible once comics artists and readers take it as a given that the medium has aesthetic value, an artist like Crumb can be reevaluated from within the context of print culture.

Much of what we know about R. Crumb and the underground comix movement of the 1960s and 1970s that he is so closely identified with has come from those who were a part of it. From R. Crumb and Trina Robbins, to Gary Groth and Patrick Rosenkranz, the history of underground comix has been written, in interviews, exhibition catalogs, coffee table books, reprint editions, and anthologies, by those who lived through their emergence.[6] For comics studies scholars, the underground movement in comics—the period in the late 1960s and through the 1970s, when comics artists began making and publishing work outside of the confines of the US Comics Code Authority—remains something like the bedrock of the field. The underground made possible the comics that many of us teach in the university classroom, and that many of us have written about in academic journals and books, because those comics depart from established popular genres and embrace individual styles. Yet, underground comics themselves do not fit easily into the matrix of aesthetic and literary value that defines comics today. As made evident in MICE's announcement about the Crumb Room, many underground comics are deeply offensive today. They celebrate violence, misogyny, and racist caricature. The comics that we value from the postunderground moment, even when created by artists like Alison Bechdel and Joe Sacco who claim to have been influenced by figures like Crumb, emphasize humanistic and progressive politics.

Bart Beaty and Benjamin Woo have discussed this curiosity in their book *The Greatest Comic Book of All Time*, a meditation on how our comics canon has been shaped by institutional forces like the reading habits of literary studies and the relative prestige of book-length works. About Crumb, and underground comix more generally, they note that these works are not often book length, so they don't fit easily into the literary studies framework that has dominated comics studies:

> While literary studies itself is not necessarily biased toward long works—as hundreds of years of the study of poetry clearly demonstrates—the case of Crumb highlights how comics studies is keenly attuned to the study of individual works, and of longer-form works in particular.... [B]ecause his work has not been composed primarily of graphic novels and because he lacks the single exemplary work that can be made to stand metonymically for his entire oeuvre, Crumb has been difficult for scholars of literature to take up in a serious manner. (Beaty and Woo 2016, 31)

Moreover, the content of many of Crumb's comics is troubling: "Crumb isn't simply not-feminist but his work is antifeminist to the point that it has been widely condemned for its misogyny. Themes of sexualized violence run rampant within Crumb's comics, where rape and incest are commonly foregrounded" (Beaty and Woo 2016, 31–32). As Beaty and Woo speculate, an alternate universe where "comics studies developed under the aegis of art history rather than literary studies" might have projected Crumb as being much more central to the comics studies canon, since a more formalist frame might have been less preoccupied with narrative content (40).

And indeed, that formalist framework is mixed with a redemptive narrative in Hillary Chute's book *Why Comics?* In her chapter about sex in comics, she details Crumb's channeling of his psyche onto the comics page, focusing on how his masterful line work captures the messiness and violence of sex and taboo in the midcentury United States:

> Crumb is one of the most virtuosic, if not *the* most virtuosic, draftspersons in comics. He is acknowledged across the board, and worldwide, as a master of drawing. Part of his renown as a cartoonist resides in his content—what [comics artist] Lynda Barry identifies as his game-changing demonstration by example that "you could draw *anything*" in comics, however dark, unpleasant, goofy, or private. But a large part of his appeal is how this content appears, which blends comfort and discomfort together on the page. (Chute 2017, 109)

Even Crumb's most problematic comics are redeemed as fantasy, in Chute's analysis, by the cartoonist's marriage to Aline Kominsky-Crumb. As Chute notes of Crumb and Kominsky-Crumb's collaborative comics: "[T]he depicted sexual activity of Kominsky-Crumb and Crumb is violent, but it's always consensual—Kominsky-Crumb draws eccentric sex as part of her daily domestic routine" (126). Kominsky-Crumb's acceptance and encouragement of Crumb balances the misogyny and violence in Crumb's comics with a feminist viewpoint, and their pairing offsets Crumb's sexually violent comics through the couple's consent to a kinky, married sex life.

Yet in this chapter, I am interested in what one might make of Crumb's early underground comics through the lens of print culture, not biography. That is, since many of Crumb's comics are, by today's standards, callously offensive and privileged, a reading of these comics in their original publications provides the kind of context that the organizers of MICE claimed necessary to understanding the artist. Much comics scholarship in the past has been focused on celebrating the medium—making it legitimate in the eyes of our fellow scholars who sit on graduate, hiring, and tenure committees; making it seem like an area to invest in for university administrators who are interested in attracting and retaining students; making the case to librarians that archival editions of comics are worthy of being included in a university's research library; and making it clear to students that comics merit close analysis and attention. As comics studies has moved beyond a first wave of comics scholarship that sought to legitimize the field, perhaps the kinds of redemptive narratives that would explain Crumb's comics via his later marriage or the differences between an art historical and literary studies approach to his work can only reveal part of what makes his comics meaningful. Perhaps there is something to his comics that can be encountered in the print culture archive that is no longer resonant with contemporary comics culture.

ZAP COMIX AND CONTEXTUAL READING

To explore this idea, I will analyze not the work of Crumb alone but instead the periodical *Zap Comix*. A landmark underground comics series, *Zap Comix*'s first issues in 1968 (issue #1 and #0, published in that order) contained only works by Robert Crumb. Starting with issue #2, other artists appear in *Zap*: S. Clay Wilson, Victor Moscoso, Rick Griffin, Gilbert Shelton, Spain Rodriguez, Robert Williams, and eventually Paul Mavrides. From 1968 to 1978, the *Zap* artists would publish nine issues. Issues 10 to 15 would appear between 1988 and 2005, with a final issue published in 2014 by Fantagraphics—the last issue was originally packaged as part of a deluxe reprint edition of *Zap*, which retails for $500. Thus, *Zap* still exists today as a periodical, in the rarefied form of the high-quality reprint edition.

Instead of isolating the work of Crumb—which has been collected in *The Complete Crumb Comics*, published in seventeen volumes by Fantagraphics—looking at *Zap* itself gives an interesting context to Crumb, and the problems that Crumb poses for comics studies. One of the things that immediately stands out in early *Zap* comics is the paratextual ads. In "I'll Bet This Happened to You When You Were a Kid," published on the back cover of *Zap* #0, Crumb uses comics' bad reputation, reminiscent of the 1950s comics panic, as well as a representation of motherly femininity as cruel, to imagine the reader of *Zap*. That reader is a young adult, white and male, who is on the one hand attached to the notion that comics are artistically interesting, but who is also nostalgically attached to the idea of comics as antidomestic, hostile to family norms. In classic American symbolism, then—after all,

Fig. 3.1. R. Crumb, "I'll Bet This Happened to You When You Were a Kid,"
Copyright © Robert Crumb, 1968. All rights reserved.

Leslie Fiedler's account of antidomesticity and homosociality in *Love and Death in the American Novel* was published in 1960—Crumb imagines *Zap* as addressing a homosocial community, united by rebellion against domestic and feminine norms.

This mode of imagining readership continues in other paratextual material. One fake ad in *Zap* #1 mimics bodybuilding and fashion ads, championing the transformation one can experience by getting stoned. Another in *Zap* #6 advertises suicide as a solution to the overpopulation problem. In these fake ads, with the promise of sexual attraction through the use of drugs and with the self-loathing endemic to *Zap*'s characterization of everyday masculinity, championing suicide as a social good, the reader of *Zap* is projected as a straight white male, seeking social and sexual relevance.

In one Crumb comic, "Dirty Dog" (1968), an anthropomorphized dog visits a newsstand and buys a porn magazine. In the magazine, the viewer learns through panels with thought balloon borders, Dirty Dog's violent sex fantasies are played out. Ineffective in his attempt to talk to a woman at a crosswalk, Dirty Dog looks to the magazine to provide a fantasy in which he is an object of desire. The comic concludes with him smiling, on his way home with his porn. This is similar to how Crumb himself is represented in a parodic Gilbert Shelton comic, "Wonder Wart-Hog Breaks Up the Muthalode Smut Ring" (1969). Wearing a beanie, Crumb, named "Robert Scum," gives a comic to a young woman, who doesn't find his "funny book" to be funny at all. Instead, she is disgusted by the graphic sexual content in Crumb's comic. Crumb slinks away.

In both of these comics, *Zap* is figured as an explicitly heterosexual male fantasy space, a substitute for communication and intercourse with "real" women. *Zap*'s indulgence of male sexual violence—seen even more explicitly in S. Clay Wilson's comics than in Crumb's—projects a vision of the comics reader as a sexually dissatisfied, emotionally immature, and socially awkward white heterosexual male, and comics are akin, if not equal to, pornography. I think it's important not to deny this key element of *Zap*, but instead to view it as the central feature that it is. The context of *Zap* is white heterosexual male desire and sociality. The limits and elisions created by this emphasis are clear, yet that context itself has some explanatory power that can be absent when individual comics from *Zap* are viewed in isolation.

Crumb's representation of race, especially his caricatures of African American and African figures, is notorious. His Angelfood McSpade character is a variation on the sexualized African female, while his urban African American figures look like minstrel caricatures. In Crumb's "Ooga Booga" comic (1969), his racial caricature and racialized dialect become a kind of

Fig. 3.2. R. Crumb, "Ooga Booga," Copyright © Robert Crumb, 1969. All rights reserved.

formal exercise. Going back to Beaty and Woo's claim that Crumb's art world prominence might mean that an alternate comics studies universe, where art history championed the medium and not the English Department, would have read Crumb differently, one can imagine what a crude formalist analysis would have done here. Like Gauguin paintings of Tahitian nudes, Crumb's "Ooga Booga" displays otherness as a formal mode. That is, in this frame of analysis, the comic is less about people than it is about caricature as a form. Like a Cindy Sherman film-still photograph, the comic makes a form out of content. In so doing, the inherent violence and brutality of racist representation is transformed into an object of formal study. At once critical of how racist caricature contributes to the language of comics storytelling in its ironic distillation of narrative sequence to rhythm, the comic also presents it as a necessary formal element of comics making. It is no wonder, then, that critics interested in the variability and flexibility of the comics medium find in Crumb a troubling essentialism not just about comics form but about its representational capacities.

Yet *Zap*'s relation to the discourse of fine art is uniquely complicated. In one Robert Williams comic, "Masterpiece on the Shithouse Wall" (1973), a Neanderthal makes a cave painting with feces of another Neanderthal having sex with an elk. That painting is later seen in a museum alongside a Venus of Willendorf with added nipples. A docent speculates about the symbolic meaning of the work. Williams's character Coochy Cooty leans against this cave painting and is magically given a ray gun that can destroy "pictorial decadence." He goes about destroying images of all kinds, until he encounters a bathroom stall covered in graffiti. The bathroom graffiti's collective force undoes the power of the iconoclastic weapon wielded by the comics' protagonist. His failure results in his own incorporation into the art museum. These valences are particularly apt for thinking about *Zap* and its cohort. The art museum misinterprets the visceral, literal meanings of illustrations. Yet, the line between illustrations worthy of being in the art museum (cave paintings) and those not worthy (bathroom graffiti) is inherently unstable and arbitrary.

In conversation with me in 2018, Crumb himself expressed a similar ambivalence. He recounted an experience at the David Zwirner Gallery in New York City, when a dealer was explaining to a prospective buyer that the Wite-Out visible on a piece of his original art was a sign of the "artist's hand." Crumb was baffled that this Wite-Out would be a valuable selling point to the artwork—to him, it was just a mistake that he had covered up so it wouldn't show up on a printed page. According to Crumb, his goal was always to make comic books in this period. He has sold much of his original

Fig. 3.3. Robert Williams, "Masterpiece on the Shithouse Wall," 1973.

comics art because he views it as intermediary material—it is not the work in and of itself. So hanging original art in a gallery does not capture the final product of his work. Instead, the printed pamphlet, with all of the problems it poses for the art gallery, is the final product.[7] Any docent explaining a piece of original comics art on a museum wall would be in the same position as the docent explaining the cave painting in Williams's comic. Thinking of single images as autonomous works, out of a larger print or social context, turns the viewer and critic into a fool, in the comic's view.

Yet many of Crumb's works are single-page comics that make use of a kind of formal clarity and autonomy well suited to the gallery wall. For example, in two one-page comics in the early issues of *Zap*, a single male figure is shown in different states of crisis. In one, "The Desperate Character" (1973a), he reads the newspaper, and his head explodes. In another, "No Way Out" (1973b), he is trapped in a panel, unable to get out. These two pages capture something of the formal dexterity of Crumb's work—his line work, use of the page as a compositional space, clarity of movement—as well as his major theme: white male heterosexuality in crisis. On the one hand, these are formal exercises in using the panel as a frame. On the other, these are meditations on the irresolution of white male heterosexuality—the way in which there seems to be no place to go for Crumb.

COMICS AND RELATIONAL READING

As outlined earlier, *Zap* and Crumb's comics are both difficult to fit into comics studies due to the field's emphasis on book-length, single-author works, and also works that highlight pressing questions about how we read comics and what we want to read when we read comics. The mode of relationality these comics imagine is very narrow, owing to their moment of publication and mode of address. In one panel of "Mammy Jama" (Crumb et al. 1973), one of *Zap*'s jam comics, with a panel drawn in part by Crumb, a seated female figure says that she doesn't like underground comix.[8] These comics, like the porn magazines for men to which they are likened, largely address a male readership that the comics imagine as sexually frustrated, dissatisfied with middle-class office work, and desirous of the sexual rapacity and pleasures imagined in both racial others and outlaw groups like motorcycle gangs.

To use a more recent example, Ben Passmore's *Your Black Friend* (2016) has a similar mode of critical address—the title alone addresses the comics reader as a white person. Yet Passmore's comic tells us something about contemporary comics culture, and what makes that culture different from the culture that produced *Zap*. In *Your Black Friend*, Passmore details the microaggressions, cultural appropriations, and threats of police violence that constitute the everyday reality of being Black in the United States. *Your Black Friend*'s primary interest is in relationality. Rather than trade in caricature as a formal strategy, as in many of Crumb's comics, Passmore's concern is predominantly ethical, and Passmore's own blackness informs his perspective, just as Crumb's white heterosexuality informs his own. Yet, the comic concludes with a moment of irony—the "black friend" who narrates the comic approaches a white female customer at a café, to talk to her about her offensive characterization of their neighborhood as dangerous (i.e., not entirely white). Before he speaks, he is told by the barista that he's not allowed to be in the café since he brought in a sandwich from elsewhere. While *Your Black Friend* is narrated from a point of alterity—it is drawn and written by "your black friend" for a white reader—it nonetheless hinges on frustrated masculinity, a male figure whose desire, however righteous, is thwarted by femininity. I am not presenting *Your Black Friend* as a positive counterpoint to *Zap*, but to account for how *Zap*'s framework travels, even in a text that has a very different approach to cartooning and messaging. Indeed, Passmore's approach to figure drawing and color drastically differs and departs from the style of a cartoonist like Crumb, whose work is steeped in nostalgia for the funny animal cartoons of artists like Carl Barks and Walt Kelly. With his sophisticated coloring palette for skin tone, and his attention to simple expressivity rather than caricature-based consistency in his figures, Passmore's comics move beyond the cartooning tropes that informed Crumb's imaginary.

In another recent comic about race, Medar de la Cruz's collection *MDL Comics* (2018), single-page comics about race have a hostile, yet parodic tone—these comics feature a Black protagonist who directly speaks to and about white supremacy. On the comics' interior cover, de la Cruz prints: "It's supposed to be funny," which both presents the comics as comedy and also, like *Your Black Friend*, gives the reader permission to laugh at what might seem offensive or not for them. Jenn Woodall's *Magical Beatdown* (2018) engages in a two-color fantasy of female retaliation against street harassment, as a schoolgirl transforms into a warrior and brutally murders the men who harass her on the street. Like Passmore's and de la Cruz's comics, Woodall's comic engages in the tropes refined in underground comix to make a political argument and engage in political fantasy in a way that is uniquely suited to the hyperbolic, exaggerated style of comic-book art.

These contemporary examples reinforce a basic point about print culture and comics—but one that is important when thinking about comics like

Crumb's that are more often, now, viewed outside of the comic book form. When hung on a gallery wall or reprinted in an anthology, the modes of address apparent in a comic book's editorial matter, marginalia, and range of contributors are often erased or absent. Understanding comics that embrace the comics form entails reading comics themselves, treating the comics as the object of analysis.

The *Zap* archive, then, might be where Crumb's comics, and underground comics more generally, are best studied and understood—not in anthologies that isolate individual comics from their context. Curiously, in conversation, Crumb refers to his sex comics and his comics about race as things that "needed to come out." I think that part of the print culture tradition that *Zap* plays in expects that these printed materials should emanate as artifacts from the past, as historical expressions. The late 1960s is a context we can no longer inhabit. And reprint editions of these comics incline a reader to think of these texts as contemporary. Instead, they should be read as print artifacts—on yellowed paper that crumbles as you turn the page, making it clear that these are artifacts from a different time. That perspective doesn't apologize for Crumb's work, but it conditions and tempers the ways in which his work can be read, in a way that hopefully moves beyond the modes of condemnation and celebration that constitute his reception for the past twenty years, and allows an emerging generation of comics scholarship to think in more nuanced and less binary ways about the value of the medium.

NOTES

1. Along with longer-standing organizations like the International Bande Dessinée Society, the International Comic Arts Forum, and the Popular Culture Association, recent years have also seen the emergence of the Canadian Society for the Study of Comics, the Comics Studies Society, and the Comics and Graphic Narratives MLA Discussion Group as well as scholarly journals and book series at academic presses devoted to comics. This shift has accompanied the broader circulation of (mostly) book-length comics in mainstream bookstores and libraries, as well as the proliferation of television and film adaptations of comics properties.

2. Institutions such as Columbia University's Graphic Novels Collection, Michigan State University's Comics Art Collection, and Ohio State University's Billy Ireland Cartoon Library and Museum have collections of print artifacts, original art, and archival material.

3. Early works on *Maus* and related texts include Witek 1989, Hirsch 1992–1993, and Orvell 1992. Articles about *Maus* would steadily appear in academic journals after 1992. As of this writing, the MLA International Bibliography lists ninety-eight journal articles and sixty book articles with the subject headings "Spiegelman, Art" and "*Maus.*"

4. For an anecdotal history of comic-book stores, see Gearino 2017.

5. Passmore's remarks can be viewed at @shannondrewthis 2018. For an account of the event and Crumb's status in independent comics culture, see Leblanc 2018.

6. See, for example, the autobiographical work by Robbins (2017); the interview-based history of underground comix by Rosenkranz (2003); and the collections of interviews by Dean (2015) and George (2004).

7. For accounts of the complicated relationship between comics art and the art gallery/museum, see Beaty (2012) and Molotiu (2007).

8. The "jam comics" in *Zap* were collaboratively drawn and scripted by the *Zap* collective of artists.

WORKS CITED

Beaty, Bart. 2012. *Comics versus Art*. Toronto: University of Toronto Press.

Beaty, Bart, and Benjamin Woo. 2016. *The Greatest Comic Book of All Time: Symbolic Capital and the Field of American Comic Books*. New York: Palgrave Macmillan.

Chute, Hillary. 2017. *Why Comics? From Underground to Everywhere*. New York: HarperCollins.

Crumb, R. 1968. "Dirty Dog." *Zap*, no. 3.

Crumb, R. 1969. "Ooga Booga." *Zap*, no. 4.

Crumb, R. 1973a. "The Desperate Character," *Zap*, no. 6.

Crumb, R. 1973b. "No Way Out." *Zap*, no. 6.

Crumb, R., et al. 1973. "Mammy Jama." *Zap*, no. 6.

Dean, Michael, ed. 2015. *The Comics Journal Library*. Vol. 9, *Zap: The Interviews*. Seattle: Fantagraphics.

De la Cruz, Medar. 2018. *MDL Comics*. http://www.mdlcomics.com/.

Gearino, Dan. 2017. *Comic Shop: The Retail Mavericks Who Gave Us a New Geek Culture*. Athens, OH: Swallow Press.

George, Milo, ed. 2004. *The Comics Journal Library*. Vol. 3, *R. Crumb*. Seattle: Fantagraphics.

Hirsch, Marianne. 1992–1993. "Family Pictures: *Maus*, Mourning and Post-Memory." *Discourse* 15, no. 2 (Winter): 3–29.

Leblanc, Philippe. 2018 "Rounding Up the 2018 Ignatz Award Winners and SPX Controversies." *Comics Beat*, September 21. https://www.comicsbeat.com/rounding-up-the-2018-ignatz-award-winners-and-spx-controversies/.

Massachusetts Independent Comics Expo (MICE). 2018. "MICE is Retiring the Name of the 'Crumb Room.'" March 26. http://www.micexpo.org/2018/crumb-room/, accessed May 25, 2019.

Molotiu, Andrei. 2007. "Permanent Ink: Comic Book and Comic Strip Original Art as Aesthetic Object." *International Journal of Comic Art* 9, no. 2 (Fall): 24–42.

Orvell, Miles. 1992. "Writing Posthistorically: *Krazy Kat*, *Maus*, and the Contemporary Fiction Cartoon." *American Literary History* 4, no. 1 (Spring): 110–28.

Passmore, Ben. 2016. *Your Black Friend*. San Francisco: Silver Sprocket.

Robbins, Trina. 2017. *Last Girl Standing*. Seattle: Fantagraphics.

Rosenkranz, Patrick. 2003. *Rebel Visions: The Underground Comix Revolution, 1965–1973*. Seattle: Fantagraphics.

@shannondrewthis. 2018. "Things are changing and it's not on [sic] accident . . ." Twitter, September 17, 9:22 a.m. https://twitter.com/shannondrewthis/status/1041724181866536960.

Shelton, Gilbert. 1969. "Wonder Wart-Hog Breaks Up the Muthalode Smut Ring." *Zap*, no. 4.

Singer, Marc. 2019. *Breaking the Frames: Populism and Prestige in Comics Studies*. Austin: University of Texas Press.

Williams, Robert. 1973. "Masterpiece on the Shithouse Wall." *Zap*, no. 6.

Witek, Joseph. 1989. *Comic Books as History: The Narrative Art of Jack Jackson, Art Spiegelman, and Harvey Pekar*. Jackson: University Press of Mississippi.

Woodall, Jenn. 2018. *Magical Beatdown*. Vol. 1. San Francisco: Silver Sprocket.

Part II

POLITICAL
IMAGINARIES

Chapter 4

HOW MANY TREES HAD TO BE CUT DOWN FOR THIS ESSAY?

Crumb as Ironic Eco-Elegist

JOSÉ ALANIZ

Robert Crumb's "A Short History of America," first published in 1979 in the environmentalist journal *CoEvolution Quarterly*,[1] unfurls over twelve stately page-wide panels to build a devastating portrait of ecological doom. The first frame shows what some might consider a "pristine" unpeopled woods and meadow: deer calmly amble, flocks of birds fill much of the sky. In the following panels, train tracks cut through the terrain, tearing a diagonal wound that steadily widens as grass and trees disappear. Telephone wires spring up. Roads are paved and repaved. Fences sprout. And street lights, signs, buildings, cars, gas stations, and every sort of urban detritus take over from horizon to horizon, all nonhuman animal and plant life long gone. The concluding text box—"What next?!!"—betokens even worse to come.

Crumb's relentlessly pessimistic before-and-after (panel 9, in which the last tree vanishes, has always hit this reader especially hard) functions, among other things, as a literalistic parody of Ralph Waldo Emerson's contention that

[n]ature is thoroughly mediate. It is made to serve. It receives the dominion of man as meekly as the ass on which the Saviour rode. It offers all its kingdoms to man as the raw material which he may mould into what is useful. Man is never weary of working it up. He forges the subtile and delicate air into wise and melodious words, and gives them wing as angels of persuasion and command. More and more, with every thought, does his kingdom stretch over things, until the

79

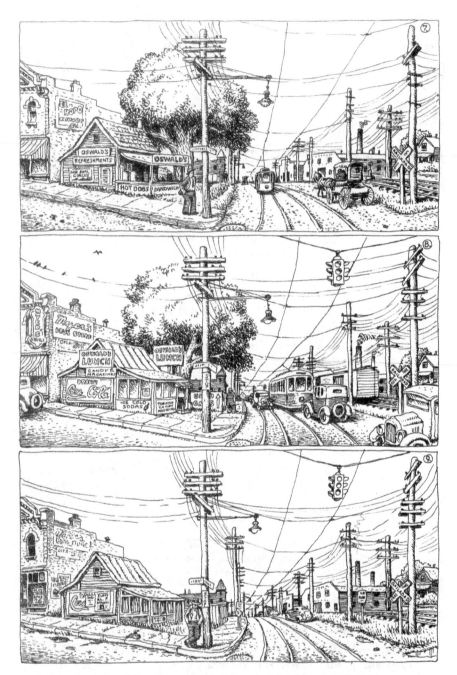

Fig. 4.1. R. Crumb, from "A Short History of America," Copyright © Robert Crumb, 1978. All rights reserved.

world becomes, at last, only a realized will,—the double of the man. (Emerson 2015, 51)[2]

More directly, it incarnates in comics form the much-bemoaned postwar mania for development, which Russell Baker, in a 1963 op-ed for the *New York Times*, dubbed "The Great Paver":

His dream, which we would dismiss as implausible if concocted by one of Ian Fleming's villains, is to pave the entire United States with concrete and asphalt. He envisions a nation buried under six-lane, limited-access turnpikes. When the last blade of American grass is buried, he plans to go on to pave Europe. Then Asia. And on and on until the whole planet is coated in cement. Today America—tomorrow the world. (Baker 2008, 378)[3]

Furthermore, "A Short History of America" stands out from Crumb's oeuvre—and certainly belies his reputation as a "raunchy" provocateur—for its avoidance of overt references to sex and drugs and for its seemingly "serious," even tragic, mood. The only "rape" here is of the landscape.[4] Such a sobering, easily understandable, and unimpeachable message perhaps helps to explain why this work stands alongside "Keep on Truckin'" (1968) and Crumb's cover for Big Brother and the Holding Company's album *Cheap Thrills* (1968) as his most reproduced and anthologized.[5] "Short History" has appeared as a poster;[6] in several Crumb-themed collections, including a color version near the beginning of *The R. Crumb Handbook*, setting the tone; more recently in innumerable internet iterations;[7] and even in the Library of America's *American Earth: Environmental Writing since Thoreau* (2008), edited by 350. org founder and environmental activist Bill McKibben. In his introduction, McKibben notes that "in the years around the first Earth Day [in 1970], every radical expressed themselves on the ecological crisis, and Crumb [. . .] was no exception" (McKibben 2008, 590).[8]

It turns out that it's not so easy to pin down Crumb's message, even in so relatively straightforward a piece of environmentalist agitprop as "Short History." For one thing, the people in it all seem equally to blame—or equally blameless—for nature's extirpation. We see no one picketing or protesting the tearing up of the land and banishment of the birds; no government steps in to regulate and conserve at least some of the original setting (as actually happened). Instead, a nameless force (Baker's "Great Paver," perhaps) drives the ineluctable process of uglification to an apocalyptic end. "Short History" thus amounts not to history, exactly, but more to a dramatically satisfying work of misanthropy. We may boil down its message to: "Humans suck, they ruin everything; a plague o' both your houses."[9]

Such an outsider stance virtually defines Crumb, seriously compromising the efficacy of any progressive politics his comics might advance. As Brandon Nelson argues in a 2017 essay:

> Rather than appealing to a revolutionary artistic and political mode by condemning the social and political establishment, or scoring points at the other end of the spectrum by propping up traditional power structures, Crumb criticizes and destabilizes the utopian ideals inherent in both reactionary and radical aesthetics of his and previous eras. (Nelson 2017, 140)

Gary Groth has likewise identified "an unresolved conflict between Crumb's serious attitude toward his art and his attitude toward seriousness," which Crumb himself confirms: "There's a tension between wanting to get as close to the truth in some form of expression as you can, and being too serious" (Groth 2012, xi).

And yet, few things seem more serious than the ecological devastation, disappearing species, unsustainable population growth, and human-induced climate change of the Anthropocene. To address them, even satirically, is to confront one of the greatest ongoing disasters of planetary history—deemed by most scientists, in fact, a sixth mass extinction.

This chapter will suggest a resolution to the perceived conflict and tension between Crumb's "serious" concerns and his politically inert disavowal of action as it pertains to the environmental crisis: a resolution that I will propose by thinking of Crumb as an ironic eco-elegist. As discussed by Jessica Marion Barr, Patricia Rae, and other scholars, the contemporary eco-elegy descends from the modern, post–World War I elegiac form, with its resistant politics couched as grief over unjust losses and dread of more to come. Similarly, the eco-elegist proleptically expresses anticipatory grief when she "mourn[s] past losses such as habitat destruction and species extinction, and [...] also warn[s] against the kind of absences we will be mourning in the future should present losses be allowed to continue" (Barr 2017, 197). Crumb does comparable work, addressing these losses in characteristic style: with snark, scatological humor and ironic detachment premised on contempt for *Homo sapiens* as a species.[10]

Crumb's expressions of irreverent "ecological angst," an underexplored strain both in his work and in underground comix in general, appear in explicit as well as figurative form throughout his oeuvre, although most scholars have seen it as a subset to larger themes like the Cold War nuclear threat and his attack on modernity. While drawing on such insights, this chapter maintains focus on Crumb's environment-themed comics from an ecocritical perspective, with an emphasis on one of his longest stories, "Whiteman Meets Bigfoot" (1971). Examining material from roughly four decades of Crumb's cartooning, noting such influences on his thinking as Deep Ecology and postmodernist discourses, I aim to trace the development of the artist's bleak (albeit tongue-in-cheek) expressions of postwar environmental dread—Robert Crumb as ironic elegist for the death of nature—and suggest that such a stance need not diminish the eco-elegy's power to "spur an ethical impulse to act" (Barr 2017, 195).

THE ECOLOGICAL CRISIS, UNDERGROUND COMIX, AND CRUMB

In the late 1960s, during a period that saw the launch of the *Whole Earth Catalog* (1968); the founding of Friends of the Earth (1969); and the first Earth Day (1970), San Francisco State University graduate student Ron Turner discovered underground comix. Turner was an "ex–Ceylon Peace Corps member/ex–Bakersfield engineer/ecology freak" (Green 2004, 93). Patrick Rosenkranz, in his *Rebel Visions: The Underground Comix Revolution, 1963–1975* (2002), recounts how Rod Frieland, a printer at the Berkeley Ecology Center, suggested that Turner start a "comic book on ecology" as a benefit venture for the center (128). Turner launched his company, Last Gasp Eco-Funnies, and published the first issue of its anthology, *Slow Death Funnies*,[11] shortly before the first Earth Day, which took place on April 1, 1970. The series, which lasted eleven issues published through 1992, would become the underground's most prominent and striking example of environmental consciousness-raising, tackling issues such as pollution, cancer, the AIDS crisis, nuclear energy, and climate change.[12]

The cover of *Slow Death Funnies* #1 shows that Turner was willing to go far beyond Walt Kelly's *Pogo* (a newspaper strip then notable for its ecological focus): a ravenous monstrosity, with a cityscape for a back, straddling the globe, gouges out great chunks of earth and pops them into its maw, while greedily reaching for the moon. Inside the comic, the reader discovers that the cover reproduces the final panel of Greg Irons's three-page comic "It Grows," a blend of essay and EC Comics horror featuring an unstoppable contagion. The fourth panel on page 1 declares: "Like a terrible tidal wave, it spread over the earth, leaving behind it bleak, ravaged desolation. It found it could eat anything. It spawned and ate and grew, and the delicately balanced wheel of life began to grind to a shuddering halt." Irons continues, "In seeking the 'good life' we have created a toxic, alien environment which threatens our very existence," and concludes, "Even as our choked planet shudders and gasps for it's [sic] life breath, it reaches out into space, expanding, seeking more raw material to appease it's [sic] insatiable appitite [sic] . . . Will the festering cancer of western civilization[13] consume all life?"[14]

A Crumb story in the inaugural *Slow Death Funnies*, "Smogville Blues," replaces Irons's humorless approach with tragicomic farce. Introduced with the phrase, "And now for a little pep-talk . . . ," the opening panel shows straight man Flakey Foont traversing a crowded, smog-choked city, griping, "Everything has become such a fucked-up mess . . . I can't stand it anymore . . . I really can't . . ." A despairing Foont decides to help reduce the population by committing suicide—but jumps off a bridge with no water under it (we see trash and a dead fish on the ground), and sinks into mud. As a cavalier Mr. Natural explains, "Hey, Flakey! Don't you know they've drained the bay to quench th' parched throats of th' citizens of Los Angeles?" a reference to California water diversion schemes.

Enraged, Foont demands concrete solutions for the environmental crisis, but Mr. Natural responds only with a plethora of platitudes ("Mother nature will prevail"; "Behind every cloud there's a silver lining"; "Life will go on somehow") in text-heavy speech balloons extending over three panels. The white-bearded guru concludes: "Now get out of my sight and don't come back until you've cleaned up this goddamned hell-hole!!" giving Foont a kick in the posterior for good measure.

The story, however, concludes with a cynical twist. A thought balloon reveals Mr. Natural's true feelings: "Poor Flakey! Bless his heart! Thank god somebody's worrying about it!!" The "pep-talk," then, serves not to solve anything (nature is still doomed) but only to sardonically appeal to the reader's sentiment over Foont's "good heart." "Smogville Blues"—subtitled "How many trees had to be *cut down* for this comic book? A moot point!"—depicts environmental disaster as no less apocalyptic than Irons's grotesque earth-straddling "cancer," but where "It Grows!" ends with a question, challenging the reader to engage with the problem, Crumb's piece forecloses hope. Mr. Natural patronizes squares like Foont ("Poor Flakey!") who think we can actually make any difference at all. We might as well just have a laugh as the planet burns.

Nuclear planetary annihilation[15] likewise serves as grist for a send-up of real-world anxieties in an earlier Crumb one-pager, "Mr. Sketchum" (*Hydrogen Bomb Funnies*, 1967). The eponymous bespectacled hero, while mailing his cartoons to Bertrand Russell,[16] falls victim to an H-bomb attack on his city. Plans ruined—along with, presumably, much of humanity—a vaporized Sketchum complains, "Now I'll never know if Bertrand Russell liked my cartoons . . ." (Crumb and Poplaski 2005, 151). The Dr. Strangelove–like buffoonery in the face of atomic doom both mocks and confirms fears of the ultimate Cold War catastrophe. Crumb vents and defuses them at one stroke.

As Hillary Chute points out: "Underground cartoonists, including founders of the movement such as Crumb, made comix the arena in which they could visualize disaster" (2016, 149) through what she calls "an atomic haunting" (151). However, she downplays the role humor and irony played in such expressions, seeing "the atomic reality" (151; emphasis in original) not in the undergrounds but rather in such "serious" autobiographical works as Keiji Nakazawa's *I Saw It* (1972), an autobiographical comic about the author's experiences as a child during the Hiroshima bombing. Despite accounting for the frequency of nuclear-anxiety imagery in Crumb's works, Chute here overly discounts the potent ways parody and absurdity—as opposed to more "realistic" approaches—capture the particular madness of the atomic age.[17]

Similarly, Crumb's double-edged treatment of the environmental theme in "Smogville Blues" and "Mr. Sketchum" (his lampooning of a dead-serious subject) may seem facile compared to more "weighty" approaches, but to argue so is to overlook the central, multivalent, politically charged, in short revolutionary role irony played in underground comix. As Les Daniels wrote in the early 1970s:

> If some underground comix are pure propaganda, the best of them are distinguished by an irony denoting skepticism at the notion of any simplistic solution. Such comics are equally likely to overstate their case for the purpose of shock, a type of exaggeration that the undergrounders use as a major comedy device, gleefully secure in the belief that it will pass over the heads of the uninitiated. (Daniels 1971, 166)[18]

Charles Hatfield has written the most incisively on this facet of the undergrounds; although he does not define precisely what sort of irony he means, he is describing a fundamental tension between form (comic book) and content (adult material) when he writes: "[M]any of the comix books were awash in irony, based on the appropriation of popular (or once-popular) characters, styles, genres, and tropes for radically personal and sometimes politically subversive ends" (2005, 18).[19] Furthermore, he identifies Crumb's comix in particular as "inherently ironic, in a manner not unlike that of the Pop artists before him. Indeed, this is his signal contribution to American comics: the ironizing of the comic book medium itself" (12).

Thus Crumb, along with other underground artists—including Gilbert Shelton, Trina Robbins, Larry Welz, Denis Kitchen, and Ron Cobb[20]—took on the ecological crisis with varying degrees of irony, despair, satire, and sobriety, though always with an anti-authority bent reflecting their disdain for government. Such a radical stance proved rather misplaced, given that in this very era (the Richard Nixon and Gerald Ford administrations), "the federal government was moving most quickly, strongly and effectively to address environmental problems" (Rifas 2019, xx), with the passage of the Clean Air Act (1970); the formation of the Environmental Protection Agency (1970); the passage of the Clean Water Act (1972) and Endangered Species Act (1973); and other measures.[21]

CRUMB AND "DEEP ECOLOGY"

Crumb articulated his well-known contempt for postwar modern life—and its toll on the natural world—as early as 1959, in the letters he wrote as a fifteen-year-old. Corresponding with a friend on July 9, he describes a journey from New York to visit an acquaintance, Stan Lynde:

> It took about half an hour to get to Massapequa Park, which is a typical "suburbia," USA! Miles and miles of modern ranch style homes with neat little lawns between neat little streets, with convenient little shopping centers neatly distributed throughout. Frightfully boring set-up, although most people like it that way, men out with their power-mowers whistling as they walk them along . . . The wives lazily reading magazines and sipping drinks while relaxing on contour chairs , etc. . . . (Thompson 2012, 40)[22]

In this and throughout his oeuvre, Crumb associates "real" nature with blessed isolation, an escape from the loud chaos of cities and the flipside to his hatred of "progress."[23] A March 8, 1961, letter in the form of a first-person comics story depicts the young Crumb's ruminations on his beloved jazz records and art as he ambles through a calm wooded area, encounters speeding traffic ("voom"), and eventually gets run over by a train ("splat")—all encroachments into an otherwise peaceable natural setting (Thompson 2012, 141–44).

The middle-aged author, now living in rural France, would later elaborate on these lifelong feelings in a 1999 interview:

In America, it's very difficult to find, unless you own thousands of acres of land yourself, it's hard to get away from people. You have to go to national parks. You drive, you pay, you go in. All the trails are marked; there are other people. Campsites are full of people. You really have to work hard to get away from people in the United States. As big a country and as wide open as it is, it is hard to get out to the wilderness. You have to go in your car and drive a long distance, and be really committed. When we lived in California, it was sort of out in the country, yet all the land around us was private property.[24] Here, I just walk up there . . . Unique! What a country! (Laughs)[25] I tried very hard to find a place like that in California, where I could go out to nature, but it was too difficult! I used to go down along this creek, and these farmers would come and chase you out: "Whaddaya doin' down here?" "Oh, just walking around, is that OK?" "Eh, naw, not rilly." "Why not?" "Well, ya know, we have to pay a lot of insurance, if you get hurt or something like that, we gotta pay, blablabla." (Laughs) (Mercier 2004, 222)

Such lamentations resonate with a strain of late twentieth-century environmentalist thought broadly labeled ecocentrism or Deep Ecology,[26] which couches a radical critique of modern life within its defense of "wilderness" (a highly subjective term). Note, for example, how Crumb's grousing over the difficulties of getting away from people find their correlate in Bill McKibben's writing:

There's no such thing as nature anymore—that other world that isn't business and art and breakfast is now not another world, and there is nothing there except us alone.

At the same time I felt lonely, though, I also felt crowded, without privacy. We go to the woods in part to escape. But now there is nothing except us and so there is no escaping other people. (McKibben 2006, 76–77)

Discourse like this has deep roots, from Emerson and Thoreau with their writings on wilderness to George Perkins Marsh and John Muir in the nineteenth century to Aldo Leopold and Dave Bower in the twentieth, as well as to the modern environmentalist movement launched in the 1960s with the publication of Rachel Carson's *Silent Spring* (1962).[27] As refracted through countercultural expressions such as underground comix, such thinking amounted to the blunt "demonization of modern machines" (White 1995, 178) and economic expansion, which its detractors felt had severed an ancient and benign relationship with nature. At its worst, Deep Ecology thinking could descend into outright nihilism and misanthropy.[28]

Apart from the danger of such self-defeating rhetoric and acts, Jeffrey Stark argues, movements like Deep Ecology suffer from an antiscience, fundamentally postmodernist stance, which offers "quaint spiritualistic assertions about nature" instead of ethical reasoning (1995, 270). He goes on:

> For postmodern environmentalism, the essential connection to existence is manifest in the authentic individual who resists participation in all repressive and externally imposed contexts, including social interaction operating under taken-for-granted norms of daily life. This includes a rejection of all conventional restrictions or obligations, whether or not the individual agrees with them. In this framework, community *is* repression, community *is* inauthentic. At best, what postmodernism implies is communities without unity in which all persons are united in their alienation and isolation and can do little more than pursue private virtues. (272)

While he has never come out as a Deep Ecologist, it is striking how well this description applies to the uber-nonconformist, modernity-despising, alienated artist Crumb. Related themes and imagery appear with considerable regularity throughout his career, even in incidental or unpublished works. "Leave the City" (a color drawing in a 1967 sketchbook) shows a besuited urban "schlub" figure walking astride tram tracks on a smoggy metropolitan street, about to fall victim to a train, while his thought balloon depicts presumably longed-for trees, sun, and a meadow (Crumb and Poplaski 2005, 126). Urban detritus and the polluting, filth-spewing smokestacks of factories often form a backdrop, as in "King of Motor City?" (one factory boasts the banner, "Great United Shitworks, Inc.") in *Motor City Comics* (1969) and the *Mr. Natural* strips Crumb produced for the *Village Voice* in 1976.

They appear too in the one-pager adorning the back cover of *Home-Grown Funnies*, "The Desperate Character Writhes Again" (1971), with its naked neurotic "who sheds bitter tears for the human race!!" Against a dark industrial landscape, with bulging eyes and scraggly hair, he harangues:

> The dum shits! The stupid fucking sons of bitches!! Those fucking assholes!! sob They're ruining it for all of us! They're destroying our planet! Those blind, arrogant bungling fools! Those viscious [sic] power-hungry

insane maniacs! They should all be killed! Even now they continue to create even more and greater methods of destruction!! Why? Why? How can we stop them? Or is it . . . is it . . . *Is it too late?*

Underscoring the sardonic, half-serious tone, the homunculus-like "Desperate Character" walks off in the last panel, concluding his tirade with "I don't know . . . I just don't know . . . Fuck it!"[29]

Two Crumb projects from the 1980s in particular exhibit his environmentalist proclivities. Early in the decade he joined the staff of the Yolo County, California, alternative ecological newspaper *Winds of Change*, working as art and layout editor (Holm 2004, xix). There, he produced a number of striking, ecologically themed illustrations, including a skeletal farmworker directing a crop-dusting bat in a field.[30] In general, however, as Crumb told Fantagraphics publisher Gary Groth in a 1988 interview, he felt artistically stifled:

> I couldn't go along with doing creative work that's decided by some dour bunch of politicos at this point in my life, even if I believed they were right. When every decision is made by a committee or consensus it becomes hard to do anything interesting or exciting, because when it comes down to it, this one objects to something, that one objects to something, and when you come to an agreement all that's left is the most bland piece of mashed potatoes. It was like that when I worked for *Winds of Change*. They always wanted to present what they thought were positive alternatives to the ways things are. It always had this dreary, goody-goody aura of we're-gonna-eat-tofu-and-sit-around-singing-folk-songs-together. Politically I agreed with those people, but working with them was so tedious and annoying, and they were utterly humorless. [. . .] I tried to do these really strong political cartoons, like Thomas Nast, putting down agribiz and stuff, and everybody said I was too negative. General agreement that I was too negative (Laughter). (Crumb, qtd. in Groth 2015, 32–33)

Another venture, more in keeping with Crumb's anarchist politics and poetics, involved his illustrations for the tenth anniversary edition of author Edward Abbey's *The Monkey Wrench Gang* (1985).[31] A cult favorite among radical environmentalists that may have even inspired the early development of the advocacy group Earth First!, Abbey's ecoterrorist novel gave Crumb a much freer hand in his renderings of industrial sabotage (Woodhouse 2018, 185). In one illustration, of the nighttime partial dismantling of a soil compacting machine, the artist even took license to show the gang's one

Fig. 4.2. R. Crumb, "The Desperate Character Writhes Again," Copyright © Robert Crumb, 1971.

Fig. 4.3. R. Crumb, cover of *Winds of Change*, vol. 2, no. 4, Copyright © Robert Crumb, 1980.
All rights reserved.

female wrecker, Bonnie Abzug, bent over her work, derrière prominently displayed (Abbey 1985, 83). In this illustration, Crumb's anarchist politics intersect with his sexual thematics.

Taking into account, along with the foregoing, Crumb's much-celebrated 2009 *The Book of Genesis*, especially the early chapters with their detailed renderings of an ecotopian Garden of Eden, the reader may agree with Marc DiPaolo that "environmentalist themes permeate [Crumb's] body of work" (2018, 273). In the next section, we discuss Crumb's longest and most sustained comics exploration of this recurring preoccupation.

"WHITEMAN MEETS BIGFOOT"

Imagery of satyrs (goat-human hybrids) and "wild men" (civilization's others) goes nearly as far back into the European past as history documents. The wild man, according to Timothy Husband and Gloria Gilmore-House, reflected wide-ranging beliefs in "aberrational human forms" and "monstrous races" described by, among others, the fifth-century BCE historian Herodotus, and played a role in the formation of highly ordered Christian social structures in early modernity, which a savage "shadow figure" helped to define (1980, 5–6).

Similarly, "wild man" lore took shape on the late nineteenth-century US frontier as an emblem of "freedom" and counterpoint to advancing "civilization" from the continental East. Increasing industrialization exacerbated the process. Since the 1950s, alleged sightings and media depictions of yetis, abominable snowmen, and related "Sasquatchiana" have represented a "modern update of the traditional wildman," writes folklorist Joshua Blu Buhs (2011, 196).

Such a cultural idée fixe betokened postwar anxieties—in particular over changing definitions of manhood. The "wild man" motif functions as a way of

> grappling with this new world, of resisting the cultural arrangement, and of accommodating oneself to it. The magazines, books, and movies in which the wildman appeared flattered the mostly male, mostly working-class audience's sense of self-worth, denigrating the womanly art of shopping and championing traditional notions of character. (Buhs 2011, 200)

We should not underestimate the enduring centrality of such myths to the US national character, pervading even children's literature. An especially stark example: Maurice Sendak's "psychoanalytical" picture book *Where the*

Wild Things Are (1963), a fantasy of escape from domesticity to a community of monsters in a faraway land, in which the young protagonist Max dresses like a wolf.

But no "wild man" gripped the country more immediately than that US pop culture obsession of the 1960s and 1970s: Bigfoot. Purportedly sighted by loggers in northern California as early as 1958 (Buhs 2011, 198), the shy, hirsute giant saw an explosion of media coverage after the release of Roger Patterson and Bob Gimlin's faked Bigfoot footage, shot in 1967 near the California-Oregon border (200). We could indeed call the 1970s the Bigfoot decade, when the figure came to dominate popular discourse.

Tapping into the national mood, "Whiteman Meets Bigfoot" portrays as only Crumb can modern man's deteriorating link to nature, a process intersecting with questions of race, sex, the nonhuman, and male inadequacy. Taking up the majority of *Home Grown Funnies* #1 (1971), extending even onto the inside back cover, the twenty-two-page epic represents Crumb's most detailed, tragicomic statement on the ecological crisis, and it is uncharacteristically a statement not without hope.

Rooted in the author's childhood memories of watching Irish McCalla in the *Sheena, Queen of the Jungle* television series in the summer of 1956,[32] the story imbricates femininity, nonwhite identity, and animality in a sort of raunchy ecofeminism *avant la lettre*.[33] As Maria Mies and Vandana Shiva write:

> An ecofeminist perspective propounds the need for a new cosmology and a new anthropology which recognizes that life in nature (which includes human beings) is maintained by means of co-operation, and mutual care and love. Only in this way can we be enabled to respect and preserve the diversity of all life forms, including their cultural expressions, as true sources of our well being and happiness (2014, 6).

By personifying a dying environment in the form of a gigantic, furry, sexually voracious "abominable snowgirl," Crumb brings together most of his major themes (with the exception of drugs, which he implies people in cities consume precisely because of their alienation from nature). As he told an interviewer: "Angelfood McSpade was a goddess, a vision of perfect, primitive sexuality ... The 'Yeti' in 'Whiteman Meets Bigfoot' is a further development of this theme ... The lusty Amazon sex goddess who lives naked in the jungle ... You figure it out ..." (Duncan 2004, 121).[34]

Crumb contrasts this prelapsarian vision with Whiteman, a modern, straight-laced, barrel-chested male citizen (seemingly modeled on his ex-Marine father) plagued by violent erotic urges. When first introduced in "Whiteman" (*Zap* #1, 1967), the figure can barely keep these drives in check: "My real self deep down inside . . . The raging, lustful beast that craves only *one* thing! *Sex!*" (Crumb and Poplaski 2005, 120). But in "Whiteman Meets Bigfoot," we see a more benign version: younger, thinner, more "puny." The "lovable honky" is taking "his yearly two weeks from the salt-mines" with his wife and family, driving his "spankin'-new '71 Winnebago Renegade." Yet even here, at the beginning, Whiteman vaguely longs for something beyond the twentieth-century city: "Ah, the life of an explorer! I tell you what, Louise, if we didn't have so many bills, I'd just quit my job and hit th' road 'n' just be a nomad, wanderin' from place to—" "*Fergit it*, Marco Polo," his wife interrupts. "We owe enuff on this goddamn jeep to keep us in debt 'til doomsday!"

That evening, the family hooks up "at a campsite in one of America's great national forests," and although the kids, Dick and Jane, prefer to watch *Mission Impossible* on TV, their father insists that they go on a hike. While on this trek in the woods, Whiteman gets separated from the children and kidnapped, tossed into a sack by a hulking, hirsute anthropoid. Text boxes over the next two panels, echoing the stereotypical speech of "primitives," inform us that "Bigfoot run like the wind for hours!" and "Bigfoot take Whiteman to his home deep in the mountains . . ." The next morning, this creature presents Whiteman to his "tribe." They immediately react with their form of laughter ("Horch horch!"; "Guhunk hilk hilk!"), rolling and farting on the ground. A female then rubs her overflowing genitalia all over the human's face, almost gagging him ("No! Please! I'm a happily married man! I—blub blb!").

Soon, as a text box notes, "Bigfoot gives his daughter to Whiteman as a mate. The family says goodbye and the newly wedded couple goes off to make their own nest . . ." With escape impossible, Whiteman settles in for the night, straddling his furry "bride" for warmth. One thing leads to another, and when our hero discovers that he has an erection ("C-could I actually be sexually aroused by this mountainous hairy ape-like beast?"), nature takes its course. In the act, Whiteman has his epiphany: "Wow! Louise was never like this!! Yetti, you're incredible!! Ya make me feel like a real man!" As Brandon Nelson notes, Crumb here promotes the act of sex "as an aesthetic tool, so base and animalistic that it can exist outside the realm of social hierarchies, consumerist impulses, and political posturing" (2017, 144).[35] Whiteman literally fucks his way back to nature—or so the story claims.

Six weeks later, a long-haired, bearded, bedraggled Whiteman (resembling the hippies he routinely despises) lounges with "Yetti" in the woods. He wears rags and has lost his glasses, another marker of civilization. To his grinning, oblivious mate he soliloquizes:

I've learned so much! More than I ever learned in ten years working for General Dynamics! When I think of the *shit* I used to take from those jerks! How useless and futile it all was! [...] Living here in the woods hasn't been easy for me ... I've never had to fend for myself in the wilds like this ... But it's surprisingly simple, once you learn how ... So much simpler than life back there ... I feel so much more alive than I've felt in years!

Notably, in Whiteman's journey, smell plays a determining role from the very first panel. In the title, the word "Whiteman" appears in a sleek, bespoke typeface connoting modernity and perhaps superheroics, with our hero's face as an accent (looking hyperpolished, as if made of metal). In sharp contrast, the word "Bigfoot" below presents as furry, pockmarked flesh that reeks with curvy "smell lines" and hovering flies. These "stink flies" also accompany the Bigfoot who abducts the human, while Whiteman himself often makes remarks such as "Ugh! What a stink! Gag!" (as Yetti introduces herself by presenting her genitalia) and "Phew! She sure *smells!!!* Kind of like it almost ... musky animal odor ..." (as Whiteman starts to get aroused on his wedding night).

Like sex, then, the olfactory forms an atavistic link to our animal nature, as it did for early sexologists like Havelock Ellis, Richard von Krafft-Ebing, and Sigmund Freud, who, as David Huebert notes, surmised that "the human species' ascension up onto hind legs and the subsequent turn away from olfactory eroticism might in fact have caused the proliferation of human neurological disorders [Freud] encountered in the modern populace." In fact, Huebert concludes, "a more mentally healthy creature might be one that engaged more deeply with smell" (2018, 132). Here, the father of psychoanalysis and the obstreperous undergrounder see eye to eye.

The rest of "Whiteman Meets Bigfoot" recounts our hero and his paramour's return to civilization, which immediately misjudges their relationship: "rescuing" him so he may resume his previous life, incarcerating her in the Abominable Snowman Research Center for scientific study. After only two weeks back in modern America, though, Whiteman, now dressed in slacks and a long-sleeve shirt, is reduced to sitting passively before a television, when a fortuitous call from Dr. Greyface at the ASRC reunites him with the forlorn Yetti, imprisoned in a dungeon-like cell. "Oh, God," he laments when he sees her, "... sob choke ... It's all my fault! What a fool I was to bring you back here! sob whimper ... In six short weeks I'd forgotten what a fucked-up mess civilization is!! Sob ..." Yetti is soon fellating Whiteman, who is still wearing a coat and tie.

Although Dr. Greyface sees a rich research opportunity in Whiteman—
"We've got to have him put under psychiatric care immediately!! [. . .] I'm
afraid his whole experience with the snow-woman has had a traumatic effect!
He should prove a most interesting case study, I should say!!"—the interspe-
cies couple escapes, with Yetti bounding over traffic, her lover in tow. Not
long after, we see a key image for Crumb's intersectional representation of
his "wild woman." In a large panel taking up more than half the page, the
"hot chick" Yetti clop-clops down a city street in tight jeans, a wig, sweater,
and boots, to stares and catcalls. Whiteman, spewing sweat drops and gazing
round nervously, mutters, "This is embarrassing! I can't stand to be conspicuous!" In disguising his animal-wife to more easily traverse the city, Whiteman
visualizes Crumb's sexist, racist fantasy: an amalgam of urban and pastoral in
the striking figure of a nonwhite, steatopygic woman of limited intelligence
who stirs the envy of other men ("Man, that dude sure has his hands full!
Haw Haw!!").

The image invites comparison with "Whiteman Meets Bigfoot"'s only
other panel of comparable size:[36] the splash page that begins the story. Here,
our man finds himself at the wheel of his Winnebago, relaxed, unashamed,
with his bored-looking wife. He travels in the opposite direction—left to
right—of what Crumb draws in the later picture of the bewigged Yetti. Here,
too, a male passerby, also in the southeast quadrant of the panel, expresses
his admiration—but not for Whiteman's woman. Instead, he digs the wheels:
"Jeezo! What a rig! Lucky guy!" The two scenarios set up a telling contrast
between different modes of manhood and libidinal engagement: one public,
conventional, industrial, and observing the proprieties, another private, deviant, amalgam, blurring nature and culture and thus prompting shame—yet all
the more alluring for it. Significantly, one of the leering dudes in the second
panel resembles the *Zap* version of Whiteman himself: he wears a fedora-like
hat, yet another marker of the civilized self, while our hero by this point has
long abandoned his, getting around bareheaded.

The direction of travel in the panels discussed above bears additional
comment. Just as Thomas Cole's painting *The Oxbow* (1836) and other protest
landscapes of the westward expansion era represent the encroachment of
white populations from right to left (east to west) to denote the conquest of
the North American continent and, as artists like Cole saw it, the despoilment
of nature,[37] so do Yetti and Whiteman's traveling left to right in the aforementioned image, as well as in the work's penultimate panel as they make
their final break for freedom, signal a return to the—swiftly receding—wild.[38]
Conversely, the opening splash with its right-to-left direction of movement
marks the opposite: constraint, narrowness of horizons, confinement—an

Fig. 4.4. R. Crumb, from "Whiteman Meets Bigfoot," Copyright © Robert Crumb, 1971. All rights reserved.

effect enhanced by showing Whiteman and Louise's tiny bodies looking out from inside the metal "prison" of the Winnebago (we see even less of the man admiring the RV; he looks positively cramped in his smaller car). Modernity means life in boxes (cars, buildings), watching boxes (televisions).

The "snow woman's" physical struggle with the Winnebago over six panels, as Whiteman tries to help her board—"C'mon Yetti! Squeeze yer big butt through there!"—underscores the antagonistic relationship of animal and machine. Her large frame gets stuck in the door, her weight almost tips over the vehicle, and finally she leaves it ruined, its wheels bent. The clamor attracts a livid Louise, who poses to her husband the story's climactic moral dilemma. As Whiteman agonizes in a thought balloon, "I can't just get up and walk out on my family . . . Oh, Lord, what'll I do? What'll I do?"

In the end, Yetti makes the choice herself, absconding with him by foot—again, right to left, breaking the panel borders—and making good their escape ("Whew! That was easy!"). A final panel shows the couple in an idyllic forest, Yetti lolling lazily on her back. She cools her head in a stream, a newly "hippified" Whiteman astride her, scratching her neck: "*And so, Bigfoot took Whiteman back to the woods where they lived happily ever after!!*" Apart from repeating the sexually accessible prostrate female pose noted earlier, the scene recalls nothing so much as Pieter Bruegel the Elder's *The Land of Cockaigne* (1567) and related "paradise of plenty" imagery, with Crumb substituting love and sex for food.

Nelson, through a feminist lens, sees the conclusion of "Whiteman Meets Bigfoot" as rehearsing a familiar Crumbian fantasy in which "the straight men are granted a sexual trophy at the end, seemingly as compensation or consolation for the humiliations they have been made to endure, provided usually in the final panel by an inert, purely accommodating female who receives his sexual attention with unawareness or slobbering gratitude" (2017, 144). With its long-haired, half-dressed Whiteman and the ever-naked Yetti, the final panel also represents a utopian, Garden of Eden–like fusion of human and animal. Whiteman's torn remnants of shirt and pants signify that the vital transformation proceeds apace, away from domestication and back toward the "wild."

MUST WE BURN CRUMB?

This chapter has tried to show that despite a reputation for unsentimental, sardonic, sexist satire, Robert Crumb has consistently voiced distress over the state of the natural world, especially the role of modern consumerism in its destruction. As he told an interviewer in 2015: "[A]ll that stuff, the whole ecological crisis and all that. That worries me" (Limnios 2015). This preoccupation led Crumb, in 1988,[39] to return to his most straightforward statement on the issue, "A Short History of America," and add three new panels depicting a trio of possible futures: "Worst-case scenario: ecological disaster"; "The FUN Future: Techno Fix on the March"; and "The Eco-Topian Solution."

Like the original twelve-panel version, this extended "Short History" functions among other things as a parody and update of Thomas Cole's *The Course of Empire* (1833–1836), a five-painting cycle tracing the evolution of an imperial power from its "savage" origins to its arcadian/pastoral state to "consummation" and collapse. A key difference between Cole's sequence and Crumb's is that Crumb's added panels dare to envision the possibility of a livable future, even if that future is compromised.[40]

At times, racist, sexist, misanthropic, and pessimistic works on the environment such as "A Short History of America," "The Desperate Character Writhes Again," and "Whiteman Meets Bigfoot" viciously mock and ironize postwar anxieties about modernity's zero-sum approach to the natural world. But I submit that they hardly evince the notion, voiced here by Nelson but shared by other critics, that Crumb presents "a borderline nihilistic assertion that all ideology and social persuasion is ruinous and devoid of ethical value" (Nelson 2017, 140) or that "[t]here is an intellectually inert quality to Crumb's representation, an outrage expressed in grotesquery and surrealistic exaggeration, but with no implied interpretation, and, perhaps thankfully, no proffered solution" (143). We need, it seems to me, to differentiate between irascibility, contrarianism, curmudgeonliness, and nihilism. Problematic and noncommittal as they are, the noted works come from a place of outrage, even melancholy, not a "moral vacuum" (Nelson 2017, 140). As Kristine McKenna better captures it: "Crumb's concern about the bigotry, pollution, illiteracy and corruption that he feels are poisoning this country is mirrored in his Expressionist depiction of America as a country in the process of decay, a corroded, withered and gnarled place" (2004, 162).

Such concerns, as this chapter seeks to demonstrate, have a long history in US culture. Most immediately we may tie them to the Deep Ecology and ecocentric discourses that emerged into public awareness at the height of the counterculture era, although their origins date to much earlier. As such, Crumb's stance is vulnerable to the critique of Deep Ecology: that among other flaws it traffics in a false urban/rural dichotomy and an essentialized vision of "wilderness" that ignores nonwhite populations that have often occupied "pristine" lands for untold millennia. (As I noted near the outset, "A Short History of America" is more about hating people than loving nature.) Rebecca Solnit in her essay "The Thoreau Problem" puts it this way:

> Those who deny that nature and culture, landscape and politics, the city and the country are inextricably interfused have undermined the connections for all of us. [. . .] This makes politics dreary and landscape trivial, a vacation site. It banishes certain thoughts, including the thought that much of what the environmental movement dubbed wilderness was or is indigenous homeland—a very social and political space indeed, then and now. [. . .] Conventional environmental writing has often maintained a strict silence on or even an animosity toward the city, despite its importance as a lower-impact place for the majority to live, its intricate relations to the rural, and the direct routes between the two. Imagining the woods or any untrammeled landscape as an unsocial place, an outside, also depends on erasing those who dwelt and sometimes still dwell there, the original Americans. (2008, 972–93)

The foregoing leads me to value Crumb's nature-themed work not for its upholding of such untenable ideological fictions as "wilderness" but for what he does so well throughout his oeuvre, what he seems almost congenitally predisposed to do: not take things so seriously. Nicole Seymour has recently hailed the rise of an "irreverent ecocriticism" that forsakes the maudlin phrasings and counterproductive hand-wringing of much environmentalist discourse. Such works, she writes, "largely reject the affects and sensibilities typically associated with environmentalism" like "gloom and doom ... guilt, shame, didacticism, prescriptiveness, sentimentality, reverence, seriousness, sincerity, earnestness, sanctimony, self-righteousness, and wonder—as well as the heteronormativity and whiteness of the movement" (Seymour 2018, 4–5). As she has also argued:

> A comedic stance entails flexibility and humility, those qualities required for humans to coexist with non-humans, or maybe even for us to contemplate our possible demise. And it might be the best stance at a point when humans suffer from doomsday fatigue, or an overload of "tragedy." A comedic, irreverent stance would thus entail adaptation on the part of ecocritics and "regular" humans alike. (Seymour 2012, 63)[41]

It strikes me that, as an ironic elegist for the death of nature, Crumb brings that gonzo, antisocial, sacred cow–tipping, and yes, often offensive irreverence that Seymour welcomes as a tonic for discussions of how we are killing our fragile environment day in, day out. In fact, as seen in his farcical interactions with the "tofu-eating" *Winds of Change* staff, Crumb can't seem to help ironizing the standard ecological narrative of utopian striving on the one hand, apocalyptic damnation on the other. This seems to me a more productive approach to the cartoonist than zero-degree critical dead ends like this:

> By couching obscene depictions of violence and sexuality in the style of American comics produced earlier in the twentieth century, and by reproducing offensive racial and sexual caricatures absent of any obvious attempt to condemn or interrogate them, the works of R. Crumb represent an aesthetic of perpetual and apolitical obscenity that favours the collision of discordant styles and themes as its method for ultimately achieving ideological nullification and correspondingly unfettered indulgence and gratification. (Nelson 2017, 140)

That said, Nelson's reading does bring to mind a colleague who once told me about discussing the work of Robert Crumb in office hours with a black female student. Holding back tears, she explained how much the work hurt her, how painfully it ripped open racial wounds, and she demanded to know why she should be required to read it in a college literature course.

Indeed, why read Crumb, whose work Nelson decries as perhaps nothing more than "personalized pornography writ large," at all? Why not burn Crumb? The reference is to Simone de Beauvoir's 1953 essay "Must We Burn

Sade?" Apart from many cutting insights on one of Western civilization's great monsters—such as this: "On the eve of his adult life he brutally discovered that a reconciliation was impossible between his social existence and his private pleasures" (De Beauvoir 2012, 47–48)—De Beauvoir answers her own question in the negative by concluding, in part: "What constitutes the supreme value of [Sade's] testimony is that it disturbs us" (95).

While it is important to vigorously critique Crumb, to acknowledge the violent reactions his work provokes, practically by design, as well as the harm it can and does do, I have chosen to champion him in this chapter precisely for his capacity to disturb; for his potent—and, crucially, irreverent—challenge to intellectual complacency about the death of nature for which each of us bears our share of blame. A satirist like Crumb, hurtful as he is, helps us feel the obscenity at the heart of the Anthropocene, its desecration of both human and nonhuman life—without sinking into mournful keening, itself a piece of that complacency.

But, you know what, screw all that. Given the artist's legendary recalcitrance, it feels most apt for me to close this chapter by giving Crumb the final word. So, on nature, from his "Litany of Hate":

> Nature is horrible. It's not cute and lovable. It's kill or be killed. It's very dangerous out there. The natural world is filled with scary, murderous creatures and forces. I hate the whole way that nature functions. Sex is especially hateful and horrifying, the male penetrating the female, his dick goes into her hole, she's impregnated, another being grows inside her, and then she must go through a painful ordeal as the new being pushes out of her, only to repeat the whole process in its time. Reproduction—what could be more existentially repulsive? (Crumb and Poplaski 2005, 386)

NOTES

1. *Co-Evolutionary Quarterly* (1974–1985) descended from Stewart Brand's *Whole Earth Catalog*. "A Short History of America" was soon reprinted in *Snoid Comics* #1 (1979).

2. Emerson here reflects a nineteenth-century transcendentalist strain in US environmentalist thought that recognized nature as resource.

3. Compare such discourse to that of Emerson and of early conservationist George Perkins Marsh, who wrote in *Man and Nature* (1864): "But man is everywhere a disturbing agent. Wherever he plants his foot, the harmonies of nature are turned to discords. The proportions and accommodations which insured the stability of existing arrangements are overthrown. Indigenous vegetable and animal species are extirpated, and supplanted by others of foreign origin" (36).

4. For more on age-old descriptions of nature as feminine and "virgin," see Merchant 1995.

5. Publisher Denis Kitchen's online store bills it as "arguably Robert Crumb's most popular and most timeless image," and Kitchen Sink Press's best-selling poster (Steve Krupp's Curio Shoppe n.d.).

6. The poster, with all twelve original panels and an additional three that I discuss at the end of this essay, was designed by Peter Poplaski in 1981 (Steve Krupp's Curio Shoppe n.d.).

7. See for example this version, to the accompaniment of Joni Mitchell's "Big Yellow Taxi" (1970): https://www.youtube.com/watch?v=mRkq595NhD0&app=desktop.

8. Many—perhaps most—post-hippie-generation Crumb fans discovered the piece in semi-animated form, as a minute-long sequence in Terry Zwigoff's documentary *Crumb* (1995). Here, "A Short History of America" unfolds in slow dissolves from panel to panel, to the accompaniment of "A Real Slow Drag" from Scott Joplin's 1911 opera *Treemonisha*, played by Crumb himself. At least, we first see Crumb playing the overture before switching to "Short History" as the music continues.

9. In this regard "A Short History of America" mirrors the three-pager "Mr. Natural's 719th Meditation," published in *Mr. Natural* #1 (1970), which preceded it by nine years.

10. As Crumb writes in his "Litany of Hate": "For me, to be human is, for the most part, to hate what I am. When I suddenly realize that I am one of them, I want to scream in horror" (Crumb and Poplaski 2005, 387).

11. Later, the anthology was simply titled *Slow Death*.

12. For more on *Slow Death*, see Witek 1989, 54–55; and Rifas 2019.

13. The wording references Stephanie Mills's 1969 valedictory address at Mills College, in which she declared: "Mankind has spread across the face of the earth like a great, unthinking, unfeeling cancer" (Mills 2008, 470).

14. All comics emphases, suspension points, and unconventional spellings are reproduced as in the original unless otherwise noted.

15. On the role played by nuclear anxiety in forming the counterculture, see Rifas 2019. Cold War environmentalists used the ecological consequences of nuclear war as an argument for denuclearization (see Hamblin 2013, 241).

16. In addition to being a major philosopher, Russell actively worked for nuclear disarmament and cofounded the Campaign for Nuclear Disarmament.

17. Off the comics page, Crumb gave voice to his nuclear dread in more "straight ways," in interviews and letters such this one, from 1961: "I don't want to be around when the bombs start falling. All my life I've had a sort of terror in me" (Thompson 2012, 152).

18. A notoriously difficult term to define, irony (from Greek *eironeia*, denoting an artful double meaning since around the fourth century BCE) "produces and implies aesthetic *distance*: we imagine some authorial point of judgment that is other than the voice expressed" (Colebrook 2004, 160).

19. Hatfield adds: "[U]nderground comix ironized the comic book medium itself: the package was inherently at odds with the sort of material the artists wanted to handle, and this tension gave the comix books their unique edge" (2005, 8); and "[T]he central irony of that most ironic of packages, the underground comix book, was the way it mimicked the very format of the corporatized comic books of yore" (11).

20. Leonard Rifas, in a useful overview, identifies such environmentally themed underground comix works as Larry Welz's cover to *Yellow Dog #17* (March 1970, a month before the first Earth Day) and Denis Kitchen's "Terry the Turgid Toad and His Sidekick Cosmic Dog" (*Snarf #2*, 1972).

21. In 1972, President Nixon also signed the Coastal Zone Management Act, the Ocean Dumping Act, the Marine Mammal Protection Act, the Federal Insecticide, Fungicide, and Rodenticide Act, and the Toxic Substances Control Act. President Ford signed the Safe Drinking Water Act in 1974. See Scheffer 1991.

22. For Crumb's opinion in a 1960 letter on the link between having children and the declining fertility of soil tenant farmers, see Thompson 2012, 112.

23. See, for example, Crumb's "Litany of Hate": "I hate the modern world. For one thing there are just too Goddamn many people. I hate the hordes, the crowds in their vast cities, with all their hateful vehicles, their noise and their constant meaningless comings and goings. I hate cars" (Crumb and Poplaski 2005, 386).

24. This recalls the scene in Zwigoff's documentary *Crumb* in which Aline Kominsky-Crumb complains about surveyors and "dream homes" surrounding their property.

25. See Crumb's two mid-1990s sketches of the French "Mer des Rochers," one of which he titles, "Getting Away from People . . . Must Be Back by Aperitif Time . . ." (Crumb and Poplaski 1998, 216–17).

26. Norwegian philosopher Arne Naess coined the term "Deep Ecology" in 1973. See Stark 1995, 260–61. Bill Devall and William Sessions published a central text of the movement, *Deep Ecology*, in 1985.

27. For a brief history of US views on the wilderness and key figures in the debates, see McCarthy 2015, 44–48.

28. For discussions of radical environmentalists as "ecofascist" and misanthropic, see Ellis 1995, 265; and Woodhouse 2018, 184 and passim.

29. Other mid-career Crumb works in this vein include the one-page "Let's Talk About This Here Modern America" (*Hipster Times*, 1976) and the back cover to *Carload o' Comics* (1976), which depicts Crumb sitting before a blank sheet of paper, poised to draw, while through a series of panels above we see a tree transformed first into raw material for a paper factory, then a commodity to deliver, argue over, and sell (Crumb and Poplaski 2005, 161).

30. A gentler, better-received illustration for *Winds of Change*, of Mr. Natural watering the "caring tree" from 1983, would go on to adorn posters and T-shirts.

31. As Crumb told the *PM Magazine* television show in 1985: "[I'm] in total agreement with the politics of it." See part of Eric Temple's feature story on the subject, https://www.youtube.com/watch?v=wldzZEUFEeA. On its frontispiece, the book bears a 1985 picture of Crumb and Abbey together in Arches National Park, Utah.

32. See Crumb and Poplaski 2005, 91–92. Crumb also addressed his childhood fetish in the first part of *My Troubles with Women* (1992).

33. Ecofeminism as a philosophy links the oppression of women to that of the earth (Laplante 2005, 166). Coined by Françoise Deaubonne in the 1970s and further popularized in March 1980 at Amherst, Massachusetts's Women and Life on Earth: A Conference on Eco-Feminism in the 1980s (Mies and Shiva 2014, 14), ecofeminism "re-examine[s] the formation of a world-view and a science that, reconceptualizing reality as a machine, rather

than a living organism, sanctioned the domination of both nature and women" (Merchant 1980, xxi).

34. The black Angelfood McSpade, whom Roy Cook calls "Crumb's most controversial creation" (2017, 37), had appeared on the arm of a figure strongly resembling Whiteman in "Angelfood McSpade" (*Zap* #2, 1968). Here called Angelfood McDevilsfood, she appears in *Home Grown Funnies* #1 in "Backwater Blues," in which a flood washes her out of her home while she sleeps. Floating flat on her back, she makes for an eerie precursor to Beyoncé's Hurricane Katrina–themed "Formation" video (2016). The feminine figure lying prone on her back, sexually available, reappears in the form of Sheena in *My Troubles with Women* (Crumb 1992) and at the conclusion of "Whiteman Meets Bigfoot," as we will discuss.

35. Nelson goes on to critique the story on feminist grounds: "The fact that 'Big Foot gives his daughter to Whiteman as mate,' or that Whiteman's first sexual act towards the female Yeti begins when she is asleep, is rendered apolitical and uncritically amoral, allowed to exist in what, in this comic at least, seems to be the only utopia Crumb will advocate in his work: the natural realm and the uninhibited sexual impulse that is presumed to accompany it" (2017, 144).

36. Crumb tells "Whiteman Meets Bigfoot" almost entirely in standard three-tier panel arrangements, ranging from six to eight panels per page. These two large panels really stand out.

37. See Carolyn Merchant's discussion of John Gast's 1872 painting *American Progress*, showing a spectral white woman towering over pioneers and settlers in covered wagons on their journey west, figured as left to right on the canvas (Merchant 1995, 147–48).

38. Of course, such a "left-to-right = freedom" depiction also reinscribes colonialist discourses, even if Yetti herself here represents the indigenous population.

39. As Denis Kitchen's website explains: "After the popular but depressing 12-panel poster went out of print, Crumb added three panels to answer the 'What next?' question posed in his original final 12th panel" (Steve Krupp's Curio Shoppe n.d.). The three new panels were printed on the back cover of *Whole Earth Review* 61 (1988) and later added to printings of the "Short History of America" poster.

40. Marc DiPaolo writes, rather unconvincingly: "The tone of a given work by Crumb is notoriously difficult to pin down, but one gets the feeling that he not only prefers the final panel, but believes it is the only way we really can proceed from here" (2018, 274).

41. Seymour adds: "[I]t's not just that an ecocritical turn to the absurd, perverse or otherwise 'unserious' texts *is itself* absurd and perverse, but that such a turn can force us to critically reexamine our own investments and strategies, in addition to those of the texts we read" (2012, 65).

WORKS CITED

Abbey, Edward. 1985. *The Monkey Wrench Gang*. Illustrated by R. Crumb. Salt Lake City: Dream Garden Press.

Baker, Russell. 2008. "The Great Paver." In *American Earth: Environmental Writing since Thoreau*, edited by Bill McKibben, 377–79. New York: Penguin Putnam.

Barr, Jessica Marion. 2017. "Auguries of Elegy: The Art and Ethics of Ecological Grieving." In *Mourning Nature: Hope at the Heart of Ecological Loss and Grief*, edited by Ashlee Cunsolo and Karen Landman, 190–226. Montreal: McGill–Queen's University Press.

Buhs, Joshua Blu. 2011. "Tracking Bigfoot through 1970s North American Children's Culture: How Mass Media, Consumerism, and the Culture of Preadolescence Shaped Wildman Lore." *Western Folklore* 70, no. 2 (Spring): 195–218.

Chute, Hillary L. 2016. *Disaster Drawn: Visual Witness, Comics, and Documentary Form.* Cambridge, MA: Harvard University Press.

Colebrook, Claire. 2004. *Irony.* London: Routledge.

Cook, Roy T. 2017. "Underground and Alternative Comics." In *The Routledge Companion to Comics*, edited by Frank Bramlett, Roy T. Cook, and Aaron Meskin, 34–43. New York: Routledge.

Crumb, R. 1971. "Whiteman Meets Bigfoot." *Home Grown Funnies*, no. 1. Princeton, WI: Kitchen Sink Press.

Crumb, R. 1992. *My Troubles with Women.* San Francisco: Last Gasp.

Crumb, R., and Peter Poplaski. 1998. *The R. Crumb Coffee Table Art Book.* New York: Back Bay.

Crumb, R., and Peter Poplaski. 2005. *The R. Crumb Handbook.* London: MQ Publications.

Daniels, Les. 1971. *Comix: A History of Comic Books in America.* New York: Bonanza Books.

De Beauvoir, Simone. "Must We Burn Sade?" Translated by Kim Allen Gleed, Marilyn Gaddis Rose, and Virginia Preston. In *Simone de Beauvoir: Political Writings*, edited by Margaret A. Simons and Marybeth Timmermann, 44–102. Urbana: University of Illinois Press.

DiPaolo, Marc. 2018. *Fire and Snow: Climate Fiction from the Inklings to "Game of Thrones."* Albany: State University of New York Press.

Duncan, B. N. 2004. "A Joint Interview with R. Crumb and Aline Kaminsky-Crumb." In *R. Crumb: Conversations*, edited by D. K. Holm, 117–32. Jackson: University Press of Mississippi.

Ellis, Jeffrey C. 1995. "On the Search for a Root Cause: Essentialist Tendencies in Environmentalist Discourse." In *Uncommon Ground: Rethinking the Human Place in Nature*, edited by William Cronon, 256–68. New York: W. W. Norton.

Emerson, Ralph Waldo. 2015. "Nature (1836)." In *Ralph Waldo Emerson: The Major Prose*, edited by Ronald A. Bosco and Joel Myerson, 34–73. Cambridge, MA: Harvard University Press.

George, Milo, ed. 2004. *The Comics Journal Library.* Vol. 3, *R. Crumb.* Seattle: Fantagraphics.

Green, Keith. 2004. "What's a Nice Counter-Culture Visionary Like Robert Crumb Doing on a Secluded Farm in California?" In *R. Crumb: Conversations*, edited by D. K. Holm, 92–104. Jackson: University Press of Mississippi.

Groth, Gary. 2012. Introduction to *Your Vigor for Life Appalls Me: Robert Crumb Letters, 1968–1977*, edited by Ilse Thompson, vi–xii. Seattle: Fantagraphics.

Groth, Gary. 2015. "A Marathon Interview with Legendary Underground Cartoonist Robert Crumb." In *The Comics Journal Library*, vol. 9, *Zap: The Interviews*, edited by Michael Dean, 11–45. Seattle: Fantagraphics.

Hamblin, Jacob Darwin. 2013. *Arming Mother Nature: The Birth of Catastrophic Environmentalism.* New York: Oxford University Press.

Hatfield, Charles. 2005. *Alternative Comics: An Emerging Literature.* Jackson: University Press of Mississippi.

Holm, D. K., ed. 2004. *R. Crumb: Conversations.* Jackson: University Press of Mississippi.

Huebert, David. 2018. "Scenting Wild: Olfactory Panic and Jack London's Ocular Dogs." In *Seeing Animals after Derrida*, edited by Sarah Bezan and James Tink, 127–44. Lanham, MD: Lexington Books.

Husband, Timothy, and Gloria Gilmore-House. 1980. *The Wild Man: Medieval Myth and Symbolism*. New York: Metropolitan Museum of Art.

Laplante, Kevin de. 2005. "Making the Abstract Concrete: How a Comic Can Bring to Life the Central Problems of Environmental Philosophy." In *Comics as Philosophy*, edited by Jeff McLaughlin, 153–72. Jackson: University Press of Mississippi.

Limnios, Michael. 2015. "Robert Crumb: Comix Sings the Blues." Blues.gr, November 6. http://blues.gr/profiles/blogs/interview-with-american-illustrator-artist-robert-crumb-widely.

Marsh, George Perkins. 1864. *Man and Nature; or, Physical Geography as Modified by Human Action*. New York: Charles Scribner.

McCarthy, Michael. 2015. *The Moth Snowstorm: Nature and Joy*. New York: New York Review Books.

McKenna, Kristine. 2004. "Moving Day: A Visit with R. Crumb." In *R. Crumb: Conversations*, edited by D. K. Holm, 158–63. Jackson: University Press of Mississippi.

McKibben, Bill. 2006. *The End of Nature*. New York: Random House.

McKibben, Bill, ed. 2008. *American Earth: Environmental Writing since Thoreau*. New York: Library of America.

Merchant, Carolyn. 1980. *The Death of Nature: Women, Ecology, and the Scientific Revolution*. New York: Harper and Row.

Merchant, Carolyn. 1995. "Reinventing Eden: Western Culture as a Recovery Narrative." In *Uncommon Ground: Rethinking the Human Place in Nature*, edited by William Cronon, 132–70. New York: W. W. Norton.

Mercier, Jean-Pierre. 2004. "Who's Afraid of Crumb?" In *R. Crumb: Conversations*, edited by D. K. Holm, 191–222. Jackson: University Press of Mississippi.

Mies, Maria, and Vandana Shiva. 2014. "Introduction: Why We Wrote This Book Together." In *Ecofeminism*, edited by Maria Mies and Vandana Shiva, 1–21. London: Zed Books.

Mills, Stephanie. 2008. "Mills College Valedictory Address." In *American Earth: Environmental Writing since Thoreau*, edited by Bill McKibben, 469–72. New York: Library of America.

Nelson, Brandon. 2017. "'Sick Humor Which Serves No Purpose': Whiteman, Angelfood and the Aesthetics of Obscenity in the Comix of R. Crumb." *Journal of Graphic Novels and Comics* 8, no. 2: 139–55.

Rifas, Leonard. 2019. "The Politics of Underground Comix and the Environmental Crisis." *International Journal of Comic Art* 20, no. 1 (Spring): 128–50.

Rosenkranz, Patrick. 2002. *Rebel Visions: The Underground Comix Revolution, 1963–1975*. Seattle: Fantagraphics.

Scheffer, Victor B. 1991. *The Shaping of Environmentalism in America*. Seattle: University of Washington Press.

Sealts, Merton M., Jr., and Alfred R. Ferguson. 1979. *Emerson's "Nature": Origin, Growth, Meaning*. 2nd ed. Carbondale: Southern Illinois University Press.

Seymour, Nicole. 2012. "Toward an Irreverent Ecocriticism." *Journal of Ecocriticism* 4, no. 2 (July): 56–71.

Seymour, Nicole. 2018. *Bad Environmentalism: Irony and Irreverence in the Ecological Age*. Minneapolis: University of Minnesota Press.

Solnit, Rebecca. 2008. "The Thoreau Problem." In *American Earth: Environmental Writing since Thoreau*, edited by Bill McKibben, 971–74. New York: Library of America.

Stark, Jeffrey A. 1995. "Postmodern Environmentalism: A Critique of Deep Ecology." In *Ecological Resistance Movements: The Global Emergence of Radical and Popular Environmentalism*, edited by Bron Raymond Taylor, 259–81. Albany: State University of New York Press.

Steve Krupp's Curio Shoppe. n.d. "R. Crumb Poster: A Short History of America." Denis Kitchen Online. http://www.deniskitchen.com/mm5/merchant.mvc?Session_ID=029d 2a43588ad81a5c5022d127b23524&Store_Code=SK&Screen=PROD&Product_Code=P_ SHOA, accessed May 25, 2019.

Thompson, Ilse, ed. 2012. *Your Vigor for Life Appalls Me: Robert Crumb Letters, 1968–1977.* Seattle: Fantagraphics.

White, Richard. 1995. "'Are You an Environmentalist or Do You Work for a Living?' Work and Nature." In *Uncommon Ground: Rethinking the Human Place in Nature*, edited by William Cronon, 171–85. New York: W. W. Norton.

Witek, Joseph. 1989. *Comic Books as History: The Narrative Art of Jack Jackson, Art Spiegelman, and Harvey Pekar.* Jackson: University Press of Mississippi.

Woodhouse, Keith Mako. 2018. *The Ecocentrists: A History of Radical Environmentalism.* New York: Columbia University Press.

Chapter 5

THE VISUAL POLITICS OF R. CRUMB'S "BULGARIA: A SKETCHBOOK REPORT"

STILIANA MILKOVA AND LILIANA MILKOVA

I t is widely held that the 1968 publication of R. Crumb's *Zap Comix* #1
was a watershed moment for the emergence of the underground comix
movement. Shortly thereafter, Crumb was enjoying popularity so enormous that the movement gained distinct visibility in the mainstream press.
A 1972 article in the *New York Times Magazine* titled "Who Is This Crumb?"
remarked on his recent success outside of the underground market. Crumb's
visibility was evident in the ubiquitous presence of his cartoon characters
on subway walls, bumper stickers, posters, baseball caps, and sneakers, "even
in the remotest corners of the country," the article asserted (Maremaa 1972,
12). It described Crumb's pictorial universe as "a Boschian world of raunchy
cartoon characters who curse, cavort, and fornicate as if they inhabited an
X-rated Disneyland." Certainly, Crumb's visual style can be described as
grotesque and in direct violation of the taboos and bourgeois tastes of the
time. Notably, the same article heralded the twenty-nine-year-old Crumb as
an artistic equal to Toulouse-Lautrec and Picasso, who, too, had ridiculed
or defied artistic and societal norms and in the process revolutionized both
art's form and its social role. The article declared Crumb "the most important underground cartoonist—and by extension, social satirist—in America
today" (Maremaa 1972, 12).

In this chapter we examine Crumb's creative work before he gained notoriety in the United States, namely when he trained his sharp satiric eye on
communist Bulgaria in the mid-1960s. We analyze Crumb's visual politics—
the pictorial and textual strategies he employs in portraying and narrating
a country behind the Iron Curtain whose representation in America had

already been enmeshed in political and ideological discourse. In what follows, we first outline the political and cultural context of Bulgarian-American interactions in the 1960s, focusing as well on their visual and textual parameters. Then, we turn to Crumb's "Bulgaria: A Sketchbook Report," which Harvey Kurtzman published in *Help!* magazine in July 1965. Finally, we consider a few sketches not included in Kurtzman's selection for the magazine. When examined all together, Crumb's Bulgarian sketches suggest an American visitor who, perhaps unwittingly, embraces the tropes of Cold War rhetoric but is then fascinated by the attractive simplicity of life behind the Iron Curtain.

POLITICAL AND CULTURAL CONTEXT

The early to mid-1960s was an especially important era for Bulgarian-American relations. On the political front, several Bulgarian-American Cold War episodes in the 1950s and early 1960s—such as spy scandals and demonstrations in front of the US legation in Sofia—had ruptured the relationship between the two countries. In 1964, the People's Republic of Bulgaria managed to reestablish diplomatic relations with the United States and returned within the American political and cultural purview. Bulgaria's key role in Cold War politics had already been noted by *Life* magazine. This popular weekly publication was known for its binary rhetoric equating America's capitalism with freedom and democracy, and communism with conformity and uniformity, as well as for its easily accessible photo-essays with linear structures, unified narratives, and formulaic design. As an article from April 11, 1960, reporting on the reopening of the US legation in Sofia, puts it, "Bulgaria is one of the poorest countries in Europe and it has always been Russia's most dutiful satellite. But it also borders the critically strategic countries of Yugoslavia, Greece and Turkey, and Minister [Edward] Page will be in a key listening post for Eastern Europe. Just as important, Bulgaria is considered the home base of Communist operations in the Middle East" (*Life* 1960, 57). By underscoring the connection between Bulgaria and the Middle East, the article firmly situates Bulgaria in the Orient.

The effort to increase Bulgarian visibility was in fact bilateral, and by 1964 new forms of economic and cultural cooperation were inaugurated. American diplomats in Bulgaria arranged visits in 1963 to Sofia by figures such as Chief Justice Earl Warren and Secretary of Agriculture Orville Freeman. The renewed ties were endorsed by the Central Committee of the Bulgarian Communist Party as well.[1] Bulgaria "opened its doors" (*Tourist* 1965, 1) to international tourism and in 1964 alone welcomed more than eight hundred thousand foreign visitors (for reference, Bulgaria's population at the time was about eight million). A range of modern cultural establishments were built—from beach resorts and hotels to restaurants and other entertainment venues—to spur and facilitate international tourism, and to captivate the foreign imagination. A 1965 article from the Bulgarian magazine *Tourist*, published in English, presented an overview of Bulgaria's exalted coverage in the international media. Dozens of foreign publications were cited, extolling the country's natural beauty and cultural heritage (*Tourist* 1965, 15). Various committees and institutions were tasked to design and organize the foreign tourist's experience in Bulgaria, thereby regulating to a large extent how outsiders perceived the country. The 1960s politics of "opening the doors" to foreign tourists was accompanied by a softening of the regime's hold on Bulgarian culture and the arts, which also facilitated the limited but steady influx of Western literature, film, and visual arts. Still, the country's cultural production and social mores were subject to strict ideological censorship and self-censorship (Roussev 2012; Yordanov 2012).

American Cold War rhetoric positioned Bulgaria as one of the so-called captive nations or Soviet satellites that played a crucial role in the cultural politics of the Cold War. The term "captive nations" had gained currency in the political and popular discourse of the early 1950s and referred to those states behind the Iron Curtain that had fallen "victim" to a Soviet "tyrant." These words were used in public rhetoric and implied a strong polarization between the oppressor and the victimized countries. In July 1959, President Dwight Eisenhower instituted Captive Nations Week and invited Americans to observe the week with appropriate ceremonies and activities (Campbell 1965). Geographically and symbolically suspended between the monstrous system of Soviet communism and the "Free World," the captive nations of Eastern Europe came to occupy a strategic buffer zone in America's Cold War imaginary.[2] These captive nations were seen as possible sites where Soviet power could be dismantled or at least diminished through aggressive American cultural infiltration.

Cultural infiltration—or the "infection" of the Soviet satellites with the ideals of American democracy—was set into motion by the 1958 US-Soviet Cultural Exchange Agreement, which allowed for the systematic bilateral exchange in different cultural arenas between the United States, the Soviet Union, and the countries of the Soviet bloc. Of course, the agreement had a political goal that aligned with the American Cold War agenda—it was to provide the means and resources for the deployment of cultural infiltration. The countries of the Soviet bloc were to be encouraged to seek independence from Moscow and develop a greater degree of nationalism. In other words, the United States was to "infect" Eastern Europe with its democratic culture (Richmond 2003). Travel restrictions were relaxed, and writers, artists, scientists, and journalists visited different communist countries and produced narratives of life behind the Iron Curtain.

One such project was documented by *Life* magazine. A special issue from September 13, 1963, was dedicated to the Soviet Union, recording "how Soviets really live." The editorial, titled "Why We Must Put Holes in the Iron Curtain," described the curtain as "an affront to human spirit" and called for the West to "prod and perforate it at any opportunity" (*Life* 1963, 4B). The editorial demanded increased cultural contact in the form of mass tourism and student exchange, concluding that "we must push our export of culture as aggressively as they do theirs; but every such skirmish helps breach the vicious curtain with the voice of art" (*Life* 1963, 4B). In other words, the magazine saw itself, and its own artistic agenda, as spearheading the project of "prodding and perforating" the Iron Curtain. It did so by espousing a tourist's perspective and offering a detailed, instructive guide to visiting the Soviet Union replete with maps, lists of tourist attractions, and a wide range of travel tips, very much in the style of popular travel guidebooks. The *Life* magazine tour of the Soviet Union was accompanied by attractive photographs of cultural events, colorful parades, appealing seascapes, culinary specialties, singers in exotic-looking costumes, and alluring captions such as "A stylish look all over the place," "Sweet girl grads of Alma-Ata," or "The Baltic blondes of Estonia hold to their ways." Both text and images imply a fascination with the Soviet other, with life in a country at once distant and suddenly accessible.

Just two months later, in November 1963, *Life* published a photographic travelogue of Eastern Europe under the title "The Faces of the Satellites," subtitled "*Life* photographer travels unhindered through Eastern Europe." The subtitle echoes American studies scholar Wendy Kozol's description of the narrative flow of a typical *Life* photo-essay as "a journey" that progresses "visually through time or space toward a solution" (1994, 43). In the case of this photo-essay, the satellite countries transform from "anonymous puppets" under "the iron grip of the Soviet Union" into individualized nations that "try to go into their own orbit" (Schutzer 1963, 114).

Bulgaria featured prominently on the pages of the magazine: taken by the prolific and well-known photojournalist Paul Schutzer, the photographs depict a poor and underdeveloped country, while the text describes a potential tourist destination open to cultural exchange with the United States: "Perhaps the most remarkable phenomenon in present-day Bulgaria is its bashful love affair with the West.... Contacts on the official level are improving too, especially with the U.S., apparently in hopes of opening new trade relations. Several U.S. exhibits and visiting artists were mobbed this year by Bulgarians" (Schutzer 1963, 114). Yet the visual narrative of life in Bulgaria presented on the pages of *Life* differs strikingly from the tourist guidebook of the Soviet Union published in September. If the Soviet Union is represented as a place to be "prodded" and appropriated through tourism, then Bulgaria seems to occupy a space yet to be approached and cultivated. More specifically, the photographs accompanying "The Faces of the Satellites" show a dejected, run-down, static reality suspended between backwardness and moderniza-tion, as if stuck in time, or better yet, as indolent and timeless.

A photograph bearing the caption "Children play behind crammed Sofia apartment house" features a modern apartment building dominating most of the distant background, only a glimpse of open sky visible in the upper right; dilapidated old houses, rugs hanging on primitive laundry lines, and scattered furniture occupy the middle ground; in the foreground, two chil-dren play on a makeshift slide. The sense of doom and entrapment is further underlined by the low vantage point, the odd triangular shape that binds the scene from above, and the grid of recurring diagonal lines that crisscross the pictorial field. The visual rhetoric of this photograph and several others showing Bulgarians at rest (a close-up of a woman field worker taking a nap is especially striking) recalls the pictorial strategies of nineteenth-century orientalist painting that constructs the other as idle, uncivilized, backward, and in a state of decay, while also available to the scrutinizing Western eye.

Crumb collected early issues of *Life* magazine, and he was likely famil-iar with its photo-essays, along with the visual and ideological messages inscribed by the magazine (Thompson 2012, 216–17). Crumb's visual diary of Bulgaria thus can be situated within the context of the narrative created by *Life* magazine as well as within the literary discourse of the time, which also echoed the general rhetoric surrounding Bulgaria. For example, John Updike's six-week visit in 1964 to the Soviet Union, Bulgaria, and Romania functioned within the framework of cultural diplomacy and cultural infiltra-tion. Updike's travels were fictionalized in a series of short stories that not only illustrated the practice of cultural exchange but, unlike the narrative in *Life*, also intimated its futility. Updike's protagonist, Henry Bech, is a writer who gets invited to travel behind the Iron Curtain "as an ambassador of the arts, to the other half of the world, the hostile, mysterious half" (Updike 2012, 43).[3] One of those stories, "The Bulgarian Poetess," was published in the *New Yorker* in early 1965 and contributed to Bulgaria's visibility in America. The vision Updike inscribes conforms to the Western traveler's gaze con-structed by the images in *Life*: Sofia is an enchanted place of the past with singing trees and flickering electricity, barely touched by modernization but rich in mausoleums, mosques, and obsolete trolley cars (Updike 2012, 44). This opening up of the Soviet Union and Eastern Europe to the American public and the increased artistic representation of life in the Soviet satellites through a consistent visual and textual rhetoric provide the historical and discursive framework within which we examine Crumb's encounter—literal and creative—with Bulgaria.

CRUMB'S BULGARIAN SKETCHBOOK

It is precisely during this thaw in American-Bulgarian relations that the twenty-one-year-old Crumb was sent to Bulgaria by the New York–based humor magazine *Help!* to draw a diary of his stay and sketch the "horrors of Communism." Harvey Kurtzman, the magazine editor and writer-cartoonist who founded *Mad* magazine in 1952, was familiar with Crumb's work. In the January 1965 issue of *Help!*, he published Crumb's "Harlem: A Sketchbook Report" and the first appearance of Fritz the Cat (Wells and Dallas 2014, 21). Kurtzman had heard Bulgaria described as "just like in *1984*," and he dispatched Crumb, like a war reporter, to document what Kurtzman perceived as an existing Orwellian society (Crumb 1989, x–xi). Crumb was already traveling through Europe on his honeymoon and on a tight budget at that, so when Kurtzman offered him $300 to take a trip to Bulgaria, he could not refuse (Crumb 1989, x–xi). Just over half of the comics he produced appeared in *Help!* in July 1965 under the title "Bulgaria: A Sketchbook Report."[4] The visual account published in *Help!* indeed compounds an image of a daily life permeated by ideological control and censorship, a civilization impoverished by the demand for socialist realism in every form of cultural production, and a sorry spectacle of urban modernity barely concealing its rural backwardness. Nevertheless, Kurtzman was disappointed by "the lack of sharp, biting humor in the sketchbook reports Crumb sent back . . . from Bulgaria" (Mouly 2005, 282).

Why was Kurtzman disappointed? Was this novel use of comics for a travel account expected to produce a new, untapped, provocative view of Bulgaria? Perhaps Crumb's portrayal is not as singular or revelatory as that: it at once confirms and resists the dominant narrative of "communist horrors" he was sent to report on and capture in images. In addition to documenting the "horrors of Communism," the sketchbook also inscribes a vision of Bulgaria as peculiarly attractive in its allegedly horrendous reality, a vision that ensnares the Western gaze through its own familiar devices, in an act of reverse infiltration. The "sketch" as a visual form or genre suggests a drawing done on the spot, a quick preliminary study, an outline or draft that is not fully developed and awaits completion. Crumb's sketchbook portrays Bulgaria as a space that is itself sketchy, perhaps even liminal, not fully defined or delineated, suspended between urban modernity and rural backwardness, between local demands and Soviet directives, between a glorious antiquity and a bleak present. Crumb's vision of Bulgaria might be said to borrow from the familiar rhetoric and structures of other cultural institutions—those of the tourist, the travel guidebook, and the postcard. This familiarizing strategy mediates the Bulgarian communist reality for a Western (American) audience.

In other words, Crumb adopts a Western traveler's eye and at the same time defies its dominant optics. On the one hand, his vision of Bulgaria borrows from the political rhetoric and representational strategies of the tourist's gaze, the travel guidebook, and the postcard as neatly captured by the photographic reportages in *Life* magazine. On the other hand, Crumb portrays Bulgaria as containing spaces and practices that resist, if not subvert, the American reader's notions of communist ideology and Cold War reality. What is at stake in Crumb's travel sketches then is the negotiation of a double viewpoint—a Cold War vision informed precisely by the photographic essays in *Life*, and a less ironic and more sympathetic sight that at once depicts and undermines what the American public expected to see.

Published in the July 1965 issue of *Help!*, "Bulgaria: A Sketchbook Report" at first glance appears to be a random collection of scenes of life in Bulgaria in a variety of contexts—from the street to the factory to the art gallery to the concert hall. It consists of sixteen panels and one photograph, situated across six pages, designed to imitate sheets torn off from an artist's sketchbook. (An identical layout was used for Crumb's "Harlem: A Sketchbook Report," which had come out in January 1965.) The panels selected by Kurtzman for "Bulgaria: A Sketchbook Report" do not portray any of Crumb's social interactions with Bulgarians but instead capture, as in a snapshot or postcard, pictures of communist reality, annotated by Crumb's humorous captions. The reader's experience of Bulgarian society is carefully structured as an illustrated tour. The sketchbook opens with a panoramic view of Sofia and arrival information in two panels. It continues by addressing transportation in the city in two panels, then zeroes in on men and women at work, and on five episodes in daily life that highlight the lack of consumer products. The journey closes with six panels that portray culture and entertainment in Bulgaria. From arrival to transportation to work to cultural events, the sketchbook takes the reader on a predictable route.

The title page of Crumb's sketchbook, on page three of *Help!*, doubles convincingly as a postcard that prominently labels its subject as Bulgaria, distilling the whole country into a single tourist attraction (fig. 5.1). The monumental, classicizing structure in the center stands in stark contrast to the diminutive and shabby houses that flank it and that persist through several of the other panels. Crumb's image is nearly identical to an actual photographic postcard from the same time period showing the same building from the same angle and likely from a comparable distance (fig. 5.2). The building is none other than the Bulgarian Communist Party Headquarters in Sofia, erected some ten years earlier and marking the capital's very ideological, cultural, and urban center, and as such constituting a prime sight on a tourist itinerary. In fact, *Help!* begins with Crumb's sketch of the party headquarters *and* a photograph of him standing in front of it, inserted as if to authenticate the artist's vision by documenting his presence precisely next to the sight he is sketching.

Crumb's drawing presents a building that dominates its surroundings, which in their dilapidated state would not take much to be overpowered. In addition to altering the scale of the buildings adjacent to the party headquarters (as seen in the postcard), Crumb has distorted the perspective so as to emphasize the vastness of the open—and by implication underdeveloped, one might even say rural—space. In reality, the square outside the party building was a busy thoroughfare that linked the neighboring buildings. It was also framed by imposing architecture that housed the most important government, administrative, commercial, financial, and cultural institutions in the country—the seat of the government, the People's Bank main office, the Central Department Store, and the mausoleum of Bulgaria's most celebrated communist leader, Georgi Dimitrov, alongside the ancient Roman forum and magnificent medieval churches, the Archaeological Museum, and the National Gallery. Crumb elides all of these significant sites and privileges the seat of political power.

That Kurtzman included Crumb's photographic portrait on the title page of the sketchbook, despite the visual repetition (the party headquarters is doubly present), demonstrates an awareness of the spatial and architectural significance of this concrete locale. Crumb's photo also embodies the tourist's practice of authenticating the experience abroad through postcards or snapshots of recognizable sights, a practice that in turn constructs or confirms those sights as tourist attractions (Culler 1988). In fact, foreign visitors in Sofia were expected and encouraged to have their photo taken in front of the party headquarters (Yanakiev 2012), thereby turning the building into an image to be "exported" abroad by tourists as emblematic of the country and

Fig. 5.1. R. Crumb, "Bulgaria: A Sketchbook Report," Copyright © Robert Crumb, 1965. All rights reserved.

Fig. 5.2. Postcard of the Bulgarian Communist Party Headquarters in Sofia, ca. 1960.

its political order. Further, that particular sight serves as an illustration to what a 1963 travel guidebook, *All of Europe at Low Cost*, describes as Sofia's "broad streets and avenues lined by Moscow-inspired modern architecture" (Ford 1963, 271).

Crumb's specific choice of the same postcard image for both the sketchbook's title page and for his personal photographic portrait functions on multiple levels. It highlights the singular importance of the Communist Party and recognizes the magnetic ideological power emanating from the party headquarters. More importantly, the sketch is easier for the viewer to read and understand as a postcard. It transforms the party headquarters into a mere tourist sight recommended by the travel guidebook. Crumb's opening image thus already neutralizes or at least familiarizes the potentially threatening communist reality. Curiously, Crumb's main source of income prior to his trip was designing greeting cards for the American Greetings Corporation in Cleveland, so one is tempted to also superimpose a "Greetings from Sofia" or "Happy New Year" message onto Crumb's opening image.

The bottom panel on the title page (fig. 5.1), also contained within a pictorial frame, appropriates the horizontal postcard format. The nocturnal, wide-angle view of a snow-covered Sofia adopts the trope of the panoramic prospect and insinuates the viewer in a central position, clearly indicated by Crumb's own inscription into the image—the newly arrived tourist in search of a taxi, as the caption explains. The city represented in this panel is dark, menacing, and again empty. The wide expanse of unfilled, literally white space invites the viewer to populate it with his or her own fantasy of it—a kind of tabula rasa for the visitor.

Unlike the panels on the title page affording carefully framed postcard vistas of a barely populated Sofia, the following fourteen borderless panels make up individual vignettes that exhibit Crumb's characteristic short, tight, systematic hatched lines. While the panels on the title page are formally more polished as drawings, the remaining ones are much sketchier in their execution and in their subject matter, which reveals the nitty-gritty existence of the Bulgarian people. The sketchbook's captions provide seemingly informative and practical glosses on those fundamental aspects of life in Bulgaria—from arrival and transportation to cultural events and practices.

When he describes his travels through Europe, Crumb clearly identifies his source of practical information, "that *Europe on $5 a Day* book" (Crumb and Poplaski 1998, 57). The way in which the deictic "that" familiarizes the guidebook co-opts the reader into the community of American budget travelers, which by 1964 had increased significantly. Arthur Frommer's *Europe on $5 a Day* had been published in 1957 and then updated and published again almost every year after that. The guidebook thus becomes an important intertext to Crumb's account of his European trip. Interestingly, Frommer's *Europe on $5 a Day* does not include any information on Bulgaria. It is another guidebook, Norman Ford's *All of Europe at Low Cost*, published in 1963, that provides Crumb with an entryway into Bulgarian geography, culture, and mentality. The guidebook's titular inclusivity—*All of Europe*—delivers its promise by including all of the Soviet bloc countries and the Soviet Union itself, while also testifying to their newfound availability. The guidebook instructs visitors that Sofia is readily accessible to the Western traveler headed east: "Sofia, the capital, is easily reached by rail from Yugoslavia and you can go by international train via Plovdiv to Istanbul" (Ford 1963, 271). While the guidebook delineates the geographic coordinates of the traveler's arrival in Bulgaria (Yugoslavia, Plovdiv, Istanbul), Crumb condenses his trip to three personal experiences—the Orient Express, the middle of the night, and taking photographs: "Dana and I took the *Orient Express* and got off in Sofia in the middle of the night. We spent a week in ... Bulgaria, took photos and I drew in my sketchbook" (Crumb and Poplaski 1998, 57; italics in original). The iconic Orient Express connected London to Istanbul via Paris, Milan, Belgrade, and Sofia, thereby situating Bulgaria's capital as the last stop before arriving in the "Orient." Crumb perhaps identifies (and italicizes) his particular mode of travel not only because it may have been familiar to his readers, but also because of its exotic name and itinerary.[5] Indeed, *Life* had already linked Bulgaria rhetorically to the Orient by stressing its geographic position.

The images of the Orient, darkness, and the Western gaze (as implied by both photography and sketching) underlie the visual rhetoric of the sketchbook with its cluttered frames brimming with dark cityscapes, drawn with nervous, energetic vertical hatched lines of black ink, populated by clusters of things modern and primitive, and animated by people in heavy coats who look more like peasants than urban dwellers (fig. 5.3). This vision is evoked by the guidebook as well: "Sofia: was a small, half Oriental town of mosques and churches that has burgeoned into a thriving metropolis" (Ford 1963, 271). Curiously, this sentence from the guidebook reads suspiciously like Crumb's text that accompanies panel 3: "Since the revolution, Bulgaria's capital has mushroomed into a modern metropolis." This shared rhetoric underscores the affinity between Crumb's text and the guidebook's informative commentary. The affinity between Crumb's comics and the guidebook is even more evident when we consider the generic attributes implied by the full title, "Bulgaria: A Sketchbook Report." A report presupposes the objective documentation of existing conditions for an audience that has a need for that information. Crumb's graphic narrative thus claims for itself a function not unlike that of the guidebook. Crumb's sketchbook was his constant companion, a place to "draw from real life," to transcribe his lived experience: "I lived on paper. I lived through the [sketch]book" (Hanson 2012, 31).

The caption to the top panel in figure 5.3 not only calls attention to Crumb's appropriation of the guidebook's language but also replaces the guidebook's innocuous verb "burgeoned" with the more suggestive verb "mushroomed," hinting at a familiar Cold War rhetoric that had seeped through American popular culture. More specifically, the mushroom-like form of the atomic explosion pervaded the comics of the 1950s and early 1960s. Crumb's caption might thus be seen as a textual nod to American and Soviet atomic power, or the recently prevented nuclear crisis over Cuba. The panel itself corroborates this reading: apart from the toxic-looking atmosphere and soot-covered buildings, the sky's outline against the dark houses approximates the shape of a mushroom cap.

At the same time, panels 3 and 4 (fig. 5.3) neutralize the threat by presenting the urban metropolis as an innocuous or laughable hodgepodge of the modern and the antiquated. The two borderless panels together present an absurdly anachronistic picture of modern life in Sofia, a picture already insinuated by *Life* magazine's photo-essays and John Updike's short story.

Fig. 5.3. R. Crumb, "Bulgaria: A Sketchbook Report," Copyright © Robert Crumb, 1965. All rights reserved.

Smokestacks and industrial buildings rendered in a thick, dense black in the background relegate the Western viewer to a nineteenth-century industrial cityscape, while in the communist visual lexicon they signal socialist progress: "the more smoke, the bigger the progress" (Botusharov 2012). In the foreground in panel 4, two steam trains, a freight train, an agricultural vehicle, and a horse-drawn carriage compete as modes of transportation and signs of progress. People in the two panels are dressed in a similarly motley and anachronistic manner—from a military coat to peasant outfits to a smoking suit and a top hat. The only space spared from the black appears in panel 4—the white arched structure likely exemplifies Sofia's ancient architectural heritage, which punctuates the city's actual center. This image gestures to an old and rich culture behind the modern veneer. It is, however, just as absurdly located—stuck between industrial buildings and steam trains; imprisoned between foreground and background, it serves as a visual pun on Bulgaria's own position between the Soviet Union and the West, as a kind of buffer zone. This visual pun is reiterated textually in the caption to panel 4: "Bulgaria is a poor country, but one can find a wealth of beautiful relics and ancient objects . . ." The caption plays on the meaning of "relics" and "ancient objects" to refer to the obsolete machinery filling Sofia's urban space.

The same obsolete and primitive appliances appear in the domestic space as well as in the agricultural arena (fig. 5.4, panels 7–10). Panel 7 on the top left side of the page, for example, depicts three women, seen from the back and in profile, as they stare at a display of domestic appliances, their spines bent to better examine the goods. The ironic caption "A wide variety of home appliances have been made available to the Bulgarian housewife" underscores the poverty and backwardness of a country whose "housewives" ogle primitive-looking housewares. Crumb's drawing, however, perhaps unwittingly, repeats both the visual and textual rhetoric of contemporary Bulgarian advertising and self-promotion to the West. In 1964–1965, *Resorts*, a Bulgarian magazine published in English and intended for a Western audience, featured on its pages precisely the domestic appliances drawn by Crumb: centrifugal dryers, washing machines, electric kitchen ranges, and electric hot plates. The image Bulgaria exported seems to have been exactly what Crumb saw and sketched.

Likewise, the bottom panel in figure 5.4 (panel 10) portrays women workers in a grain field, raising shovels above their heads, a dilapidated tractor or similar agricultural machine in the vicinity. Crumb's picture echoes that of *Life* photographer Paul Schutzer, who documents Bulgarian men and women resting after harvesting a grain field. Schutzer's text could in fact work perfectly as the caption to Crumb's drawing: "They had been working since dawn, the men scything, the women raking" (Schutzer 1963, 111). But while the

Fig. 5.4. R. Crumb, "Bulgaria: A Sketchbook Report," Copyright © Robert Crumb, 1965. All rights reserved.

Fig. 5.5. R. Crumb, "Bulgaria: A Sketchbook Report," Copyright © Robert Crumb, 1965. All rights reserved.

Life photographer traveled in Bulgaria during the summer and photographed the ongoing wheat harvest, Crumb visited for a week, in the dead of winter, as he states on the title page showing the snow-covered Sofia cityscape. The anachronism of this panel is obvious: Crumb could not have witnessed and reported on the harvest of a grain field. But such imagery—workers in a field—was prevalent in the communist propaganda of the period. As in the case of women ogling domestic appliances, Crumb again produces not a unique vision of Bulgaria but rather an image he is intended to see and capture. Crumb was perhaps in a way seduced by the experience designed and organized for him as a foreign visitor.

Next, the American traveler turns to the cultural realm, and his drawings become more incisive. Crumb's sketches take the reader on a tour of Bulgarian cultural establishments: a classical music recital, a bookstore, an art gallery, a ballet performance, a social dance, and a group of female fans of the Beatles. This panorama of cultural activities not only exposes the way in which ideology seeps into all forms of art but also reveals a civilized communist society that values culture and education. The caption to panel 11 reads: "Much of the culture of the new People's Republic is imported from the U.S.S.R." (fig. 5.5, panels 11–13). The panel itself depicts a classical music recital where the audience seems to not pay any attention to the performance. Comically, even the portrait of Karl Marx on the wall is turned away from the singer. Similarly, the gallery in panel 13 is filled with exemplary socialist realist artworks, among which is a painting of field workers with shovels in hand—not unlike the workers in Crumb's own panel showing women harvesting. The gallery visitors, however, are bored or indifferent: a woman on the left yawns as she goes by. In other words, these panels suggest a public not especially enthusiastic about the manifestations of communist ideology or Russian cultural influence, yet simulating support for it.[6]

In these panels, Crumb also depicts a Bulgarian who is capable of carving his or her own private space, perhaps temporarily relieved from ideology, within the public environment underpinned by formulaic slogans, official directives, and prescribed behavior. This space is suggested by the animated conversations taking place during the music recital in panel 11, as well as by the vibrant, cheerful dancers enjoying themselves in panel 15 (fig. 5.6, panels 14–16). Notably, a couple in the middle seems to be doing the twist despite the lack of space and despite what the caption states regarding the dance's acceptability. "We danced the twist freely," asserts the illustrious Bulgarian poet, playwright, and publicist Nedyalko Yordanov, who was in his mid-twenties at the time of Crumb's visit (Yordanov 2012). But he also recalls Communist Party leader Todor Zhivkov's circa 1963 public denunciation of

Western dances, especially the twist, and the song that people would chant in response, using Zhivkov's nickname: "Tosho the communist banned the twist" (Yordanov 2012). In Crumb's vision, the Bulgarian social body comes alive in private—a not so horrendous or unattractive portrayal of communism, and perhaps even an admiring observation of a people who make the best out of their bleak reality. As the art editor of the *New Yorker*, Françoise Mouly, says, "Crumb *loved* Bulgaria behind the Iron Curtain" (Mouly 2005, 282; italics in original). Crumb himself admits that he really liked Bulgaria. As he puts it in an interview:

> I guess what appealed to me was the lack of that constant, relentless commercial hype that you live with in the West. The oppressive aspect of the communist government was somewhat invisible to me, but they were clearly free of the commercial sales pitch that we are constantly subjected to in the West. The absence of that was refreshing. . . . People didn't look particularly happy but they didn't look any more miserable than the average run of proletarians in New York or Philadelphia, or any other place. (Wood n.d.)

Similarly, in an interview with the Bulgarian journalist Veneta Nikolova, Crumb explains that he enjoyed Bulgaria's rather different, devoid of consumerism, proletarian reality (Nikolova 2017).

Indeed, the final panel ends the sketchbook not with Crumb's departure but instead with his literal entrance into the frame and his figurative infiltration of Bulgarian culture as a Western presence. The panel depicts Crumb's own figure directing a lingering gaze at three smiling female Bulgarian students, with the suggestive caption, "Anyway, some Western influences do seep in . . ." This last panel adds a frivolous nuance to the idea of cultural infiltration, but it also suggests that the reverse mechanism might be at work as well. After all, it is the Bulgarian women who have caught the American's eye. Crumb's conclusive gaze trained on Bulgaria, and on women in particular, exposes the serious, political Western view of Bulgaria as a possessive and lascivious gaze. The ending of the sketchbook is consistent with Crumb's own sex-obsessed visual poetics as manifest in his character Fritz the Cat, who also appeared in several issues of *Help!* in 1965.

THE OTHER SKETCHES

The sketches that did not make the final selection for *Help!* depict the pervasiveness of communist ideology and political control. These sketches feature Crumb conversing with various state officials, students, and young professionals. A few sketches focus on the large-scale building enterprises intended to provide housing for Sofia's increasing population. One such panel presents a cityscape of modern high-rise apartment buildings next to one-story houses, laundry lines, wells, and outhouses, repeating almost exactly the imagery in Paul Schutzer's photograph of a "crammed" Sofia apartment building in *Life*. Another sketch comments on the uniformity of life under communism. The caption reads: "They really like uniforms. Everybody wears a uniform. There are two kinds," and then the panel shows a worker's uniform, a military uniform, and a child's. Strikingly, the child's uniform is not a school uniform, as was common, but a replica of the military. That the state controls even private lives becomes evident from a sketch ostensibly depicting a wedding, with the caption "I was invited to a wedding reception paid for by the state." The panel shows a large group of men and two women with low-cut dresses cavorting around a long table laden with bottles and wineglasses. Crumb himself observes the scene from the liminal space of a doorway, embraced by his guide, who pronounces: "You see? Communism is heaven on earth!" What Crumb sees and draws are no ordinary workers or mere statesmen but the faces of Stalin, Brezhnev, and other communist leaders (Stalin is dancing the Russian *kazachok*). The message of this panel is chilling—even weddings are not exempt from the regime's panoptic eye.

Another set of sketches excluded from *Help!* figure Crumb in dialogue with Bulgarians in different social situations. He meets with an art student who publicly exalts the "great opportunities available to artists in Bulgaria" but in private explains to Crumb that she has to comply with official party discourse about art in Bulgaria. Then the American visitor meets a young electrician who admits that people's lives are controlled and that he would get out if he could. At that moment a policeman walks by, and the young man begins praising the wonderful, happy life under communism. These strips reveal a younger generation of Bulgarians aware *and* critical of the regime's oppressive nature. That young men and women could see through ideological propaganda and simulate support for it subtly invalidates the idea of American (or Western) cultural infiltration and questions the victimization of the "captive nations" behind the Iron Curtain. It is not surprising then that these panels were omitted from the sketchbook—they certainly fail to tell what Harvey Kurtzman likely expected from a travelogue inflected by Cold War and Orientalist tropes.

A brief juxtaposition between *Life*'s 1963 photo-essay and Crumb's Bulgarian sketchbook will make evident Crumb's uniquely reflexive approach to representation, one that would inform his later autobiographical and quasi-autobiographical comics. *Life* presents a visual narrative in a grid format, supplemented by the photographer's textual account of his travels through Eastern Europe. The photographer's vision and voice compound a documentary record, whose objectivity—indeed witnessing power—is underscored by his absence from the photographs, save for one at the very start in which he poses portrait-style with a family in a Romanian village. Schutzer's absence from the rest of the pictures suggests that he has kept the distance necessary to remain objective and truthful to reality. Unlike Schutzer, Crumb inscribes his own figure multiple times, thus creating a destabilized position as viewer and chronicler, shifting vantage points between outside and inside, observation and participation, official ideology and private discourse, reportage and touristic impressions. Only three of the six panels that feature Crumb's unmistakable eyeglasses and moustache were included in *Help!*, and it is tempting to see the decision to omit the others as a silent corroboration of Cold War rhetoric. Crumb's portrayal of his own participation in various events and social situations offers a view of an American visitor charmed by, even comfortable in, communist Bulgaria, seduced, as he himself claimed later, by its lack of consumer culture and the simplicity of its proletarian reality. The shifting perspective further suggests Crumb's awareness of—and attempts to escape—his own ideological conditioning as a Westerner and prescribed experience as a tourist in a country behind the Iron Curtain. In his Bulgarian sketchbook, Crumb employs techniques that would later become prominent in the works of comics journalists such as Joe Sacco, and that would frame Crumb's own critical distance yet proximity to American consumer culture in the late 1960s.

NOTES

1. For a history of Bulgarian-American diplomatic relations, see Kostadin Grozev's *100 Years of Diplomatic Relations between Bulgaria and the United States* (2003). For a succinct account of Bulgarian history in the 1950s–1960s, see Crampton 2005, 190–94.

2. A 1961 Radio Free Europe announcement published in *Life* magazine best sums up the critical import of this zone: "The fate of these 80 million [captive] people is of vital consequence to the cause of freedom. . . . Eastern Europe is . . . the area of decision between Russia and the Free World. . . . These captive people pose a major obstacle to the Communist advance" (*Life* 1961, 99).

3. Joseph Benatov (2008) has argued that Updike's stories playfully examine a representative sample of widely shared perceptions of the communist other in order to expose the political propaganda on which these images rest.

4. Other comic strips from Crumb's Bulgarian sketchbook have appeared in a motley manner. A more systematic collection of Crumb's Bulgarian cartoons appears in *The R. Crumb Coffee Table Art Book* (Crumb and Poplaski 1998), which chronicles Crumb's artistic production in a visual (auto)biography of sorts.

5. In the 1950s, as recalled by the world-famous Bulgarian-born artist Christo, he and other students at the Sofia Academy of Fine Arts were often given weekend assignments to spruce up a vast stretch of rail track used by the Orient Express. In the face of Western powers, Bulgaria broadcast news of economic progress, over-fulfilled factory quotas, and enviable standards of living, but the reality had nothing to do with this simulated prosperity. Art students such as Christo tirelessly arranged shiny farm machinery and bales of hay in an attractive manner and to the best possible visibility from either side of the train, or covered unsightly equipment or buildings with tarpaulin that was tied up with rope and sometimes painted over with scenes of a modern, cheerful socialist countryside. Christo reminisces: "We positioned the machines to look dynamic. We told the peasants they should set this threshing machine clearly outlined on a little hill—as if on a pedestal" (Laporte 44).

6. For an in-depth exploration of the intricate strategies of simulated support and adaptation, see Alexei Yurchak, "The Cynical Reason of Late Socialism" (1997) and *Everything Was Forever, Until It Was No More* (2006).

WORKS CITED

Benatov, Joseph. 2008. "Looking in the Iron Mirror: Eastern Europe in the American Imaginary, 1958–2001." PhD diss., University of Pennsylvania.

Botusharov, Lyubomir. 2012. Interview by the authors, July 6, Burgas, Bulgaria.

Campbell, John C. 1965. *American Policy toward Communist Eastern Europe: The Choices Ahead*. Minneapolis: University of Minnesota Press.

Carlin, John, Paul Karasik, and Brian Walker, eds. 2005. *Masters of American Comics*. New Haven, CT: Yale University Press.

Crampton, R. J. 2005. *A Concise History of Bulgaria*. 2nd ed. Cambridge: Cambridge University Press.

Crumb, R. 1965. "Bulgaria: A Sketchbook Report." *Help!*, no. 25 (July): 3–8.

Crumb, R. 1989. *The Complete Crumb Comics*. Vol. 3, *Starring Fritz the Cat*. Seattle: Fantagraphics.

Crumb, R., and Peter Poplaski. 1998. *The R. Crumb Coffee Table Art Book*. New York: Back Bay.

Culler, Jonathan. 1988. "The Semiotics of Tourism." In *Framing the Sign: Criticism and Its Institutions*, 152–67. Norman: University of Oklahoma Press.

Ford, Norman D. 1963. *All of Europe at Low Cost*. Greenlawn, NY: Harlan Publications.

Grozev, Kostadin. 2003. *100 Years of Diplomatic Relations between Bulgaria and the United States*. Sofia: Embassy of the United States of America in Bulgaria.

Hanson, Dian. 2012. "Underground Treasures: A Wild Ride through R. Crumb's Sketchbooks." *Taschen Magazine* (Summer): 30–34.

Kozol, Wendy. 1994. *Life's America: Family and Nation in Postwar Photojournalism*. Philadelphia: Temple University Press.

Laporte, Dominique. 1986. *Christo*. Translated by Abby Polak. New York: Pantheon.

Life. 1960. "Swank Yank in Bulgaria: U.S. Reopens Legation." April 11, 57.

Life. 1961. "'We Will Bury You,' Says Nikita Khrushchev." December 15, 99.

Life. 1963. "In This Year of Change, a Long Visit with the Soviet People." Special Issue, September 13.

Lopes, Paul. 2009. *Demanding Respect: The Evolution of the American Comic Book*. Philadelphia: Temple University Press.

Maremaa, Thomas. 1972. "Who Is This Crumb?" *New York Times Magazine*, October 1. https://www.nytimes.com/1972/10/01/archives/who-is-this-crumb-crumb-happy-hooligan.html.

Mouly, Françoise. 2005. "It's Only Lines on Paper." In *Masters of American Comics*, edited by John Carlin, Paul Karasik, and Brian Walker, 278–89. New Haven, CT: Yale University Press.

Nikolova, Veneta. 2017. "Interview: Robert Crumb on Socialism, Democracy and 'Human Nature.'" Aired on BNT1, April 3.

Resorts. 1964. Vol. 6, no. 33.

Richmond, Yale. 2003. *Cultural Exchange and the Cold War: Raising the Iron Curtain*. University Park: Pennsylvania State University Press.

Roussev, Stilian. 2012. Interview by the authors, July 1, Burgas, Bulgaria.

Schutzer, Paul. 1963. "The Faces of the Satellites: *Life* Photographer Travels Unhindered through Eastern Europe." *Life*, November 15, 102–14.

Thompson, Ilse, ed. 2012. *Your Vigor for Life Appalls Me: Robert Crumb Letters, 1958–1977*. Seattle: Fantagraphics.

Tourist. 1965. Vol. 6.

Updike, John. 1965. "The Bulgarian Poetess." *New Yorker*, March 13, 44–51.

Updike, John. 2012. *Bech: A Book*. New York: Random House.

Wells, John, and Keith Dallas. 2014. *American Comic Book Chronicles: 1965–69*. Raleigh, NC: TwoMorrows.

Wood, Alex, ed. n.d. "Crumb on the Industrial Revolution." The Official Crumb Site. https://www.crumbproducts.com/pages/about/IR.html.

Yanakiev, Alexander. 2012. Interview by the authors, July 11, Sofia, Bulgaria.

Yordanov, Nedyalko. 2012. Interview by the authors, June 25, Burgas, Bulgaria.

Yurchak, Alexei. 1997. "The Cynical Reason of Late Socialism: Power, Pretense, and the *Anekdot*." *Public Culture* 9, no. 2 (Winter): 161–88.

Yurchak, Alexei. 2006. *Everything Was Forever, Until It Was No More: The Last Soviet Generation*. Princeton, NJ: Princeton University Press.

Chapter 6

WHERE THE ACTION IS

Crumb, Semiotics, *L'Écriture Féminine*, and Taste

JULIAN LAWRENCE

Critics and scholars have linked Crumb's work with the expressionistic and introspective modes of the confessional poets, the surrealists, and to early 20th century cartoonists.[7] Crumb is "a survivor not just of his personal demons but of a culture crippled by its own materialism, racism, bigotry, and neuroses."[8] His admitted misanthropy[9] "makes any analysis of his work examine a far more individualized ideology."[10]

I'm going to shift gears here for a moment...

-- and speak from an autobiographical grounding. I suggest Crumb's work is important for comics studies, but he is also an influence on me personally and creatively.

What follows is a little story I like to call:

the AUTHOR who CHANGED my LIFE!

September 1976... I'm a twelve year-old English lad starting high school at a French Jesuit college for boys in Gatineau, Québec, Canada...

TAPETTE!   VIVE LE QUÉBEC LIBRE!

TÊTE, CARRÉE!

•Me/moi
snif

I hope Mummy and Daddy are correct and this is helping to develop my character--

Naturally, I spent many lonely hours in-between classes in the school library, drawing and reading. One day, I was flipping through an issue of the French weekly Tintin Magazine from Belgium:

tintin
HIT PARADE

"The magazine for young folk aged 7 to 77"

He's drawing himself drawing a picture of a woman being squished by a bus!

Is this allowed?

Inside was an interview with a comic book artist I had never seen before: R. Crumb!

Fig. 6.1. R. Crumb, "The Phonus Balonus Blues" with "Where the Action Isn't,"
Copyright © Robert Crumb, 1968. All rights reserved.

Two weeks after discovering Crumb, I hunted for and bought my first underground comic from an Ottawa head shop. It didn't smell like the ones I bought from the local corner store... it smelled subversive.

Is this Crumb? It looks like Crumb, sort of...

I think it smells like marijuana!

I am going to analyse Crumb's one-page comic *The Phonus Balonus Blues/Where the Action Isn't.*[11]

Fabulous Furry Freak Brothers #1

I have chosen a one-page comic for two reasons: It's short; and the methodologies for analysis can also apply to multi-page narratives.

Following a broad overview/scan[12], Crumb's comic can be read as a multi-layered coded text by analysing it with the *Integrative Multisemiotic Model* (IMM). To begin, the *Space of Integration* holds the *Expression* and *Content Planes* together.

On the *Expression Plane* are *Language* (English) and *Images* (cartoons)...

-- as well as *Typography* (hand-lettered) and *Graphics* (hand-drawn).

SPACE OF INTEGRATION

LANGUAGE

IMAGES

TYPOGRAPHY

GRAPHICS

LEXICO-

VISUAL

Crumb's hand-drawn *Typography* and *Graphics* raise questions of practice. Investigations into the material handling [13] of the medium's writing, pencilling, and inking subvert theory whereby "(t)heory and text have been privileged as more valid and rigorous in articulating and constituting knowledge than 'practice.'"[14] As such, Crumb's visibly hand-drawn typography bridges the divide between language and image.

Thus, cartooning practices of singular authorship (l'auteur complet)[15] provide new openings of investigation...

-- within the liminal cross-hatchings of a thousand hash tags on the page.

On the IMM's *Content Plane* are the *Lexico Grammar* (slang, onomatopoeia) and the *Visual Grammar* (exaggeration, graphiation). Lexico and Visual Grammars operate together in Crumb's comic to "account for the activities and interactions that go on in each frame."[16]

Crumb's comics can present dual viewpoints of character and narrator, and this focalization[17] functions on the **Discourse Semantics** level.[18]

Portrayals of character and narrator provide two perspectives whereby authorship can be studied.

The language in the first panel's **Discourse Semantics** introduce the "calls to order"[19] that portray the protagonist as:

The **Discourse Semantics** for images, such as flies, contain clues the outsider smells bad, and is thus "disgusting" and "despicable".

Moving down deeper into the **Context Plane** is **Register**. This level answers questions such as "who is communicating (tenor), about what (field), and by what means?"[20] As such, Crumb is transmitting an urban fiction in the comics medium, and communicates "a world of contemptible and immoral human behaviour that might otherwise only be insidiously implied in media and culture."[21]

The *Genre* level can be defined as "cultural types of unfolding social action... which have features appropriate to their current social situation-- register."[22] The "goddamn animal" chasing a cartoon prey, as in the *Phonus Balonus* comic, brings to mind a *Tom & Jerry* or *Coyote & Road Runner* cartoon.

SPACE OF INTEGRATION

TYPOGRAPHY
LEXICO-GRAMMAR
DISCOURSE SEMANTICS

GRAPHICS
VISUAL GRAMMAR
DISCOURSE SEMANTICS

REGISTER

GENRE

IDEOLOGY

I suggest the comic also satirizes themes of unrequited love, such as *Krazy Kat & Ignatz Mouse.*

In a work of comics "the choices imply contextual motivations, consequences, and ideology: Even as we speak 'about' someone else, we are representing ourselves, our values, our desires, the ways we want to tell our story."[23] Indeed, the *Phonus Balonus Blues* is signed "by Crum the bum."

POW!

The comic ends with a surprise as the "sickening" character screeches to a halt. Confronted unpredictably by the girl, he flop-takes with a "plop" out of the panel; and the introduction of a third leering character creates circularity.

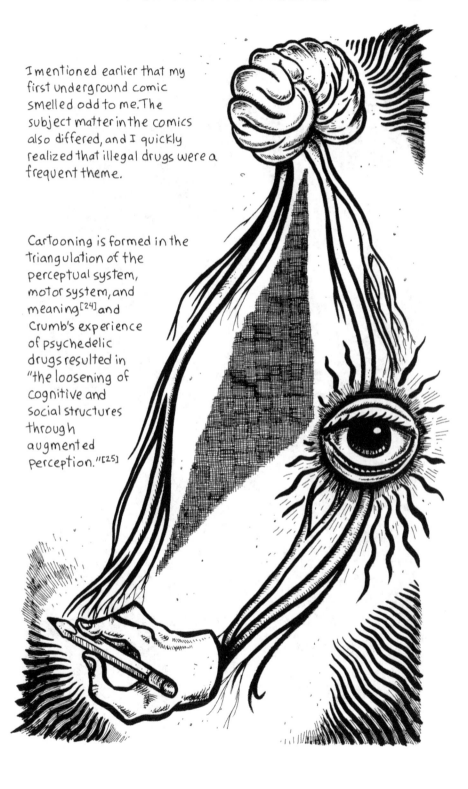

I mentioned earlier that my first underground comic smelled odd to me. The subject matter in the comics also differed, and I quickly realized that illegal drugs were a frequent theme.

Cartooning is formed in the triangulation of the perceptual system, motor system, and meaning[24] and Crumb's experience of psychedelic drugs resulted in "the loosening of cognitive and social structures through augmented perception."[25]

A six-panel strip titled **Where the Action Isn't** runs along the bottom of the *Phonus Balonus Blues*.

Where the Action Isn't presents at least five areas for discussion:

- Prediction of the future;
- Digitization of cartooning;
- The breakdown of the State's constructed order;
- Destruction of the father;
- Charles Crumb's fatal mental collapse.

Crumb's brother Charles kept journals that, by the end of his life, contained writing that resembles the short vertical lines that replace dialogue in *Where the Action Isn't's* penultimate panel.[27]

I will shift gears here once again, as discussions of dialogue and family lead to the mother tongue of l'écriture féminine (the feminine writing).[28]

It can be said that a certain irony emerges when analyzing Crumb's work through a feminist lens.

At a conference panel in 2012, scholar Hamza Walker said,

"There is an indoor place, a conscious and unconscious, where the gears are grinding... Drawing is a very conspicuous site of activity."[29]

BARRY   PANTER   BRUNETTI   CRUMB

L'auteur complet...

--artistic freedom...

-- and unconscious gestures...

-- open practices of l'écriture féminine (the feminine writing) whereby "ideas converge performatively through material production in ways that are not always fully knowable."[30]

Crumb says,

"A lot of this stuff I didn't realize when I was doing it what it was really about, you know, what it was connected to in my mind."[31]

The subjective semiotics of Crumb's cartooning unfold as narratives that disclose unconscious negotiations of identity.

In an interview with publisher Gary Groth, Crumb says that people have a

"fear of being abnormal. I am abnormal, but I've been copping to it for so long that it no longer has any liar quotient for me at all."[32]

THE STATE

He avoids "the sturdy but apparently banal perch of a moral stand"[33]...

-- and "equates consumerism, complacency, and conformity...

OUGHTA LOCK TH' SUN OF A BITCH UP!

OBVIOUSLY MALADJUSTED!

SICKENING!

MOTHER OF GOD!!

GODDAMN ANIMAL!!

-- with fascism and totalitarianism."[34]

OUGHTA LOCK TH' SUN OF A BITCH UP!

MO OF

A reading of *The Phonus Balonus Blues* that delves no further than the *Expression Plane* can be summed up as:

SPACE OF INTEGRATION

EXPRESSION PLANE

TYPOGRAPHY

GRAPHICS

VISUAL GRAMMAR

DISCOURSE SEMANTICS

"Crumb is fucking repulsive."[35]

Analysis interrupted by subjective standards of good taste ignores "the larger patterns of cooperation that allow these picture-stories to come into existence and be circulated."[36]

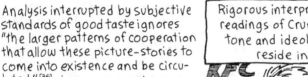

Rigorous interpretations and readings of Crumb's register, tone and ideology cannot reside in taste.

Bourdieu writes, "the dominant class constitutes a relatively autonomous space whose structure is defined by the distribution of economic and cultural capital among its members, each class fraction being characterized by a certain configuration of this distribution to which there corresponds a certain lifestyle." [37]

Thus, it can be suggested that a reader's perceptions of *The Phonus Balonus Blues* as degenerate will adhere to the conditions dictated by the class fraction they belong, aspire, or want to transfer out of. Reactionary rejection repeats "the calls to order ('who does she think she is?''That's not for the likes of us!') which reaffirm the principle of conformity --the only explicit norm of popular taste."[38]

In fact, the aforementioned "calls to order" are visible in panels one and two of *The Phonus Balonus Blues* when the crowd ("dominant class") accuse the outcast of being "twisted", "sickening", and a "goddamn animal." Crumb performs his identity "through images and consumption, rather than assigned by societal roles."[39] Crumb is a non-conformist who transcends class and taste and, as such, requires readings, analysis, and studies that go beyond social norms and hierarchies of taste.

TH'END

NOTES

Page 1

1. Fei 2007, 198.

2. Sabin 1996, 90.

3. Groensteen 2007, 119; and Uidhir 2012, 47.

4. Cixous 1995; and Taylor 2014.

5. Crumb 2013a, viii.

6. Crumb 2013b, viii.

Page 2

7. Nelson 2017; Rifas 2004; and Walker 2014.

8. Shannon 2012, 647.

9. Groth 1993; and Shannon 2012.

10. Nelson 2017, 147.

Page 3

11. "The Phonus Balonus Show of Some Really Heavy Stuff" was also the name of a 1969 art show featuring R. Crumb and other underground cartoonists. Additionally, Phonus Balonus was the name of the Roman general in the English-language animated version of René Goscinny and Albert Uderzo's *Asterix the Gaul*.

Page 4

12. Groensteen 2007; and Karasik and Newgarden 2017.

Page 5

13. Bolt 2007, 29.

14. Taylor 2014, 303.

15. Groensteen 2007, 119; and Uidhir 2012, 47.

16. Fei 2007, 208.

Page 6

17. Nelson 2017.

18. Fei 2007, 200.

19. Bourdieu 2010, 381.

20. Hofinger and Ventola 2004, 194.

21. Nelson 2017, 150.

Page 7

22. Hofinger and Ventola 2004, 194.

23. Hofinger and Ventola 2004, 196.

Page 8

24. Cohn 2012.

25. Jones 2007, 285.

Page 9

26. Jones 2007, 286.

Page 10

27. Zwigoff 1995.

28. Cixous and Calle-Gruber 1997; Cixous and Clément 1986; Cixous and Sellers 1994; and Taylor 2014.

Page 11

29. Walker 2014, 237.

30. Taylor 2014, 306. While it might seem, at first glance, that Crumb is a strange fit for this kind of analysis, it is notable that Cixous makes a distinction between meaning and author: "Speaking about 'male' authors, Cixous distinguishes the writing from its author, in line with foundational poststructuralist thinkers like Foucault and Barthes, and then removes physical sex/gender from what she considers to be the *femininity* embodied in and enacted by the text. If for Cixous the works of authors like Kafka or Joyce are examples of 'feminine writing,' then she can be seen as extending the concept and practice of 'femininity' beyond binary structures to take advantage of its plasticity as a flexible and pliable term whose tangibility does not simply gesture towards sex/gender but lies elsewhere" (Varino 2018, 294). Crumb discusses the affinity he developed toward Kafka while working on the book *Introducing Kafka*: "The more I worked on it, the deeper that affinity became until it almost got spooky after a while; I felt so close to him after a while, it was almost like I knew him" (Groth 1993, 134).

31. Zwigoff 1995.

Page 12

32. Groth 1991, 78.

33. Nelson 2017, 153.

34. Shannon 2012, 644.

35. Anonymous email correspondence, 2018.

Page 13

36. Rifas 2004.

37. Bourdieu 2010, 257.

Page 14

38. Bourdieu 2010, 381.

39. Bonnstetter and Ott 2011, 356.

WORKS CITED

Bolt, Barbara. 2007. "The Magic Is in Handling." In *Practice as Research: Approaches to Creative Arts Enquiry*, edited by Estelle Barrett and Barbara Bolt, 27–34. New York: I. B. Tauris.

Bonnstetter, Beth E., and Brian L. Ott. 2011. "(Re)Writing Mary Sue: *Écriture Féminine* and the Performance of Subjectivity." *Text and Performance Quarterly* 31, no. 4 (October): 342–67.

Bourdieu, Pierre. 2010. *Distinction*. London: Routledge.

Cixous, Hélène. 1995. "Castration or Decapitation?" In *Authorship: From Plato to the Postmodern; A Reader*, edited by Seán Burke, 162–77. Edinburgh: Edinburgh University Press.

Cixous, Hélène, and Mireille Calle-Gruber. 1997. *Rootprints: Memory and Life Writing.* New York: Routledge.

Cixous, Hélène, and Catherine Clément. 1986. *The Newly Born Woman.* Minneapolis: University of Minnesota Press.

Cixous, Hélène, and Susan Sellers. 1994. *The Hélène Cixous Reader.* New York: Routledge.

Cohn, Neil. 2012. "Explaining 'I Can't Draw': Parallels between the Structure and Development of Language and Drawing." *Human Development* 55: 167–92.

Crumb, R. 2013a. *The Complete Crumb Comics.* Vol. 3, *Starring Fritz the Cat.* Seattle: Fantagraphics.

Crumb, R. 2013b. *The Complete Crumb Comics.* Vol. 5, *Happy Hippy Comix.* Seattle: Fantagraphics.

Fei, Victor Lim. 2007. "The Visual Semantics Stratum: Making Meaning in Sequential Images." In *New Directions in the Analysis of Multimodal Discourse*, edited by Terry D. Royce and Wendy L. Bowcher, 195–212. Mahwah, NJ: Lawrence Erlbaum.

Groensteen, Thierry. 2007. *The System of Comics.* Jackson: University Press of Mississippi.

Groth, Gary. 1991. "A Couple of White Guys Talking: An Interview with Robert Crumb." *Comics Journal*, no. 143: 77–92.

Groth, Gary. 1993. "Robert Crumb Interview." *Comics Journal*, no. 180: 115–38.

Hofinger, Andrea, and Eija Ventola. 2004. "Multimodality in Operation: Language and Picture in a Museum." In *Perspectives on Multimodality*, edited by Eija Ventola, Cassily Charles, and Martin Kaltenbacher, 193–210. Philadelphia: John Benjamins.

Jones, Matthew T. 2007. "The Creativity of Crumb: Research on the Effects of Psychedelic Drugs on the Comic Art of Robert Crumb." *Journal of Psychoactive Drugs* 39, no. 3 (September): 283–91.

Karasik, Paul, and Mark Newgarden. 2017. *How to Read "Nancy": The Elements of Comics in Three Easy Panels.* Seattle: Fantagraphics.

Nelson, Brandon. 2017. "'Sick Humor Which Serves No Purpose': Whiteman, Angelfood and the Aesthetics of Obscenity in the Comix of R. Crumb." *Journal of Graphic Novels and Comics* 8, no. 2: 139–55.

Rifas, Leonard. 2004. "Racial Imagery, Racism, Individualism, and Underground Comix." *ImageTexT* 1, no. 1. http://imagetext.english.ufl.edu/archives/v1_1/rifas/.

Sabin, Roger. 1996. *Comics, Comix and Graphic Novels: A History of Comic Art.* London: Phaidon.

Shannon, Edward. 2012. "Shameful, Impure Art: Robert Crumb's Autobiographical Comics and the Confessional Poets." *Biography* 35, no. 4 (Fall): 627–49.

Taylor, Jacqueline. 2014. "From 'Or' to 'And': *L'Écriture Féminine* as a Methodological Approach for Fine Art Research." *Arts and Humanities in Higher Education* 13, no. 3: 303–11.

Uidhir, Christy M. 2012. "Comics and Collective Authorship." In *The Art of Comics: A Philosophical Approach*, edited by Aaron Meskin and Roy T. Cook, 47–67. Chichester, W. Sussex, England: John Wiley and Sons.

Varino, Sofia. 2018. "Liminal Politics: Performing Feminine Difference with Hélène Cixous." *European Journal of Women's Studies* 25, no. 3: 293–309.

Walker, Hamza. 2014. "Panel: Lines on Paper Lynda Barry, Ivan Brunetti, R. Crumb, Gary Panter." *Critical Inquiry* 40, no. 3 (Spring): 237–54.

Zwigoff, Terry, dir. 1995. *Crumb.* Sony Pictures.

Part III

CARTOONS OF SCRIPTURE, SELF, AND SOCIETY

Chapter 7

"AND ABRAM LISTENED TO THE VOICE OF SARAI"

R. Crumb's Pro-Feminist Interpretation of Sarah in the Bible

ZANNE DOMONEY-LYTTLE

The *Book of Genesis Illustrated by R. Crumb* purports to be a faithful, graphic interpretation of the book of Genesis from the Hebrew Bible.[1] Crumb states that Robert Alter's translation and commentary on the book of Genesis, among other sources, informed his work along with the King James Version (KJV), the Jewish Publication Society version (JPS), and a little-known academic volume by Savina J. Teubal titled *Sarah the Priestess: The First Matriarch* (1984). From those, Crumb produced his own interpretation together with annotations to explain his interpretive decisions. What resulted was a retelling of Genesis that placed women at the forefront of the narrative, subverted "traditional" readings of biblical stories, and challenged common perceptions of Crumb's troublesome history of representing women, which include accusations of misogyny, sexism, and racism.

This chapter will present an analysis of Crumb's representation of biblical women from the book of Genesis, through the lens of biblical reception history and interpretive approaches to reading text-image narratives using the work of Ann Miller, Thierry Groensteen, and Scott McCloud. I will argue that Crumb's remediation of the matriarch Sarah in his *Genesis Illustrated* presents to the reader a strong, dominant character who is cast as a potential leader in an otherwise traditionally patriarchal world, and that this treatment of Sarah is also reflected in other biblical women such as Eve, Rebekah, Rachel, and Leah. These renderings of biblical women subvert traditional biblical readings of the women of Genesis as well as expectations of Crumb as an artist. This is a result of Crumb's identification with "pro-feminism," a term that is as problematic as it is unclear.[2] However, defining Crumb's understanding of pro-feminism will illuminate his treatment of women in *Genesis Illustrated* and potentially challenge the accusations of misogyny and sexism that have followed Crumb throughout his career in two ways: first, by grounding Crumb's representation of women in his identification of pro-feminism, I demonstrate his intention to present women at the forefront of the narrative, and therefore as leaders of the story. Second, such positive representations demonstrate Crumb's nuance of thought with regard to gender and society. Where early representations of women in Crumb's work may appear sexist and misogynistic, his later work on *Genesis Illustrated* demonstrates some growth and development of his understanding of women and gender.

CRUMB'S PROBLEMATIC HISTORY WITH WOMEN

R. Crumb has often been accused of producing sexist or misogynistic work throughout his career.[3] His depictions of large, curvaceous women are often described as unflattering and unrealistic, and he is known for producing images of gratuitous sex scenes, many of which involve smaller, inferior men being dominated by strong females[4] but which also depict scenes of violence against, and sexual exploitation of, women. For example, Roger Sabin notes that of the underground comix culture prevalent in America during the 1960s and 1970s, the works of Crumb, S. Clay Wilson, and Spain Rodriguez frequently expressed misogynistic and sexist views, which resulted in those "three names being singled out for feminist criticism in this respect" (Sabin 1993, 224). Of those three names, Sabin continues, Crumb was the creator most likely to be criticized: "[I]ndeed, it has been argued that by example he set in motion a vogue for misogynist comix featuring violence against women" (224n12). In his defense, Crumb has often described his most lurid works as "all fantasy" (Arnold 2005) and has previously addressed such claims of propagating violence against women as follows:

> When I started doing it in '68 or '69, the people who had loved my work before that, some of them were shocked and alienated by it— especially the women, of course. I lost all the women. I'm not antifeminist. I like strong, independent women, like the matriarchs of Genesis—they ordered the men around. The sex-fantasy thing was a whole other side of myself, and when that started coming out, I could no longer be America's best-loved hippie cartoonist. (Widmer 2010)

In the same interview, Crumb describes women as "powerful and predatory," and in a later interview with National Public Radio, he explains that depictions of sex and women have, for him, always been personal and fetishistic, and only meant for his own enjoyment (Conan 2013). Quite what this means is unclear, but for many, reading depictions of women in Crumb's works of the 1960s and 1970s has been particularly challenging because his work draws upon the problematic issue of the male gaze, through which Crumb depicts women as subservient and objectified rather than as independent characters in their own right. Sabin notes that Crumb's work including women has "mellowed over the years" (1993, 224n12), and it also appears that Crumb has, for his part, reframed his understanding of women, gender, sex, and power in his comics by identifying as pro-feminist (Hignite 2006, 22).

As noted above (see endnote 2), Crumb does not clearly unpack what he means by the title "pro-feminist," although it is a term he uses to identify himself. He was also vocally critical of feminist movements in his earlier years,[5] suggesting that pro-feminism is not deeply connected to feminist perspectives. This is a perspective that, I argue, can be seen in some of his more recent work, *Genesis Illustrated* included. By identifying as pro-feminist, Crumb suggests that he understands masculinity to be oppressive to women (although he does not mention nonbinary/LGBTQ+ members of society), and he sympathizes with many of the causes associated with feminism, such as challenging unequal status between men and women; however, it does not appear that he actively pursues or involves himself in campaigns to further the feminist agenda.[6] Generally speaking, it is normally men who identify as pro-feminist, as they argue that feminism is a movement created by and for women, and to identify as a feminist for a cis-het male would be to colonize a women's movement and remove power and agency from the very group of oppressed people fighting to claim rights. For Crumb, then, identifying as pro-feminist is expressed through his visualizations of women in comic books, such as showing women in leadership roles and through positive characterizations. How well he expresses such representations is somewhat debatable and potentially reveals his misunderstanding or even basic understanding of gender politics.

Clearly, this definition and understanding of feminism (and, by extension, pro-feminism) is highly problematic: there is not one form of feminism but many, including liberal, radical, black, queer, and postmodern feminisms, and this diversity is reflected in the beliefs of men who identify as pro-feminist as well (Burrell and Flood 2019). However, one of the overarching viewpoints of pro-feminism is that it is a movement concerned with antisexism and antipatriarchalism. This is a view that, more recently at least, Crumb agrees and identifies with, and arguably has tried to incorporate into his remediation of Genesis.

In particular, Crumb has concentrated on depicting women as strong, story-leading figures in *Genesis Illustrated*, a move that is influenced in part by his dependence on Savina J. Teubal's *Sarah the Priestess*.[7] It is worth noting that within the circle of biblical hermeneutics, Teubal has been widely critiqued for failing to provide supporting evidence for her claims, as well as for situating modern feminist concerns onto ancient texts. The veracity of her work is not the concern of this chapter; however, Crumb's understanding and use of Teubal's work is important in ascertaining the context of his remediations.

TEUBAL, CRUMB, AND SARAH, THE FIRST MATRIARCH OF GENESIS

In her work published in 1984, Savina Teubal offers a perspective on the matriarch Sarah (who appears sporadically in Genesis 11:29–23:20) garnered from an archaeological, historical-sociological, and to an extent literary approach (Teubal 1984, xiv). Arguably based on a feminist reading of Sarah and the matriarchs, Teubal's thesis attests that Sarah is descended from a line of high priestesses and a matriarchal society, elements of which she brought with her when she left her homeland to marry and travel with Abraham (xv). Teubal reads Sarah as being of equal stature to and equal in importance with Abraham. Moreover, she contends that it is the narrative of Sarah (and later the matriarchs Rebekah, Rachel, and Leah) that propels the story forward, rather than that of their male counterparts:

> In the story of Abraham the narratives begin with an account concerning Sarah and Pharaoh and continue with this woman's trials in securing progeny. Finally, a whole chapter is dedicated to her place of burial. Of the forty-eight years of Abraham's life after Sarah's death there is no detail whatever. In other words, it is Sarah's role that furthers the story. (Teubal 1984, xv)

Within the book, Teubal revisits key scenes of Sarah's story that seem to be missing information or that are inconsistent with the rest of the narrative. In some cases, Teubal's approach is convincing and attractive, and it is easy to see why Crumb became so interested in this nontraditional approach to the matriarchs. In most cases, however, Teubal's thesis makes assumptions about inconsistencies in the biblical text without providing historical or literary evidence for support. By highlighting such inconsistencies, problems, and moments of erasure in Sarah's story, Teubal gets to her overarching hypothesis: that such gaps exist because the stories of the matriarchs and patriarchs of Genesis were written at a time when a patriarchal society was developing strength and power and was challenging and diminishing the power of the matriarchal culture that preceded it, and that this can be read in the texts of Genesis pertaining to the matriarchs/patriarchs. While the theory has not gained much academic support, Crumb was captivated by the ideas in Teubal's book (Conan 2013). As such, my analysis is concerned with Crumb's representation of the matriarchs, how he uses the tools of comics to construct their characters and stories concerning motherhood, and how this can be contextualized within the scope of biblical scholarship about women in Genesis.

SARAH THE PRIESTESS IN *GENESIS ILLUSTRATED*

Sarah first appears in Genesis 11:29, and her story is told sporadically across the next twelve chapters, ending with her death and burial in Genesis 23:20. She is introduced to the reader as Abraham's wife, and it is noted that she is barren (11:30). One of the most notable arguments in Teubal's study on Sarah is that the matriarch *chose* not to have children and was not barren. According to Teubal, this decision was linked to Sarah's role as a high priestess, details of which are vague but include representing a goddess in the ceremony of *hieros gamos*, as well as playing a part in the ecclesiastical community in her area. Traditionally, the role of high priestess in ancient Near Eastern traditions also encompasses certain political and social obligations such as acting as the spiritual head of the temple. However, because of Teubal's reading of the historical context of this story reflecting a time when matriarchal traditions are being usurped by patriarchal ideologies, Sarah's role as high priestess is erased from the biblical text to better reflect contemporary social situations; ergo, Sarah is described as barren rather than choosing not to have a child.

The first image we see of Crumb's version of Sarah reflects her barrenness and does not suggest Teubal's ideas of decision-making (see fig. 7.1). Taking center position on the page, the panel frames Abraham embracing his brother Nahor, with Sarah on the right holding a bowl of food, which appears to be bread, and on the left, Nahor's wife Milcah nursing a newborn baby surrounded by excited people. The symmetry of the panel contents

Fig. 7.1. Genesis 11:27–32, in R. Crumb, *The Book of Genesis Illustrated by R. Crumb*,
Copyright © Robert Crumb, 2009. All rights reserved.

suggests that this is a harmonious affair, but the look on Sarah's face suggests otherwise. Outside of the panel, in the hyperframe, is the text from 11:29. Within the panel in its own caption box is the text from 11:30: "And Sarai was barren. She has no child."[8] The panel is designed to emphasize the contrast of situation and emotion that the text indicates. The embracing brothers act as a divider between a scene of a happy family situation on the left, and the lack of one on the right.

Sarah is the opposite of Milcah, who wears her hair behind her neck and a dress with a geometric design on it. Sarah wears her hair over her shoulders and a dress with an organic, waved line. Where Milcah nurses a child, Sarah holds a bowl of bread close to her body. Where Milcah shows happiness and a concentrated gaze on her child, along with the people surrounding her, Sarah looks away, showing no interest in the scene. The caption box above Sarah's head, declaring her inability to bear a child, is in contrast to the unboxed text of 11:29, introducing the rest of the family.

Of special note here is Ann Miller's description of speech bubbles as "non-diegetic elements that intrude into the space of fiction" (2007, 97). The caption box is not a speech bubble, but Crumb has incorporated it in such a way that it visually intrudes upon the space of the visual story, signifying the intrusion of the newcomer in Sarah's space. The position of the text box above her head is also reminiscent of a thought bubble, as if her supposed barrenness is on her mind. To the reader, it might as well be a neon sign above Sarah screaming "infertile."

The panel with Milcah and Sarah is larger than the others on the page and is in a central position. The deliberate configuration of panels conveys what Crumb considers to be the most important point: the introduction of the family of Abraham, and the fact that Sarah is barren and childless. Further, the position of that panel, which is themed around family and new life, contrasts with the contents of the panel beforehand, which is the scene of Haran's funeral and bereaved mourners, and of the succeeding panel, which shows a departure: both from the happy family scene just witnessed, and from the hometown of Abraham and his family.

Crumb has configured this page to imply that the introduction of Abraham and his family is of central importance. Most importantly, however, Crumb has composed this introduction to Abraham and Sarah in such a way that the reader is left under no illusion that (a) Sarah is barren and childless; (b) this contrasts Sarah with the rest of the family; and (c) Sarah is not pleased about her situation. The scene marries the issues of fertility and child-rearing to Sarah, so that every time Sarah appears in Genesis from this point until the birth of Isaac, the reader sees that neon sign above

her head screaming "childless." To reinforce this, this page is partnered with
the beginning of Genesis 12, when Abraham is first promised descendants.
Crumb is using the perifield[9]—the field of vision within the viewer's periphery—to contrast themes of fertility and infertility against each other
in panels and across pages. Moreover, the focus on Sarah's infertility over
Abraham's narrative is the beginning of Crumb's attempt to locate Sarah
at the center of the Abrahamic narrative in general, a move that continues
across Genesis 16 and 18.

Genesis 16

Sarah does not reappear in any significant part of the story until Genesis 16
(see fig. 7.2). The chapter starts with a reminder that Sarah is childless: "Now
Sarai, Abram's wife, bore him no children" (16:1). The story concentrates
on Sarah's alleged quest for a child and the consequences of her decision
to fulfill that quest through her slave girl, Hagar. It also contains the first
record of Sarah speaking (16:2). Of note here is the visual contrast between
Sarah and Hagar: Sarah is old, stern, and powerful. Her head and body are
covered; in contrast, Hagar is young with short black hair on show, and
her simple robes show her figure, especially when pregnant. The simple
garment is a visual reminder of Hagar's subservient status to Sarah but is
also a visual marker that Hagar is the opposite of Sarah in status, looks, and
childbearing abilities.[10]

   Maintaining a structure wherein the narrative directs the design of the
panels, rather than the panels dictating how the story unfolds,[11] Crumb uses
the principles of spatio-topical coding to his advantage: in other words, the
pattern of frame shapes and sizes is designed to reflect the emotional content
of this chapter—one of the clearest ways to embed emotion in a comic book
(McCloud 1993, 94–117; Eisner 2008, 24–26). For example, the first panel is
a close-up of Sarah. Her eyes are looking behind her, creating a diagonal
that the reader follows to the figure of Hagar, who is on her knees working
behind Sarah.

   The composition in this panel indicates Hagar's subservient status to
Sarah, her mistress. It is repeated in the second panel, where Hagar stands
at a distance behind Sarah, making her appear smaller than the dominant
matriarch and her husband. In almost every panel where Sarah appears
with Hagar, Hagar appears smaller than her mistress. Also of note, Hagar is
kneading bread in a large bowl in the first panel, which is a recall to when
the reader first meets Sarah, who likewise holds a bowl of bread. In this panel
it is Hagar who makes the bread, which is symbolic of her conceiving and

Fig. 7.3. Genesis 16:3–6, in R. Crumb, *The Book of Genesis Illustrated by R. Crumb*,
Copyright © Robert Crumb, 2009. All rights reserved.

carrying a child for Sarah to own, another example of *tressage* or weaving visual connections across the story.

In the third panel illustrating *Genesis* 16, narrative voice-over dominates the text, as the narrator describes Sarah giving Hagar to Abraham "as a wife" (fig. 7.3). The pairing of panels on this page signals that this "marriage" should be understood as ritualistic in the sense that, in the initial panel, Sarah stands over the joining of Abraham's and Hagar's hands, as if presiding over a marriage ceremony, and physical in the sense that, in the next panel, Abraham and Hagar are pictured in a sexual embrace, consummating their "marriage." In the background, there is a large, rounded vase, which is often associated with the womb, pregnancy, or fertility in general. In both panels, Hagar is submissive, as indicated by her smaller stature, her dropped gaze, and the physical dominance of Abraham in the consummation scene.

Some time has passed between the scene of conception and the following panel. Hagar is clearly pregnant, and in a reversal of the opening panel of this chapter, this time it is Sarah in the background and Hagar who is physically dominant. Pregnancy and fertility in Crumb's eyes are enough to elevate a woman's status in the texts of Genesis. Crumb has purposefully drawn Sarah smaller. She sits in the doorway of a tent as Hagar proudly walks past, holding her pregnant stomach. This panel is captioned with 16:4, "and when she saw that she had conceived, her mistress seemed diminished in her eyes."

Again, Crumb includes an empty basket, similar to one used to carry food or bread. It hangs above Sarah's head, in a callback to the first two panels of Genesis 16 and Genesis 11:29. Crumb uses this as a symbol to signify Sarah's lack of child, and it continues to pop up. He depicts Sarah's indignation by a white aura around her body against a dark background, as if her anger were emanating from her frame, when Sarah confronts Abraham. This aura is drawn negatively in spikes that point toward Abraham.

The background then turns to total blackness when an angry Sarah exclaims at an annoyed Abraham, "Let the Lord judge between you and me!" There is no light or joy in Sarah's tone. Abraham's eyes are squeezed tightly shut in this panel, as if by not being able to see Sarah, he cannot hear her. Sarah's final appearance in this chapter also closes the page and contrasts with the marriage scenes that opened the page. Sarah blessing the union of Abraham and Hagar after he "heeded the words of Sarai" has turned to become Sarah harassing Hagar, forcing her to flee from the union and her home.

The design of the whole page neatly showcases the emotional aspects of the narrative.[12] It moves from a place of giving/security, to physical touch/intimacy, to distress (from Sarah) and contempt (allegedly, from Hagar), to anger (from Sarah) and frustration (from Abraham). It ends in Sarah venting her emotions, "harassing" Hagar and banishing her. Hagar's own situation is upended across the panels, moving from a place of marriage and security to isolation and a quest for survival. Crumb has successfully utilized the resources of comic-making by using the page as a single unit to tell the emotional cycle of the story of Sarah and her initial solution to providing Abraham with a child within the perifield for the reader. Furthermore, it again positions Sarah as the central character of this arc who is given agency and direction, subverting the original texts of the biblical Genesis wherein Sarah is often read as no more than a passive character.

Genesis 18

In Genesis 18, the narrator begins by describing Abraham's location at the door of his tent in the heat of the day, when three men appear before him (fig. 7.4). Abraham springs to his feet, offering hospitality to the strangers and ordering Sarah to make bread (18:1–5). Sarah has visibly aged after her appearance in Genesis 16; she sits on the floor, working at what might be a loom. The rounded vase makes an appearance in the corner of the panel, next to which sits a basket, similar to the one held by Sarah in previous panels.

The same vase and basket appear in the panel relating to Genesis 18:8, which shows the strangers sitting down to eat. Similar to their appearances in earlier chapters, Crumb uses the items as symbols that the promise of a child for Sarah and Abraham will be fulfilled—the basket will be filled and the vase will hold water, or life. The pronouncement of a child for Sarah is divided over three smaller panels that appear in the second row, the central position of the panel grid, centering the promise of a child on the page. Once the visitor has declared that Sarah shall bear a son within a year, Crumb depicts Abraham's surprise using exclamatory marks that emanate from his shocked facial expression. In complete contrast, Sarah is shown in the next panel, in the bottom row of the grid, with a hand to her face as if in deep thought. She shows little emotion—certainly not shock like Abraham; instead, her body language is such that her arm is curled protectively over her stomach, indicating that there is truth in the pronouncement. Once again, the corner of a basket appears in the edge of the panel.

In this panel, Crumb uses a thought bubble to identify Sarah's thoughts: "Now that I'm withered, shall I have pleasure, and my husband so *old*?!" The thought bubble positions the reader in a unique position to comics, because the text implies that Sarah speaks the words out loud, to herself (the NRSV, for example, states: "So Sarah laughed to herself, saying, 'After I have grown old, and my husband is old, shall I have pleasure?'"), but with the use of a

Fig. 7.4. Genesis 18:1–6, in R. Crumb, *The Book of Genesis Illustrated by R. Crumb*,
Copyright © Robert Crumb, 2009. All rights reserved.

thought bubble, Crumb implies that Sarah thinks these thoughts to herself. Therefore, the reader is involved in her thought process, and we become privy to Sarah's innermost voice. When this is paired with the next panel, where the visitor questions why Sarah laughed and said "shall I really give birth, old as I am??" the implication is that the visitor can also read her thoughts, or in fact hear them. If the visitor is, as suggested, an embodiment of God, then the reader is given the same status as the divine by being allowed to read Sarah's thoughts.

On the next page, the visitor continues to respond to Sarah's reaction. In a callback to 16:5, Crumb replicates the use of an angry aura, white on black emanating from the figure as he speaks, directed toward Abraham, who cowers into the frame, diminished against the tall, angry visitor. Although his reprimand is directed toward Abraham, it is Sarah who is shown in full profile in the next panel, visibly shaking as she denies laughing. She is not seen again in Genesis 18. The arc of childbearing is completed in Genesis 21, which is the fulfillment of the promise to Sarah and Abraham from God to provide them with a child.

REPRESENTATIONS OF SARAH IN *GENESIS ILLUSTRATED*

Initially, the overriding portrayal of Sarah in Crumb's interpretation of Genesis is one of a dominant, powerful woman and not a domineering, controlling woman. Visual and textual analysis of Sarah's story in relation to motherhood presents a character who is strong willed, forceful, and clever. She understands the importance of her role in God's covenant with Abraham but also harbors her own ambitions to become a mother. While this is not always the case, the narrative of Sarah's quest for motherhood between Genesis 16 and 21 is certainly told with Sarah at the forefront of the dialogue, action, and power relations between herself, her husband, and her slave Hagar.

This representation of Sarah, Abraham, and Hagar is a nontraditional reading of the texts of Genesis, and it reflects Crumb's interpretation of the text as well as the sources he used to shape his text. Most significantly, his remediation reflects the influence of Teubal, especially in terms of presenting Sarah as a dominant character and Abraham as a passive, weak character. Even so, I do not think that Crumb presents Sarah as a high priestess throughout these passages in any way, shape, or form. Being a strong, dominant leader does not equate to being a high priestess, but Crumb's reluctance to depict Sarah in that role is probably connected to his desire to faithfully reproduce the text of the Bible. Because Sarah never appears as a high priestess in the biblical text, it is almost impossible for Crumb to present her as such in his remediation without offering further explanation to the reader, which would go against his aim of allowing the text to stand as it is and would demonstrate external influences to the reader much more obviously than Crumb would want.

The idea of Sarah as dominant and Abraham as passive also goes against the more traditional idea of Abraham as the patriarch, the father of nations, who is supported by his wife, nominally a secondary character in the text. Another challenge to traditional interpretations of Genesis is the fact that Hagar is also portrayed in a more significant light in Crumb's work than elsewhere, especially in terms of giving a face and a prominent visual role to a slave, who ordinarily occupies and represents the margins of society. While Hagar is still somewhat marginalized within the visual representation of her story, Crumb attempts to depict her as a woman who has a happy ending despite the wrongs done to her by visually connecting her to Sarah at the end of Genesis 21:20–21, where she presides over Ishmael's marriage. The visual links suggest that as everything turned out well for Sarah, it also turned out well for Hagar.

One topic that I have not yet discussed is whether or not Crumb can be accused of adhering to a particular stereotype of a Jewish woman in his representations of Sarah, a question that would apply to other women in his remediation of Genesis as well. Has Crumb drawn Sarah as dominant and in control, or is she domineering and controlling? If the latter, can Sarah's character be read as that of an overbearing Jewish woman or, indeed, a stereotypical Jewish mother? As Lois Braverman notes, the stereotype of a Jewish woman (and a Jewish mother in particular) brings to mind ideas of women who are heavily involved in their children's lives; who are controlling, domineering "pushy, loud, seductive, materialistic, guilt-inducing," especially with respect to their sons (1990, 10). Given that in American popular culture this is a stereotype created and propagated during the 1960s, when Crumb began his career in California, it is safe to surmise that Crumb would have been aware of it (Ravits 2000, 4).

In that respect, it is not impossible that he consciously or subconsciously drew the matriarchal characters in adherence to those stereotypes. Sarah and the successive matriarchs Rebekah, Rachel, and Leah were, after all, the first Jewish mothers in the Bible. Because Crumb has not distanced himself from the stereotypes he knows to exist, this allows readers to engage with those stereotypes should they interpret the characters that way in *Genesis Illustrated*. I do not read the matriarchs as stereotypes of Jewish women; rather, I read them through the lens of Teubal's theories, which means they are powerful, in control, and dominant as pro-feminist visions of women. Crumb's eagerness to represent the matriarchs as dominant creates a tension in which these representations can also be interpreted as perpetuating stereotypes of Jewish women. This tension is underscored by Crumb's suggestions of Jewish ethnicity in his representations of the matriarchs and originates partly through the history of Christian reception of the biblical texts, in which the ethnicity of the characters—assumed to be historical figures—has been a source of anxiety.

DRAWING CONCLUSIONS

Crumb's pro-feminist portrayal of the matriarchs contradicts what many believe him to be: he has often been described as misogynistic, sexist, racist, and sexually perverse. He can also be accused of adhering to stereotypes of strong women by often portraying Sarah as a domineering and controlling figure rather than a dominant figure in control. However, the fact that her character can be read in both ways highlights Crumb's ambiguous idea of pro-feminism, in which he draws women through a man's eyes rather than stepping into a woman's shoes.

In this sense, Crumb's unwillingness to identify as feminist and his sympathy with the feminist cause encourages readers of his *Genesis Illustrated* to believe that women had more control than they actually did, and it is a reminder that even if we want to read them as women in control of their own destinies, their stories are still bound by the patriarchal system in which Genesis was originally written, and in which it is still received.

Crumb's *Genesis Illustrated* in particular shows the power that image has over word. As was his intention, Crumb remains "faithful" to the biblical texts—he does not leave out any story, character, or image presented in the versions of the Bible that he consulted as sources. However, while Crumb has not changed anything textually, he has added layer upon layer of suggestion, emotion, and interpretation through the addition of images. In that respect, he has literally given a face and voice to each character, and they have come to life, bringing the text with them.

As with any adaptation or interpretation of a sacred text, Crumb's *Genesis Illustrated* and other biblical comics should be considered cultural markers. *Genesis Illustrated* documents what its creator holds to be of value, and also often reflects societal perceptions. For example, Crumb wanted his Genesis to portray Sarah as a strong woman from a high priestess tradition, but instead he has presented us with a woman who often appears vulnerable, upset, angry, and unsure of her status in Abraham's world. This ambiguous portrayal of a feminist reading of the Bible arguably reflects Crumb's own understanding and interpretation of pro-feminist ideology, which is itself a problematic notion that truly fails to take into account intersectional identities or power dynamics between genders. Perhaps the ambiguity of pro-feminism as an ideology is why Sarah is herself an ambiguous character, unsure of her place in a man's world.

One might argue that credit should be given where credit is due to Crumb because *Genesis Illustrated* is at the least an attempt to re-present biblical women in stronger positions than the text actually suggests. However, by attempting to refashion Genesis in response to a shift in cultural notions of gender, Crumb's depiction of women is somewhat confusing to the reader, who is never sure if they are strong, independent women or nagging, mouthy matriarchs.

Finally, the tools of comics used by Crumb open Genesis to layers of interpretation that text alone cannot support. Comics creators are in that respect simultaneously interpreters and open to interpretation (Alderman and Alderman 2011, 36), and depending on how they are read, text-image narratives allow for different readings of the text to emerge that are as meaningful as other critical readings of ancient texts such as the Bible.

On that point, Crumb's *Genesis Illustrated* is not just a cultural marker but a marker in biblical reception. The history of the interpretation of the Bible has shaped our culture profoundly, and ignorance of the Bible leads to ignorance of significant cultural products from Renaissance art to Victorian novels, and now to biblical comics. Along with other biblical comics, Crumb's remediation of *Genesis Illustrated* continues the work of interpretation and reception in biblical exegesis, exploring the boundary crossings between ancient text and modern popular culture and regenerating what is, after all, a very old text indeed.

NOTES

1. "And Abram Listened to the Voice of Sarai," from this chapter's title, is taken from Genesis 16:2. Unless stated otherwise, such as when I quote from R. Crumb's *The Book of Genesis Illustrated by R. Crumb* (hereafter shortened to *Genesis Illustrated*), all biblical references are from the New Revised Standard Version of the Bible (NRSV).

2. Crumb does not clearly unpack what he means by "pro-feminist," although it is a term with which he identifies (see Hignite 2006, 22). Cues from other interviews (e.g., Domoney-Lyttle 2018, appendix A) indicate that while Crumb supports and sympathizes with many of the causes associated with feminism, he does not actively pursue or involve himself in campaigns to further the feminist agenda, because feminism is a movement created by and for women. Men who partake in feminist movements can themselves be

deemed to be taking power from or colonizing women's movements, a move that some men wish to avoid. Identifying with pro-feminism is one way to do this.

3. For example, Crumb canceled a scheduled attendance at a comics/film festival in Australia in August 2011 after newspaper reports emerged in which Crumb was accused of being "sick and deranged" by several groups, including sexual assault crisis groups. For a fuller picture and an interview by Crumb on the incident, see Groth 2011b.

4. More recent examples include a two-page strip of Adam and Eve entitled "Our First Parents," which depicts Eve as an object in Adam's gaze as soon as he consumes the forbidden fruit. This strip was one of the triggers for Crumb deciding to draw the entirety of Genesis because he was "never fully satisfied with the results of those drawings and so experimented with the idea of drawing Adam and Eve in a straightforward way" (Domoney-Lyttle 2018, 74). See also Crumb and Poplaski 2005, 46–47.

5. Sabin notes that Crumb responded to accusations of sexism by suggesting that feminism was "analogous to fascism" and arguing that he had a right to present his opinions on any matter through text and image (1993, 224n12).

6. For a general overview of the qualities of "pro-feminism," see Burrell and Flood 2019.

7. For a more thorough discussion on Crumb's reading of Teubal, see Groth 2011a, 17–69.

8. Prior to Genesis 17:5–15, Sarah is called Sarai and Abraham is called Abram in the biblical texts. Unless quoting biblical text, I will refer to both characters as Sarah and Abraham to avoid confusion.

9. The perifield, or *périchamp*, is a term introduced by Benoît Peeters that describes how each panel is read with other panels in visual periphery. Therefore, panels are not read alone but along with neighboring panels (Peeters 1998, 41–42).

10. Athalya Brenner-Idan (2015) points out that often, pairs of women in the Bible are written in such a way that they complement each other—one woman has something the other does not—so that the two women when combined make a perfect, whole woman. Crumb's treatment of Sarah and Hagar is a visual representation of this.

11. Narrative-dominant forms of comic books are either "conventional use" (a regular grid of frames) or "rhetorical use" (a pattern of frame shapes and sizes that reflect the demands of the story being told in the comic book). Crumb makes use of conventional narrative-dominant grids in *Genesis Illustrated* that lend the story a systematic and logical framework through which to read the characters (Miller 2007, 86).

12. Thierry Groensteen's understanding of the multistage multiframe is that the page itself constitutes a single unit with the narrative of the comic book (hyperframe) but that other units of information—strips, panels, double-page spreads, and the comic book as a whole—are multiframes. Multistage multiframes are "systems of panel proliferation that are increasingly inclusive," and "the multiframe is the sum of the frames that compose a given comic," which include the sum of the hyperframes within each comic book (Groensteen 2007, 30–31).

WORKS CITED

Alderman, Isaac M., and Christina L. Alderman. 2011. "Graphically Depicted: Biblical Texts in Comic Form." *ARTS: The Arts in Religious and Theological Studies* 22, no. 4: 22–36.

Arnold, Andrew D. 2005. "R. Crumb Speaks." *Time*, April 29. http://content.time.com/time/arts/article/0,8599,1055105,00.html, accessed May 28, 2019.

Braverman, Lois. 1990. "Jewish Mothers." *Journal of Feminist Family Therapy* 2, no. 2: 9–14.

Brenner-Idan, Athalya. 2015. *The Israelite Woman: Social Role and Literary Type in Biblical Narrative*. London: Bloomsbury T&T Clark.

Burrell, Stephen R., and Michael Flood. 2019. "Which Feminism? Dilemmas in Profeminist Men's Praxis to End Violence against Women." *Global Social Welfare* 6: 231–44.

Conan, Neal. 2013. "Genesis: R. Crumb Illustrates the Bible." *Talk of the Nation*, National Public Radio, June 17.

Crumb, Robert. 2009. *The Book of Genesis Illustrated by R. Crumb*. London: W. W. Norton.

Crumb, Robert, and Peter Poplaski. 2005. *The R. Crumb Handbook*. London: MQ Publications.

Domoney-Lyttle, Zanne. 2018. "Drawing (non)Tradition: Matriarchs, Motherhood and the Presentation of Sacred Texts in *The Book of Genesis, Illustrated by R. Crumb*." PhD diss., University of Glasgow.

Eisner, Will. 2008. *Comics and Sequential Art: Principles and Practices from the Legendary Cartoonist*. New York: W. W. Norton.

Groensteen, Thierry. 2007. *The System of Comics*. Translated by Bart Beaty and Nick Nguyen. Jackson: University Press of Mississippi.

Groth, Gary. 2011a. "R. Crumb: The Genesis Interview." *Comics Journal*, no. 301: 17–69.

Groth, Gary. 2011b. "Robert Crumb, Live Online: The Interview That Didn't Happen." *Comics Journal*, October 31. http://www.tcj.com/crumb-and-groth-live-online/, accessed May 28, 2019.

Hignite, Todd. 2006. *In the Studio: Visits with Contemporary Cartoonists*. New Haven, CT: Yale University Press.

McCloud, Scott. 1993. *Understanding Comics: The Invisible Art*. New York: Harper Perennial.

Miller, Ann. 2007. *Reading Bande Dessinée: Critical Approaches to French-Language Comic Strip*. Chicago: Intellect Books.

Peeters, Benoît. 1998. *Case, planche, récit: Lire la bande dessinée*. Paris: Éditions Casterman.

Ravits, Martha A. 2000. "The Jewish Mother: Comedy and Controversy in American Popular Culture." *Jewish American Literature* 25, no. 1: 3–31.

Sabin, Roger. 1993. *Adult Comics: An Introduction*. London: Routledge.

Teubal, Savina J. 1984. *Sarah the Priestess: The First Matriarch of Genesis*. Athens, OH: Swallow Press.

Widmer, Ted. 2010. "R. Crumb: The Art of Comics no. 1." *Paris Review*, no. 193 (Summer). https://www.theparisreview.org/interviews/6017/the-art-of-comics-no-1-r-crumb, accessed May 28, 2019.

Chapter 8

COMPETING MASCULINITIES IN THE WORK OF R. CRUMB

IAN BLECHSCHMIDT

If there is any clear-cut "message" in the work of Robert Crumb, it can be difficult to locate. Crumb's work rarely relies on coherent narrative structures, developed characters, or, often, even punchlines in the commonly understood sense of the word. There is no setup, beat, or payoff in a strip like "Keep On Truckin'," which appears merely as a series of unconnected moments in the lives of unconnected characters. Despite its focus on a single titular character, there is not much of a character arc in a strip like "Whiteman." The descent of an uptight, middle-class American salaryman into despair may present a horrifying funhouse reflection of American middle-class reserve, but with so little in the way of an arc or resolution, it is difficult to know what the strip wants of the reader, except, perhaps, simply to be offended.

Some might say that Crumb's emphasis on style and referentiality, along with his agnosticism toward content with any kind of coherently constructed "message," is exactly the point of his work. It could be plausibly argued that the real message in Crumb's work is not what he said but merely the fact that he said it. Its fantasy world is, as Crumb once put it, one of "total liberation from censorship, including the inner censor!" (Crumb and Poplaski 2005, 256). The specific content does not really matter—the only message is the performative one of an artist defying social convention.

This chapter, however, argues that the fantasy presented by Crumb's work is not limited to the life and practice of the unflinchingly uninhibited artist, nor to the unfettered expression and gratification of Crumb's own sexual impulses. It disagrees with Brandon Nelson's assessment that Crumb's work nearly exclusively favors "representation over analysis," or that it proffers neither critique nor alternative to what it observes in the Bizarro-land of midcentury US culture. Instead, the chapter argues that focusing on the *content* of Crumb's comics reveals a recurring preoccupation with masculinity and masculine hierarchy and a distinct impulse to imagine alternative formations. But although it presents a limited alternative to, say, the hypercompetitive masculinity of what Michael Kimmel has described as the ideal of "the Self-Made Man," Crumb's fantasy world stays largely within the bounds of the existing gender system, in which men are sorted into a hierarchy on the basis of their successful performance of masculinity (Kimmel 1996, 16–17). The only difference in Crumb's world is that it is self-consistency and "authenticity" that determine one's place in the hierarchy, rather than manly strength or the ability to compete on the market. And, as in conventional hierarchies, women serve as the bottom rung—or, more often, as a mere medium through which masculine success is achieved or rewarded. Far from a nihilistic or politically disinterested sexual indulgence, Crumb's work actually exhibits a persistent and ambivalent concern with masculinity that engages in productively disruptive critique, but ends up right back in the hierarchical imaginary in which it started, only with slightly revised rules of engagement.

Although masculinity as a theme is understudied in discussions of Crumb's work, questions of gender more broadly have certainly played an important role in them. Conversations about gender in Crumb's work have often centered around whether his depictions of sexual violence ought to be celebrated for their unmasked honesty about Crumb's deepest, darkest impulses and/or as free expression for its own sake, or condemned as a normative reassertion of heteromasculine dominance and the violence—however cartoonishly depicted—that serves to maintain it in the real world. But focusing on the comics' moments of representational excess can make it easy to miss the broader gender imaginary at work in them. Gender in general and masculinity in particular play no less a role in the relatively tame encounters between Mr. Natural and Flakey Foont than they do in the brutal scenes of sexual violence in "Jumpin' Jack Flash." Taking a broader view of where "gender" is located in Crumb's comics can reveal much about how the comics present a critical reimagining (however incomplete) of a particular corner (i.e., white and middle-class) of midcentury American masculinity.

Attempts to locate Crumb's work within a history of US comics tend to celebrate its importance in launching and sustaining the underground comix movement in the United States, as well as the resultant alternative and literary comics scenes. Artistic and aesthetic histories like those by James Danky and Denis Kitchen (2009), Mark James Estren (1993), Patrick Rosenkranz (2002), Roger Sabin (1996), and Dez Skinn (2004) celebrate underground comix' radical approach to the comics medium and their function as a catalyst for more "mature" work in comics.[1] Charles Hatfield points specifically to Crumb's "appropriation of the comic *book* that proved to be the decisive break with the past" (2005, 8; emphasis added). Hillary Chute likewise draws a direct line from Crumb and underground comix to Justin Green's influential *Binky Brown Meets the Holy Virgin Mary* and Art Spiegelman's groundbreaking work *Maus* (Chute 2017, 15). Chute also notes Crumb's influence on many of the women who have created important comics, including Aline Kominsky-Crumb, Alison Bechdel, Phoebe Gloeckner, and Lynda Barry (Chute 2010, 16).

Other artists, critics, and scholars have criticized Crumb's work for its frequent use of misogynistic and racist images. Trina Robbins has been among the most vocal, lamenting Crumb's and other comix artists' penchant for "panels of rape, torture, and murder" of (usually) female characters by male ones (2009, 31). Estren's 1993 account of underground comix includes a chapter on "Sex & Sexism," in which he and Robbins acknowledge that the "underground and straight media are almost equally inept" at depicting gender and gendered relationships, with Crumb's work in particular highlighted for its contribution to a wider trend of sexism in the male-dominated underground (127).

Yet other critics have argued that there is virtually no content to the sex and violence of Crumb's work, aside from its performance of uninhibitedness. Brandon Nelson, for example, characterizes Crumb's work as best understood through its emphasis on style and referentiality:

> By couching obscene depictions of violence and sexuality in the style of American comics produced earlier in the twentieth century, and by reproducing offensive racial and sexual caricatures absent of any obvious attempt to condemn or interrogate them, the works of R. Crumb represent an aesthetic of perpetual and apolitical obscenity that favours the collision of discordant styles and themes as its method for ultimately achieving ideological nullification and correspondingly unfettered indulgence and gratification. (2017, 140)

In other words, Crumb's comics are—to borrow from the title of Nelson's article, and echoing Crumb himself—"sick humor which serves no purpose" (139).

Crumb's work is also sometimes characterized as a mere chronicle of the wider culture and its effects upon Crumb's own mind, his comics merely "a catalogue of obsessions and indulgences" (Nelson 2017, 139). Crumb's work,

Nelson further argues, is more concerned with "capturing [these obsessions and indulgences] on the page, pinned and preserved like butterflies on cork" than with offering any kind of sustained critique (139). But even if we treat Crumb as little more than a conduit for the transmission of free-floating cultural threads, or perhaps a blank slate upon which those threads act, his vision is still a curated selection of those threads that reflects a particular set of priorities and interests. Crumb's work certainly does not capture *everything* its creator sees—no work possibly could. Crumb's comics, then, are the product of what he *notices*, not what he sees. More importantly, given the astonishing and lasting popularity of Crumb's work, it clearly seems to be what large numbers of his readers through much of the twentieth and twenty-first centuries have been noticing as well. Crumb's work, like any other work, thus presents a worldview that ought to be interrogated, given its apparent resonance and durability.

Crumb himself has denied any great world-building potential for his comics (Rosenkranz 2002, 222). But to understand his work as either a mere catalog of socially inflicted impulses or an exercise in sheer, aesthetic nihilism with no effect in the real world is to ignore the many, substantial works of scholarship that trace the evolution of subjectivity through the process of reading or otherwise engaging with popular texts and forms. Works by scholars like Susan Douglas (1994), Janice Radway (1991), and Stephen Duncombe (2001), for example, have shown how popular and underground media from television, to popular novels, to zines play a role in shaping audiences' understanding of their world, their place in it, and even the contours of the world itself.

Comic books are no exception. Ramzi Fawaz's 2016 book *The New Mutants*, for example, argues that superhero comic books in the postwar United States served as a site for both readers and creators to imagine and explore new possibilities for thinking about social and political belonging. Fawaz describes comics as participating in a process of "world making" during which "cultural products facilitate a space of public debate where dissenting voices can reshape the production and circulation of culture and, in turn, publicize counternarratives to dominant ideologies" (14). *The New Mutants* conceives of popular fantasy as a resource and an opportunity to imagine responses to the challenges and changes of its present moment, not merely a means to temporarily escape from them. Although this chapter lacks the scope and scale of Fawaz's work, it too is interested in comics' ability to review and revise the world in which they circulate and to imagine alternatives to that world. Given the overtly satirical sensibilities of Crumb's work, it is not hard to think of it as a "re-visioning" of its present. This chapter agrees with Edward Shannon's assertion in his article comparing Crumb to the confessional poets, in which he argues that, "to the extent that Crumb and the confessionals both respond to cultural and political forces, their work should be seen in at least implicitly political terms, regardless of how much they seem to be merely looking inward" (2012, 628).[2] Rather than treating Crumb's observational comics as nihilistic retreats into aesthetics, performance, or self-indulgence, however, this chapter proposes a reading of Crumb's work that locates within it a fantasy alternative. The chapter thus asks what kinds of material Crumb's comics provide for reimagining the world, with a particular focus on how they address masculinity. It investigates these questions in two ways. The first is to examine how Crumb's comics challenge or interfere with existing gendered social structures by exposing the untenability of their contradictions. The second is to investigate what alternative visions the comics present for imagining those same structures, finding the alternative to be, in the end, not really much of an alternative at all.

Both of these approaches, along with others, have been represented in important works in comics studies in recent years, particularly those similarly concerned with how comics can both disrupt and reinforce existing gender systems. Scholars like Hillary Chute, Ramzi Fawaz, and Ariel Kahn (2016) have investigated the ways comics and comics artists have challenged existing gender norms by claiming space for marginalized authors, imagining new modes of queer belonging, or "feminizing the gaze." Importantly, a number have also addressed the ways in which comics have *reinforced* patriarchal gender norms, including Carolyn Cocca's investigation of the "broke-back pose" (2014), and studies by Deborah Chavez (1985), and Jack Glasscock and Catherine Preston-Schreck (2004), of gendered portrayals in newspaper comic strips. These discussions have also extended to how comics depict masculinity in particular. Fabio Parasecoli's study of the comic book series *Chew* (2014) and Jeffrey Brown's studies of Milestone comics (2001) attempt to identify alternative or subversive patterns of masculinity in comics art. By contrast, Robert Voelker-Morris and Julie Voelker-Morris (2014) show the limited set of (mostly public) roles that superhero comics imagine for male characters, arguing that this forecloses possibilities to imagine alternatives for men in the world.

This chapter makes similar inquiries into a selection of Robert Crumb's early work in the burgeoning underground comix scene that he helped create in the late 1960s, particularly as collected in *The Complete Crumb Comics*, volumes 4 and 5. This includes much of his work from 1967 to 1969, which Crumb himself considers among his best.[3] Given that it also includes much of his output for *Zap Comix* #0, #1, and #2—the comics that essentially launched the underground comix revolution in the United States—we might consider it among Crumb's most influential. This chapter, then, asks what the performance of masculinity looks like in these comix and in what ways they both challenge and reinscribe long-standing norms of American masculinity.

This chapter leans heavily on the concept of hegemonic masculinity, which is here understood through R. W. Connell's formulation (1995) and especially those elements of it that were reaffirmed by Connell and James W. Messerschmidt (2005). This model understands masculinities as both multiple and hierarchical. That is, there are multiple models or styles of masculine performance observable in a given society at a given time, with "certain masculinities . . . more socially central, or more associated with authority and social power, than others" (Connell and Messerschmidt 2005, 846). These latter are what are often referred to as "hegemonic." It is the argument of this chapter that the performance of masculinity that was hegemonic in the postwar United States (and, in many ways, remains so today) is a major target of Crumb's social critique and a mode of social organization to which it attempts to imagine an alternative.

The characteristics of hegemonic masculinity as rendered in Crumb's work are familiar, particularly to comic book readers. Jeffrey Brown summarizes this performance in his 1999 article on comic book masculinity and black superheroes:

> Classical comic book depictions of masculinity are perhaps the quintessential expression of our cultural beliefs about what it means to be a man. In general, masculinity is defined by what it is not, namely, "feminine," and all its associated traits—hard not soft, strong not weak, reserved not emotional, active not passive. (1999, 26–27)

The years leading up to the publication of Crumb's early work saw a doubling down on this version of masculinity as shifts in the economy, politics, and family life provoked anxiety about what it meant to be a man in America. As technological changes and corporate consolidation continued to reshape the economy, "work" came increasingly to mean working for someone else performing organizational and managerial labor, rather than that which directly produced goods.[4] This brought with it an attendant anxiety over decreased possibilities for exercising "manly" strength and independence in the public sphere. "In terms of sexual stereotypes," notes historian Peter Filene, "it was a feminine world. The openly aggressive individualism of a robber baron or a would-be baron was out of place and out of date. The successful worker had to use the soft arts of personal relations. To get ahead, he had to get along" (1998, 186). American men faced pressure to channel their energies into maintaining an authoritative presence in the domestic sphere, for the good of the very nation. "Foreign policy itself rested on well-articulated assumptions about masculine power," Elaine Tyler May notes, "a power drawn from sexual potency as well as the moral strength to resist temptation (2008, 94–95). Popular characters like Mickey Spillane's hard-boiled detective, Mike Hammer, "channeled . . . sexual energy into righteous violence," putting manly stamina and impenetrability to communist influence to good use by eliminating supposed communist threats (May 2008, 94). In the real world, Cold Warriors like Joseph McCarthy similarly saw "gender failures" as major threats to the United States' ability to ward off communist encroachment. As Michael Kimmel notes, McCarthy railed against "effete eastern intellectuals [and] emasculated half men" whose insufficient manly reserve, strength, and agency had put the country and the world at risk in places like China and Eastern Europe (1996, 236). In short, anxieties about the "feminization" of society wrought by political, economic, and cultural forces were met in many circles by recommitments to a masculinity that emphasized hardness, strength, emotional reserve, and active agency, not to mention the absolute rejection of anything associated with femininity. Crumb's work exhibits a distinct ambivalence about both the risk of femi-nization and the reassertion of hegemonic masculinity.

A recurring trope that illustrates the latter is the appearance and behavior of characters who embody manly strength and fortitude and who exercise authority, often through violence. "Meatball," originally published in *Zap* #0, for example, features images of burly, brawny, thick-jawed and -jowled policemen arresting "suspicious characters" (Crumb 1995, 83) and pound-ing citizens with billy clubs (84) in an attempt to prevent the spread of the "meatball." The meatball is a metaphor for an unspecified but officially unsanctioned idea or social trend, and probably a visual euphemism for taking LSD, per Robert Harvey (1996, 204). In the comic, the moment of encounter with this trend (or hit of LSD) is represented by citizens being hit in the head with a meatball of unspecified origin. The meatball, for its part, is deeply egalitarian. Anyone, including beatniks, "respected men in high places," blue-collar workers like the "machinist for Dempster Dumpmaster," and even Bertrand Russell can be blessed by the meatball. Characters gener-ally seem to benefit from the encounter, and citizens eagerly await their turn with the meatball (Crumb 1995, 84).

However, the spread of the meatball appears to generate significant anxiety among those holding the levers of power, and a crackdown ensues. The agents of the crackdown, who mostly include "Men of Government"

and police officers, are all drawn as large, brawny, male characters, visually coded as capable of dominating anyone else in the narrative with their
large physiques. The character standing in metonymically for all "Men of
Government," and thus government itself, dominates the frame in which
he is pictured, shown from a medium to low angle, as though the viewer is
standing before his microphone-lined podium. This perspective gives him
an air of authority. The microphones remind the reader that it is the Man of
Government who occupies the privileged speaking position in the meatball's
society, whose voice is amplified by government and media institutions. The
police officers who "picked up suspicious characters" and "busted heads" are
similarly huge relative to other characters, filling much of the space in their
frames, allowing them to look down over the people whose wills they are
subverting. These characters serve as abstracted—or cartoon, if one likes—
representations of the kind of hegemonic masculinity that was cast by figures
like Joseph McCarthy and Mickey Spillane as the only defense against the
feminization of society and its attendant risk of communist overrun. For
Scott McCloud, a fundamental element of comics art is its ability to abstract
images through the elimination of detail, thus boiling an image down to its
essential meaning (1993, 30). The specific details of the authority figures that
Crumb's work focuses on in these strips are the characters' strength, social
status, and agency as wielders of both political power and violence. The comic
links these attributes together in characters who are positioned as villains.

The citizens who eagerly await the meatball, by contrast, share a range
of body types, save for any resembling the broad-shouldered and -chinned
physiques of the police and Men of Government. The people pictured on that
most auspicious day on which "it rained meatballs in downtown Los Angeles
for almost 15 minutes!" range from a little old lady to a skinny everyman.
Characters in the frame are arranged in a horizontal plane, with nobody
higher—literally or figuratively—than anyone else (fig. 8.1). These are also
the people whose heads the cops bust. They are a harmless cross section
of everyday people who generally do not occupy the top spot in the social
hierarchy and, no coincidence, also do not exhibit abstracted signs for the
successful performance of powerful, agential masculinity. The crackdown
on the benign, egalitarian meatball is thus framed as an exercise in authoritarianism executed by those who occupy the top of a hierarchy of status
and power inextricably associated with the performance of a hegemonic
masculine ideal.

This animosity toward masculine authority is a recurring trope in Crumb's
work. Characters like Whiteman and Western Man even signal their commitment to hegemonic masculinity in their names, and Crumb's work is just as

Fig. 8.1. R. Crumb, "Meatball," Copyright © Robert Crumb, 1967. All rights reserved.

ambivalent toward these as he is to police officers and Men of Government. Western Man—"last of the big-time he men"—rounds up what he calls "dope takin' perverts," who, in the narrative, seem to be just about everyone in town (Crumb 1995, 77). Western Man's overzealousness and poor judgment manifest in his indiscriminate capture via lasso of just about every other character in the strip, before he hefts an "H-Bomb" in his bare hands, indicating his intent to "git them foreign comyanists straightened out" (77). He even tells off the harmless old lady who had just thanked him for his law-enforcement efforts. As with the police and Men of Government in "Meatball," Western Man's authority is visually articulated with abstracted images of masculinity, this time with added details connecting him with that timeless hero of all-American manly virtue, the cowboy. And like in "Meatball," Western Man's manliness and authority seem to generate more chaos than they resolve.

Crumb's work thus satirizes hegemonic American masculinity's connection to structures of institutional authority. It observes the tendency for the most powerful speaking positions (i.e., those who stand at podiums full of microphones and declare things on behalf of the state) and people with access to legitimized state violence (i.e., those with the ability to "bust heads," lasso "perverts," or even sling around H-bombs) also carry the most recognizable markers of masculinity. Even childhood is structured in this way, as in "Just Us Kids!!," in which large, frame-dominating bullies harass and harangue everyday schmoes like poor Bobby Trimble from Fifty-Third Street, for no apparent reason except, perhaps, the pursuit of dominance itself (fig. 8.2). All of these instances form a visual motif of hegemonic masculinity

that is signified in characters' visual style, the ways in which they occupy space, and narratively by the ways in which they interact with other characters. Crumb's work highlights and satirizes the very real ways in which masculinity was and still is structured according to relations of authority and dominance, inviting readers to examine their own relationship to such structures and consider their relation to competing ideals of egalitarianism.

Crumb also highlights the ways in which hegemonic masculinity structures the lives of individuals. Whiteman is one of Crumb's more famous characters and is clearly some kind of commentary on the hegemonic, middle-class masculinity of Cold War America (although, as above, the "message" of this commentary is not always as clear). A caricature of an "Organization Man," Whiteman embodies the same characteristics of authoritarian masculinity as the police and Men of Government. Although he does not seem to hold any significant form of institutional or government power, Whiteman similarly strives to successfully perform hegemonic masculinity as Western Man and Crumb's other masculine types. As he demonstrates to the reader, he has mastered the art of manly strength and decisive agency. He is a "hard-charger" with "know-how! A citizen on the go!" (Crumb 1995, 106). Whiteman also respects authority and hierarchy. Virtually the only object pictured in a higher-status position than he is, for example, is the American flag, which appears up and to his left in the strip's ninth frame. He demonstrates his ability and willingness to defend his status against competitors, like the unnamed man in panel 11, with whom he aggressively competes for space by thrusting his chest outward (106).

In "Whiteman," we see Crumb's work address another aspect of American masculinity. As Michael Kimmel has observed, a defining aspect of American masculinity has long been its precarity. It is not just that American men have historically been organized into a hierarchy of manhood according to their relative strength, hardness, marketplace skill, and other conditions; they must also constantly compete with each other in order to do so, or risk losing whatever status they may have managed to acquire. Kimmel traces this characteristic to the emergence of the market as the primary realm for pursuing masculine status, starting in the nineteenth century. He describes the rise of the "Self-Made Man, a model of manhood that derives its identity entirely from a man's activities in the public sphere, measured by accumulated wealth and status, by geographic and social mobility" (1996, 17). This model of manhood was disconnected from things like hereditary titles and thus was, essentially, up for grabs for those who would strive for it.[5] Kimmel argues, however, that it also introduced an element of insecurity into the pursuit of masculinity. "If social order, permanence, could no longer be taken for granted and a man could rise as high as he aspired," Kimmel reasons, "then his sense of himself as a man was in constant need of demonstration" (43).

It is not hard to see this tendency satirized in Whiteman's deterioration as a direct result of this "constant need of demonstration." As Whiteman himself says, if he doesn't "maintain this rigid position . . . all is lost!" (Crumb 1995, 106). And unfortunately for Whiteman, the maintenance of that rigid position becomes untenable, as the pressure to suppress his internal drives toward sex and violence drives him insane. Whiteman's sorry tale highlights the competitiveness of American masculinity, painting it as a completely unsustainable, if not absolutely ridiculous expectation. Connell and Messerschmidt suggest that "[w]ithout treating privileged men as objects of pity, we should recognize that hegemonic masculinity does not necessarily translate into a satisfying experience of life" (2005, 852). In "Whiteman," Crumb invites a similar observation.

And yet, it would be hard to argue that Crumb's work presents opportunities or resources to imagine a world where hegemonic masculinity or gender hierarchies more broadly are done away with or flattened out. Rather, it simply shifts the terms by which masculine status is conferred to emphasize personal "authenticity," here rendered as the ability to resist or ignore social pressures to behave in certain ways or pursue certain ends. Although Crumb's work eschews the pursuit of dominating, manly authority, it still conceives of the successful man as one who is able to resist being domin*ated*. This, too, is a long-standing concern of American men, according to Kimmel. "Manhood," he observes, "is less about the drive for domination and more about the fear of others dominating us, having power or control over us" (1996, 6). The anti-authoritarian strain in Crumb's work is proof enough of its concern with what Kimmel observes. But the alternative that it imagines is no less predicated on a hierarchy organized by manly self-consistency, agency, or the ability to resist being feminized.

Mr. Natural, one of Crumb's most iconic characters, is a prime and prominent example of this. Mr. Natural is about as close as one gets in Crumb to a recurring protagonist. He appears in strips throughout Crumb's early underground comix work and helped to announce the emergence of the underground comix movement by featuring prominently on the cover of *Zap Comix* #1. Mr. Natural is an enlightened sage-type. Bearded and dressed in robes, he is a quasi-religious figure, occasionally descending from his home high above the corrupt, "civilized" world to dispense sage advice, often for a profit. Mr. Natural occasionally finds himself in a pinch, as when imitators try to horn in on his lucrative self-help racket (Crumb 2013, 20–24). But he always comes out on top, thanks to his wit, persistence, and ability to simply let the world's expectations roll off his back.

The character Flakey Foont provides the foil to Mr. Natural's above-it-all enlightenment through his all-consuming anxiety. Foont's failures derive from his inability to free himself from the pressures to conform to a normative model of American life. He is riven by existential neurosis and a "sense of cosmic boredom" (Crumb 1995, 64). The narratives he shares with Mr. Natural position his malaise as a product of his inability to experience the world unmediated by social expectation. As Mr. Natural tells him, he "never get[s] outa [his] car" (118), with the car referring metonymically to the corrupt, consumerist, urban society more broadly from which Foont is unable or unwilling to extricate himself.

Foont's efforts to overcome his malaise are often depicted as pathetic and ineffective. Mr. Natural rebuffs Foont's entreaties to provide him with a program for achieving the state of easygoing bliss that Mr. Natural has achieved, dismissing him as "exasperating" (120) and a "degenerate" (118). It is not Foont's failure to achieve a particular mindset that makes him a "degenerate," however; it is that he so persistently turns to an external source for the answer. He is pathetic because he fails to shed his reliance on others' approval. "I can't even think without your permission!" Flakey moans in a strip from *Yarrowstalks* #3; "I'm supposed to decide for myself about something?"

The recurring Mr. Natural and Flakey Foont stories dramatize competing models of masculinity that are every bit as concerned with dominance as the hegemonic version represented by Men of Government, and every bit as willing to assign status based on dominance. Like many comic books, this recurring narrative presents, essentially, an adolescent male power fantasy. Jeffrey Brown observes that this is essentially the basis for American superhero comic books:

> [F]or nearly every comic book hero, there is a variation on the wimp/warrior theme of duality. The story of superheroes has always been a wish-fulfilling fantasy for young men. Even comic book advertisements, such as the legendary Charles Atlas "98-pound weakling" ad, often revolve around the male daydream that if we could just find the right word, the right experimental drug, the right radioactive waste, then we, too, might instantly become paragons of masculinity. (2001, 175)

Mr. Natural and Flakey Foont present exactly the same style of narrative, with Mr. Natural playing the "warrior" role to Flakey Foont's "wimp." The fantasy remains that if the protagonist—and any reader fantasizing vicari-ously through him—could just gain some kind of magic power, knowledge, or tool, then he would be impervious to the world's penetrating influence and become a proper masculine subject. The comics merely work around their ambivalence toward more "traditional" markers of successful masculin-ity, like strength, by modestly rewriting the rules of the game. Rather than status within the hierarchy accruing to the *strongest* male, the fantasy goes, it accrues to the most authentic, original, and self-consistent. The content of the fantasy may change from Western Man to the countercultural sage Mr. Natural, but the *form* stays the same.

There is perhaps an argument to be made that Crumb's work *does* present a productive reimagining of masculinity. Perhaps a masculinity that doesn't prescribe violent competition for dominance among men is an improvement over one that does. After all, Mr. Natural does not really set out to have power *over* other men; he is admirable merely because other men (and society more broadly) are unable to gain dominance over *him*. He may occupy a higher-status position in the narrative than Flakey Foont, but he seems to feel some compassion for Flakey and never seems to tire of trying to help him. But when we consider the position of women within the narrative, it is hard to see much difference, let alone improvement, in the masculine fantasy presented in Crumb's comics. As noted above, the misogyny and violence that are a common feature of Crumb's work have been well documented. It bears noting here that it is not uncommon for these scenes of violence to be preceded by depictions of challenges to male status by female characters. Eggs Ackley, for example, is another character whose "shtick" comprises unfailing and outrageous self-consistency. A 1967 strip shows what happens when Eggs is rebuffed by a strange woman on the street. Eggs attempts to get the woman's attention by shouting "Lemme introduce to you, the one and only Eggs Ackley!" The woman, however, demands that he move out of her way. He responds by tripping her. "Haw!" Ackley concludes, "Guess I showed her!" (Crumb 1995, 52). This is hardly the only example of a narrative in which a challenge to male dominance is resolved through violence.

But serving as opportunities for male characters to overcome challenges to their masculine status is not the only role that femininity plays in Crumb's comics. As Kimmel notes: "Women themselves often serve as a kind of cur-rency that men use to improve their ranking with other men" (1996, 7). This, too, is sometimes a narrative device in Crumb's comics, including in the ad-ventures of Mr. Natural. Like so many other iterations of masculinity, the reward for performing the Mr. Natural model correctly in these stories is the willingness of young, pretty women to submit to the successful male's sexual desires. This is exemplified in a 1968 strip from *Zap Comix* #2. In it, Mr. Natural is forced to outwit a profusion of phonies who are all ripping off his profitable "Holy Ned" persona. The conclusion is simple enough: Mr. Natural simply demonstrates his superior commitment to authenticity by going "back to his old self" (Crumb 2013, 24). This shift in persona is shown to be successful when "all the chicks on Haight street [who] really got their minds messed" by Mr. Natural lavish the newly dubbed "Mr. Snatcheral" with sexual favors (24). Mr. Natural wins again, and is rewarded with female attention.

Another strip from the *East Village Other* demonstrates this recurring trope even more efficiently (fig. 8.3). In "Sleezy Snot Comics," Flakey Foont complains to Mr. Natural that he is "horny," lamenting the complexity of the contemporary dating scene and all the "stupid games" one must play in order to "get laid" (Crumb 2013, 68). Mr. Natural demonstrates his characteristic unconcern with such "stupid games" by approaching the nearest strange woman and, after a brief chat, bringing her back to Flakey. "She'd like to fuck you," Mr. Natural tells Flakey. "He'll probably blow it," Mr. Natural nonetheless concludes, as Flakey stammers his way through an attempt at wooing the woman. Flakey is such a pathetically unsuccessful man that Mr. Natural, along with the reader, assumes his failure even as success seems all but guaranteed. Mr. Natural, on the other hand, is so successful in his performance that he can actually perform it on behalf of other men. His superheroic unconcern with society's expectations—with "games"—produces a surplus of manly success, symbolized by the increased willingness of women to engage in sex at his request. The comic thus imagines a world where one's ability to refuse to be dominated by social expectations ("games") results in social and sexual reward. If one fails in this task by submitting to social norms, one risks being stranded on the lower rungs of the social hierarchy among the other pathetic, failed men whom Flakey represents. Women, for their part, are again merely the currency through which success is measured and rewards allocated.

Comics scholars have often wondered what possibilities the medium provides for pursuing greater gender justice, and what opportunities it presents for "effective inversion, subversion, or displacement" of restrictive and unjust gender norms and hierarchies (Butler 2006, 44). In some small way, Crumb's work contributes to this project by highlighting and critiquing the nature and costs of hegemonic masculinity, at least for those men whom it perceives to occupy nonhegemonic social positions. But it also—somewhat ironically, given the reputation of the artist—suffers from something of a lack of imagination when it comes to envisioning alternatives. Although Crumb's

work displays a worthwhile ambivalence toward the prevailing model of authoritative manly agency and fortitude, it does little to acknowledge its own concerns about domination by others. This is to say nothing of its tendency to defray the effects of those concerns by simply pushing them on down the ladder onto women and other men who occupy a lower or abject position. As scholars continue to struggle with Crumb's legacy, it is worth always trying to assemble a more complete picture of the ways in which his work imagines and interrogates its world. Crumb's work is preoccupied with the masculine norms of Cold War America, and in so doing, his comics present the tensions attendant to imagining alternatives to gender norms within the logic of a dominant gender. "For the unravelling of hegemonic masculinity," Claire Duncanson argues, "men must be encouraged not so much to change their ways as to change the way in which they negotiate their identities in relation to others. Rather than forge their identities through relations of opposition or domination, men and subjects in general need to construct their identities through recognition of similarity, respect, interdependence, empathy, and equality with others" (2015, 233). These other-oriented characteristics seem substantially incompatible with the ideal of masculinity pictured in Crumb's work. Indeed, they seem more characteristic of Flakey Foont than anyone else. In spite of their clear ambivalence toward hegemonic masculinity as it existed in the Cold War United States, then, the alternatives that Crumb's work imagines ultimately reinforce its underlying logics, serving to reravel rather than unravel the structure of its hierarchy, if not its specific content. Although Crumb's early "magic" captures and pins a few things worth noting about this American masculinity, the fantasy it presents in response is a reinscription, rather than a rejection, of masculine norms.

NOTES

1. In the title essay of their volume, *Underground Classics*, Danky and Kitchen contrast comix' liberal expressions of sex and violence along with the sophisticated ambitions of their content with the "relatively anemic mainstream output" (2009, 20). Estren also makes a point to distinguish underground comix from the "straight mass media" based on the "irreverence" of their content and their distribution system (1993, 24). Rosenkranz (2002, 221), Sabin (1996, 92), and Skinn (2004, 11) similarly mark underground comix as an artistic revolution in the medium.

2. Indeed, in contrast to Crumb's own characterization of his work—cited above in Rosenkranz—Shannon asserts that "no other underground artist or comic book had such an impact on the wider culture" (630).

3. In his introduction to *The Complete Crumb Comics*, vol. 9, *R. Crumb versus the Sisterhood* (1992), Crumb notes: "[N]othing I've done since the 'sixties has quite the magic of that early work" (vii).

4. George Lipsitz, for example, traces how a raft of business consolidations during World War II, including the absorption of many small businesses by a smaller number of large ones, led to a reduction in small business ownership. As a result, "many Americans [were forced] to face a life of working for others" (1981, 7). As C. Wright Mills notes in his influential 1956 study on white collar work, by midcentury the increased mechanization and rationalization of work also meant that "as a proportion of the labor force, fewer individuals manipulate[d] *things*, more handle[d] *people* and *symbols*" (1956, 65).

5. That is, if one were free—meaning, white—enough to own property and compete within the public sphere and, especially, the marketplace.

WORKS CITED

Brown, Jeffrey A. 1999. "Comic Book Masculinity and the New Black Superhero." *African American Review* 33, no. 1 (Spring): 25–42.

Brown, Jeffrey A. 2001. *Black Superheroes, Milestone Comics, and Their Fans.* Jackson: University Press of Mississippi.

Butler, Judith. 2006. *Gender Trouble: Feminism and the Subversion of Identity.* New York: Routledge.

Chavez, Deborah. 1985. "Perpetuation of Gender Inequality: A Content Analysis of Comic Strips." *Sex Roles* 13, nos. 1–2: 93–102.

Chute, Hillary. 2010. *Graphic Women: Life Narrative and Contemporary Comics.* New York: Columbia University Press.

Chute, Hillary. 2017. *Why Comics? From Underground to Everywhere.* New York: HarperCollins.

Cocca, Carolyn. 2014. "The 'Broke Back Test': A Quantitative and Qualitative Analysis of Portrayals of Women in Mainstream Superhero Comics, 1993–2013." *Journal of Graphic Novels and Comics* 5, no. 4: 411–28.

Connell, R. W. 1995. *Masculinities.* Berkeley: University of California Press.

Connell, R. W., and James W. Messerschmidt. 2005. "Hegemonic Masculinity: Rethinking the Concept." *Gender and Society* 19, no. 6: 829–59.

Crumb, R. 1992. *The Complete Crumb Comics*. Vol. 9, *R. Crumb versus the Sisterhood*. Seattle: Fantagraphics.

Crumb, R. 1995. *The Complete Crumb Comics*. Vol. 4, *Mr. Sixties!* Seattle: Fantagraphics.

Crumb, R. 2013. *The Complete Crumb Comics*. Vol. 5, *Happy Hippy Comix*. Seattle: Fantagraphics.

Crumb, R., and Peter Poplaski. 2005. *The R. Crumb Handbook*. London: MQ Publications.

Danky, James, and Denis Kitchen. 2009. "Underground Classics: The Transformation of Comics into Comix, 1963–90." In *Underground Classics: The Transformation of Comics into Comix*, edited by James Danky and Denis Kitchen, 17–21. New York: Harry N. Abrams.

Douglas, Susan J. 1994. *Where the Girls Are: Growing Up Female with the Mass Media*. New York: Times Books.

Duncanson, Claire. 2015. "Hegemonic Masculinity and the Possibility of Change in Gender Relations." *Men and Masculinities* 18, no. 2: 231–48.

Duncombe, Stephen. 2001. *Notes from Underground: Zines and the Politics of Alternative Culture*. 2nd ed. Portland, OR: Microcosm Publishing.

Estren, Mark James. 1993. *A History of Underground Comics*. Scarborough, Ont., Canada: Firefly Books.

Fawaz, Ramzi. 2016. *The New Mutants: Superheroes and the Radical Imagination of American Comics*. New York: New York University Press.

Filene, Peter G. 1998. *Him/Her/Self: Gender Identities in Modern America*. 3rd ed. Baltimore: Johns Hopkins University Press.

Glasscock, Jack, and Catherine Preston-Schreck. 2004. "Gender and Racial Stereotypes in Daily Newspaper Comics: A Time-Honored Tradition?" *Sex Roles* 51, nos. 7–8: 423–31.

Harvey, Robert. 1996. *The Art of the Comic Book: An Aesthetic History*. Jackson: University Press of Mississippi.

Hatfield, Charles. 2005. *Alternative Comics: An Emerging Literature*. Jackson: University Press of Mississippi.

Kahn, Ariel. 2016. "Pursuing Paradise: Jewish Travel Comics as Feminist Spiritual Quests." *Studies in Comics* 7, no. 2: 237–64.

Kimmel, Michael. 1996. *Manhood in America: A Cultural History*. New York: Free Press.

Lipsitz, George. 1981. *Class and Culture in Cold War America: "A Rainbow at Midnight."* South Hadley, MA: Praeger.

May, Elaine Tyler. 2008. *Homeward Bound: American Families in the Cold War Era*. 20th Anniversary Edition. New York: Basic Books.

McCloud, Scott. 1993. *Understanding Comics*. New York: Paradox Press.

Mills, C. Wright. 1956. *White Collar: The American Middle Classes*. New York: Oxford University Press.

Nelson, Brandon. 2017. "'Sick Humor Which Serves No Purpose': Whiteman, Angelfood and the Aesthetics of Obscenity in the Comix of R. Crumb." *Journal of Graphic Novels and Comics* 8, no. 2: 139–55.

Parasecoli, Fabio. 2014. "Gluttonous Crimes: *Chew*, Comic Books, and the Ingestion of Masculinity." *Women's Studies International Forum* 44 (May–June): 236–46.

Radway, Janice A. 1991. *Reading the Romance: Women, Patriarchy, and Popular Literature*. Chapel Hill: University of North Carolina Press.

Robbins, Trina. 2009. "Wimmen's Studies." In *Underground Classics: The Transformation of Comics into Comix*, edited by James Danky and Denis Kitchen, 31–33. New York: Harry N. Abrams.

Rosenkranz, Patrick. 2002. *Rebel Visions: The Underground Comix Revolution*. Seattle: Fantagraphics.

Sabin, Roger. 1996. *Comics, Comix and Graphic Novels*. London: Phaidon.

Shannon, Edward. 2012. "Shameful, Impure Art: Robert Crumb's Autobiographical Comics and the Confessional Poets." *Biography* 35, no. 4 (September): 627–49.

Skinn, Dez. 2004. *Comix: The Underground Revolution*. New York: Thunder's Mouth Press.

Voelker-Morris, Robert, and Julie Voelker-Morris. 2014. "Stuck in Tights: Mainstream Superhero Comics' Habitual Limitations on Social Constructions of Male Superheroes." *Journal of Graphic Novels and Comics* 5, no. 1: 101–17.

Chapter 9

THE TORTURED ARTIST

R. Crumb's Visual Adaptation of Kafka's Iconic Ugliness

LYNN MARIE KUTCH

In the short story "Appetites" published in the 2017 anthology *Funeral Platter*, author Greg Ames imagines his protagonist accompanying Franz Kafka (1883–1924) to a bar where Kafka is "meeting a chick named Sherry" (2017, 162). In a light and humorous style, Ames climbs inside the mind of Kafka, and his protagonist's own very similar psyche, to describe why their shared evening of "boozing and brawling, picking up chicks" hardly progresses as planned (162). Kafka's repeated failure to respond to questions or attempts at conversation leads the protagonist to speculate on common characteristics that have contributed to their romantic disappointments: "Kafka and I have a checkered history with women, probably because we want them to take all of our pain away and carry it for us, while we remain focused on our special projects behind closed doors, chasing immortality"; and, less philosophically, "[Kafka] said the wrong things again and scared the chicks away" (163). Ames's entertaining short story is representative, both in theme and style, of a small but notable subgenre of literature that imagines a protagonist, artist, or even work of art interacting with Kafka or his work, often with the result of providing insight into the author's tortured professional and personal life. Writers or artists like Ames and others who engage with Kafka's works often emphasize two recurring themes: first, the author's dissatisfied and even revolting association to his own body; and second, discontented and disappointing relationships with problematic women.

One such artist whose work converses thematically with Kafka's is American comics artist Robert Crumb. In the graphic novel *Kafka* (titled *Kafka for Beginners* and *Introducing Kafka* in its first British and US editions, respectively, in 1993), a collaborative project with writer David Zane Mairowitz, Crumb does not directly place an imagined protagonist alongside Kafka.

Instead, as Ames and other writers have done using a verbal medium, Crumb uses the comics medium, infused with comic absurdity and graphic exaggeration, to portray the socially awkward and inhibition-plagued Kafka. Crumb implements his provocative and aggressive, yet amusing, signature style to render the abuse, torment, monstrousness, self-doubt, and bodily absurdity that consistently characterized and shaped Kafka's oeuvre. In his article "Comic Erudition: R. Crumb Meets Kafka," Richard Alleva describes the established artist-to-author relationship: "*Introducing Kafka* is a ... very rare example of what happens when one very idiosyncratic artist absorbs another into his worldview without obliterating the individuality of the absorbed one" (2002, 19). A central question for this chapter concerns what it means for one artist to absorb the work of another, and how exactly Crumb's work captures Kafka's tone and style. Part of the answer lies in overarching and overlapping thematic strands—namely, the troubled relationships of the artists to their own bodies and to women—that have provided consistent and mutual indexing tools for both Kafka's and Crumb's works. This is not to suggest that Crumb's personal biography makes him particularly well suited to perform Kafka's work visually. Rather, Crumb has spent his career rendering themes in his comics that are consistent with those found in Kafka's work. Thus, he has developed a professional tradition that makes him particularly proficient to capture Kafka. My method of critical inquiry will involve linking sketches in *Introducing Kafka* with parallel, antecedent, and/or analogous images from Crumb's larger body of work in order to establish analytical structures by which to read and interpret Crumb's adaptation.

In what follows, I consider to what degree Crumb's graphic style magnifies Kafka's feeling "physically and ethically impure" (Stach 2017, 239) to Crumb-like proportions of giving the viewer a "tremendous kind of impaction of lusting, suffering, crazed humanity in all sorts of gargoyle like allegorical forms" (Hughes 2005, 294). Despite or because of Crumb's highly controversial nature, he does in fact strike a visual tone that corresponds to Kafka's literary nature. Perhaps unexpected yet common fundamental thematic threads link author and artist, one of which Brandon Nelson identifies in his article "'Sick Humor Which Serves No Purpose': Whiteman, Angelfood and the Aesthetics of Obscenity in the Comix of R. Crumb": "men [who] are set up for humiliation and derision by a narrative that heaps misfortune and shame upon them" (2017, 144). As is widely known among Crumb's readers, the artist's extreme comic depictions of humiliated men throughout his career have often resulted in vehement criticism of his work as misogynist, racist, and "inherently contemptible [and] combative" (Crumb 2005h, 386). Presumably, unlike Crumb's critics, few of Kafka's readers or literary critics would label the canonized and well-respected author a creep or pervert, although he and Crumb thematize very similar concepts. In assessing Crumb's "bizarrely consistent catalogue of obsessions and indulgences," Nelson is careful to point out that the comic collection of fetishized female characters as well as humiliated and demeaned male characters is more accurately "psychological articulation, rather than analysis" (2017, 139, 150). This represents a significant common thread, as Kafka's work also presents readers with an exaggerated psychological articulation of bizarre thoughts and feelings. This chapter demonstrates how Crumb's distinct style of seeing, experiencing, and drawing reveals a supreme adeptness at articulating Kafka's biography and visually interpreting his fiction stories, in spite of the perceived collision between customarily low-art comics and the high-art realm where Kafka's writing traditionally dwells.

Throughout his work, Crumb has playfully presented his awareness of the long-established high/low divide in both literary and fine art cultures. For example, in an intentionally sarcastic faux advertisement for *Zap Comix* from 1968, Crumb references the "cheap trash" that will "ruin your mind" and the guilt that parents and society heap on comics readers (Crumb and Poplaski 2005, 242). A second example, a poster for a 2004 German exhibit of his drawings and comics, shows an exasperated illustrated version of Crumb faced with the overwhelming question (as indicated by its oversize regal cursive script): "Yes, but is it art?" The artist responds (in comparably small lettering): "You tell me, I don't know" (Crumb and Poplaski 2005, 344). Critics have told Crumb that his perceived crassness and offensiveness often relegate his comics to categories of base pop culture, where unbridled misogyny and "totalising obscenity" that "elicit[s] outrage" reside (Nelson 2017, 139). Thus Crumb's critics often have difficulty reconciling the presumably depraved depictions of mentally anguished male characters and sexually exaggerated female characters with serious art. By contrast, despite themes also common and nearly identical to Crumb's work, most contemporary Kafka critics cite Kafka's intellect, genius, erudition, and extraordinary storytelling ability as evidence that his work universally represents an extremely high literary standard (Corngold and Gross 2011).

Introducing Kafka demonstrates the ways in which Crumb has incorporated high art and literary discourse into his work, producing a hybrid image/text form. His adaptation of Kafka's life and work, with all its grotesque, monstrous, and bizarre depictions of the author's tormented existence, even achieves objectives of *Weltliteratur* as conceptualized by Goethe and paraphrased by Daniel Stein and Jan-Noël Thon in *From Comic Strips to Graphic Novels*: "Transgressing cultural borders, adapting elements of foreign cultures, and connecting them with one's proper cultural heritage, world's literatures develop in a process of mutual influence; new genres arise as well as new languages" (2013, 402). Indeed, many of Goethe's writings on world literature have to do with his somewhat politically tinged assessment of the impact of the German literary aesthetic on the literature of other European countries. He also, however, wrote in more general terms about the importance of mutual artistic influence: "Not merely what such men write to us must be of first importance to us; we have also to consider their other relationships. . . . [A]nd each [nation] is bound to find in the other something attractive and something repellent, something worthy of emulation and something to be avoided" (Strich 1949, 351). This description also contains overlapping elements of adaptation theory; and Crumb's adaptation yields a new genre that exposes aesthetically dissimilar yet thematically similar artistic traditions in dialogue with one another. Although in this case the two artists cannot personally engage in a direct process of mutual influence, it is clear that Crumb uses his comics art to converse directly with, interpret, and conceptualize Kafka's writing for a diverse and diversified audience of both Kafka readers and Crumb fans.

Exhibiting a chaotic, forceful, and emotionally dynamic design, the 175-page *Introducing Kafka* weaves biographical elements, as referenced in Kafka's private writings and letter exchanges, with visually translated interpretations of Kafka's main fiction works such as "In the Penal Colony," "The Hunger Artist," and *The Metamorphosis*. The graphic novel also contextualizes the literary works within the framework of historical events that occurred during Kafka's lifetime. Typical for the "Introducing" series, this installment offers a compact version of the author's life and key writings in an accessible visual format. Crumb's drawings in *Introducing Kafka* showcase a similar brand of the arguably obnoxious artistic style that he has been producing since his early work in the 1950s. The artistic approach draws visual attention to and isolates certain themes that unite author and artist. For example, using terms that could apply just as readily to Kafka's literature, one Crumb reviewer of the 1994 edition of Crumb's *Self-Loathing Comics* writes: "The cover image . . . is an uncomfortable depiction of the revulsion he feels inside his skin. . . . It is an iconic ugliness. . . . Crumb does not see a man, he sees a cartoon character, a monster" (Jones 2000). In his emblematic and nearly inimitable style, Crumb confrontationally provokes the reader with images of revulsion and the "iconic ugliness," with which Kafka also viewed himself his entire life. In *Introducing Kafka*, Crumb harnesses, yet also significantly modifies, the catalog of monstrous and creepy self-portraits that characterize the bodies of work of both author and artist. Crumb's adaptation consistently manifests two discernible themes: first, the broken, inadequate, ugly male body, and second, the related troubled relationships with women. Crumb's established comics tradition furnishes him with the tools to absorb and magnify these aspects of Kafka's writings.

In much of his body of work, Kafka often describes a process in which the writer must separate himself from his physical body, and in more violent terms, that an outside force performs the mutilation or dismemberment. In particular, *The Metamorphosis* (1912) and "The Hunger Artist" (1922) demonstrate notions of profound alienation from the body as well as resignation that the body must necessarily deteriorate and die. Elizabeth Boa adds an interpretive layer concerning the relationship between the author and the equivalent of physical torture that writing incites: "To explore the self is to explore the world, but . . . exploration did entail a kind of cutting off of the writer from his body and from other people" (1996, 133). Similarly, Crumb has spoken of a "defensive measure" of distancing oneself from oneself, but for the purpose of not taking oneself too seriously (Mercier 2004, 197). This would seem to contrast with, but actually complements, Kafka's seemingly paradoxical reasons for focusing on physical pain, as he states in a letter to a friend: "[Exaggerating painful things as much as possible] often seems to me the only way to drive out pain" (Begley 2008, 156). Readers can observe how the two thoughts align when Crumb exaggerates his images to such proportions that he also seeks to drive out pain through absurdity. In this way, Crumb's illustrations gesture toward Kafka's hidden system of humor, which for many readers often goes undetected.

Kafka's humor draws out the absurdity of a situation through language. Similarly, Crumb's exaggerated figures connote the absurd. Both have the effect of magnifying a real situation into one of outrageous perspective. David Foster Wallace has argued that many readers of Kafka, especially Americans, don't "get" Kafka because those particular audiences are accustomed to the concept of humor as an escape or respite from precisely those topics that the author treats (1998, 25). Throughout *Introducing Kafka*, the representations of the absurd can seem incongruous to the material. For example, Crumb proficiently executes the image of the writer's body, cut, twisted, axed, tortured, or transformed but with the subtext of a ludicrous, almost laughable existence that Kafka's original work provides. From the very first page of the graphic novel, the sketched image intensifies the sense of physical hostility and dismemberment that Kafka articulates. The text reads as follows: "The image of a wide pork butcher's knife, swiftly and with mechanical regularity chopping into me, shaving off razor-thin slices which fly about due to the speed of the work" (Mairowitz and Crumb 2007, 3). In the picture, a stunned Kafka in business suit and tie endures a meat cleaver removing the right side of his head, blood spurting and derby hat flying (fig. 9.1). His facial expression and posture indicate a passive reaction to the gross violation. He averts his eyes, his stunned expression even suggesting slapstick; and the lack of eye contact implies a passive acceptance of his mutilation. His arms remain firmly at his sides, showing no sign of fighting back and giving the overall impression that he is just waiting for the brutal ordeal to pass. Incidentally, the oversize hairy hand that holds the cleaver will reappear as the recognizable motif of Kafka's terrifying father's hands, for whom he harbored a deep-seated fear his entire life (Kafka 1974). Perhaps this repeated visual quotation also helps to explain the comic protagonist's frozen passiveness in the face of a father-like figure. The comics medium allows for a more intense magnification to absurd proportions than even Kafka's expressive prose.

As mentioned above in the brief description of method, comparing visual quotations and recognizable citations from Crumb's larger body of work assists in interpreting the comics artist's adaptation of Kafka's life and literature. A parallel motif or visual quotation, even an antecedent to the cleaver image, appears in "The Adventures of R. Crumb Himself" (1973; Crumb 2005a). In this particular example, the technique of inflating an initially normal situation to extreme proportions makes the humor transparent. In Crumb's comic, the cartoon protagonist goes in search of life's purpose and stumbles upon "the National School of Hard Knocks." After he has gone through various levels of physical torture and corporeal punishment, the school celebrates a bizarre form of graduation. A nun wields a meat cleaver that nearly chops off the comic protagonist's penis. The frame depicting this moment visually recalls the cleaver scene discussed above. Unlike the one-panel story in *Introducing Kafka* that begins and ends with Kafka's mutilation by an outside force, Crumb's protagonist takes an active stance, bares his teeth, grabs the cleaver, and beheads the nun. Aggressively tossing the nun's head at his team of torturers consequently arouses him sexually (Crumb 2005a, 183). This exaggerated projection of castration anxiety and institutional judgment is evidence of Crumb's "very powerful imagination which goes right over the top a lot of the time, but . . . very seldom lies" (Hughes 2005, 294). While the messages found in these two examples appear very similar both visually and in terms of socially critical content, Crumb does not depict an exaggerated fantasy of exacting revenge on those in authority in the Kafka version. Instead, *Introducing Kafka* suggests an internalization of fears and resignation, similar to the protagonist's fates in *The Metamorphosis* or "The Hunger Artist." In both cases, activity and passivity in the face of societal frameworks are expressed with a form of black humor streaked with desperation.

Fig. 9.1. R. Crumb, *Introducing Kafka*, Copyright © Robert Crumb, 1993. All rights reserved.

In another example from *Introducing Kafka* of Kafka's voicing criticism of an external system by showing its detrimental effect on his body, Crumb depicts the author imagining himself being dragged through a ground-floor window of a house by a noose, which then drags him through the upper floors and finally lifts him out through the roof. The page features three jaggedly framed panels of varying size, arranged vertically largest to smallest. In the first, a noose emerges from an open window and aggressively grabs the cartoon protagonist, dressed the same as in the cleaver picture in his suit, tie, and derby hat. Also as on the previous page, the derby hat—no doubt a symbol of bourgeois life—flies from his head amid drops of blood and sweat. The second frame shows his body passing through a meticulously furnished living room. It appears that the force has removed not only his clothing but also most of his flesh. The final, bottom frame shows a hole in the roof and the "last torn-off bits of [him] drop[ping] from the empty noose as it crashes through the tiles and comes to rest on the roof" (Mairowitz and Crumb 2007, 4). Of course, the depiction of physical mutilation is grotesque and extremely peculiar, but the more disturbing part about Crumb's rendition is the blank expression of the bourgeois woman who witnesses the body being pulled through her home. Crumb rightly shows with this subtle detail that Kafka interrogates his own body. Just as importantly and strikingly, however, the sketch discusses his placement within a relentless middle-class society that sets certain expectations for him, expectations that have physically dismembered him.

To return to the *Weltliteratur* concept introduced above, Crumb does not merely provide illustrations for Kafka's writings. Instead, he adapts and interprets elements of another time and culture through his own lens. *Introducing Kafka* transgresses cultural borders but strengthens common thematic frontiers by substituting "middle-class America" with "bourgeois early twentieth-century Prague." Crumb has shown key critical achievements in terms of exposing the hypocrisy of middle-class values, as Kristine McKenna summarizes in an interview with the comics artist: "Crumb brings intelligence and autobiographical candor to the form, in strips that spoof the inhibitions of middle-class America as they explore politics, sex and history" (2004, 159). Similarly, Kafka described and criticized "the chilly social milieus . . . in which altruistic solidarity occurs merely as a dream" (Stach 2017, 53). This incisive criticism of their respective societies indicates another thematic point of convergence for the two artists' dialogue.

Introducing Kafka later provides a sketch that more specifically and directly addresses the writer's battle with himself as a spiritual, psychological experience. Mairowitz describes this struggle: "The only solution was a kind of self-hypnosis or 'interior emigration' which simultaneously cut him off from the world and allowed him to take it all in" (2007, 73). Crumb's corresponding drawing of Kafka shows a feverish-looking writer with wide eyes and spiraled pupils, indicating a radical state of self-hypnosis (fig. 9.2) (73). In analogous comics, Crumb has sketched similar images of the desperate artist. Michael Dougan has described Crumb as "explor[ing] an inner world of obsessively well-crafted fantasies and blunt social satire" in his autobiographical comics (2004, 164). In one visual quotation, or 'parallel image, Crumb depicts himself in "The Many Faces of R. Crumb" (1972; Crumb 2005d) the same way that Kafka appears in the picture described above: an artist feverishly working at his desk, the angle of the artist's body sitting at the desk visually matching the Kafka image (fig. 9.3). The highly ironic tone of his caption reads: "Crumb the long-suffering patient artist-saint," and he even labels the stigmata on his hand with a large and conspicuous arrow (Crumb 2005d, 186). By the end of the strip, Crumb appears at the same desk, looking much more relaxed. In response to the question "Who is this Crumb?" he states, while waving, "It all depends on the mood I'm in. Bye all" (187), his raised hand again revealing the stigmata more prominently. Much unlike any representation of Kafka as troubled author in *Introducing Kafka*, the cynical and impudent sketched version of Crumb establishes eye contact with the viewer and, as in the example discussed above, actively responds. Multiple Crumb representations of Kafka consistently show him bent over the table, eyes crazed or averted with nervous sweat flying. Although Crumb does not depict the same authorial dispositions in the parallel images, both sets of images present the activity of art-making as an obsessive withdrawal into an inner world: "Here it is, this is it, now you see it. I've got nothing left to hide. It's all out there, everything, my darkest thoughts I've ever had are out there" (Mercier 2004, 195). Kafka's writing comes across as much more subtle and metaphorical than Crumb's, but his and Crumb's works correspond thematically by showing the writer/artist's ongoing and far-from-completed battle with himself.

Crumb continues to implement, and yet also modify, his typically aggressive style to convey not only Kafka's profound self-doubt but also the intimidating power of being an author and the creative work that existence elicits. Another image reflecting a departure both into and away from the artist's own body accompanies the following text from Mairowitz: "When he first came to Berlin, Kafka felt he had escaped from those phantoms which forced him to write. . . . But those phantoms returned and forced him one night to write" (2007, 142). In Crumb's accompanying comic, Kafka's thin, nearly skeletal body hovers above the floor, his neck gripped by a phantom

Fig. 9.2. R. Crumb, *Introducing Kafka*, Copyright © Robert Crumb, 1993. All rights reserved.

hand that emerges from the ceiling. Another hand holds a chair hovering above the floor, a third holds his chair, while a fourth presents him with a blank piece of paper (142). The indistinct phantom faces in the ceiling and bent table and chair legs, as well as a freely floating window, confirm the image's dreamlike attributes. The writer's dark-rimmed eyes take on a similar quality as those of one hypnotized, but these appear more like a skeleton's eyes, sunken deep into his apparently lifeless skull. With his words, Kafka thrusts upon the reader the writer's powerlessness to control his demons. Crumb builds upon those words with his style of art, which he maintains "is full of sweating, nervous uneasiness" (McKenna 2004, 163). He renders Kafka's words with images that "most people don't want to see . . . because it reminds them of inadequate parts of themselves" (McKenna 2004, 163). For both author and artist, the spiritual work of self-reflection reveals an anxious, uncomfortable agitation.

Along the lines of presenting nervous uneasiness, Crumb's "The Desperate Character" presents an analogous comic by which to read and analyze his interpretations of Kafka as a tortured artist. Although this comic does not directly thematize the plight of the author, it emphasizes the artist's helplessness in his own professional circumstances and in relation to perilous world events. In a series of panels, Crumb shows extreme physical reactions in the protagonist as he reads a book, the newspaper, and the daily stock report (Crumb 2005b, 366). His face takes on a more crazed look as the strip continues, until finally the head explodes, sending eyes, mouth, and teeth in all directions. He repositions the normal everyday occurrence of reading information into a bizarre moment of explosion in which such information blows up the reader's mind. On his style, Crumb has commented: "I find it more interesting to draw grotesque, lurid, or absurd pictures" (Crumb 2005g, 393). By using the technique of taking the author's or artist's existence to uncanny, certainly grotesque and absurd extremes, Crumb's work mirrors Kafka's style and tone, which also consistently contains grotesque, lurid, and absurd elements.

In addition to the sketches described above that directly portray physical harm to the body as a metaphorical response to the writer's existence, *Introducing Kafka* also presents many other examples of the author's uncomfortable and pained relationship to his figuratively and physically diseased self. A reader need only cursorily flip through the pages to encounter numerous and striking individual sketches of Kafka's troubled body, with each example contributing to a larger thematic whole. In a brief discussion of Kafka's short story "The Burrow" (1931), Mairowitz describes the affinity that Kafka felt to the story's central character, a creature who lives underground among a series of tunnels, and how that idealized existence sums up his body perception. Mairowitz links Kafka's preference for isolation with his generalized sickliness: "No ordinary, run-of-the-mill hypochondriac, Kafka used ILL-NESS, not merely as a metaphor for his troubled existence, but as yet another means of alienating himself from his family, and of course, from himself" (2007, 59). The accompanying Crumb sketch shows a naked, scrawny Kafka tightly twisted into a fetal position. His usually neatly combed hair stands on end, and he once again displays the wide-eyed look of someone entranced or mesmerized. A field of flame-like lines surrounds him as well as oversize stars, often comic shorthand for severe pain (59). The overall impression of the illustration is that Kafka is permanently and agonizingly removed from the world, all human contact, and that he takes no comfort or pleasure in his own body. As Mairowitz states elsewhere in a caption accompanying a picture of a scrawny young Kafka next to his strapping father before a swim lesson, "If Kafka was alienated from his country, his surroundings, his family, he was also a stranger in his own body. SHAME walked with him from early on. . . . His lack of self-confidence was imprinted in childhood and would remain with him to the end" (37). Crumb's sketches—parallel to Kafka's writings in effect and tone—make the anguish that Kafka expresses impossible to ignore.

Crumb's twelve-panel comic "No Way Out" is another antecedent draw-ing from Crumb's larger body of work that parallels Kafka's thematic of the problematic, inadequate body. In each of the twelve panels, Crumb depicts a naked cartoon protagonist confined to a small box, not even big enough for him to extend his arms and legs. He tries to move around in the small space and find a comfortable position, and like in the illustration of Kafka discussed above, the very thin, naked body clearly displays discomfort. In eleven dif-ferent attempts, he tries, among other things, facing the wall, climbing the wall, covering his eyes, and establishing eye contact. His facial expressions impart a deep sense of worry and distress. By the final frame, he appears less worried but still uncomfortably confined to the box (Crumb 2005e, 361). In his brief essay "The Litany of Hate," Crumb replicates verbally this theme of painful confinement, the fear that goes with it, and the causes for it: "I am constantly disgusted by reality, horrified and afraid. . . . Humanity fills me with contempt and despair." He continues, "I hate my body" (2005h, 386). On a similar note, Kafka expresses comparable disdain for his body, linking it directly to the disgust he feels when he contemptuously thinks about his family: "I doubt that I am a human being" (Begley 2008, 23). For both Kafka and Crumb, this disparagement or discomfort results from "failing to be manly" as measured by standards of their respective societies (Boa 1996, 124). For Crumb, these repeated failures manifest themselves in the explicit, and for some readers offensive, depictions of his fantasies: "All my natural compulsions are perverted and twisted. Instead of going out and challenging myself against other males, all these impulses are channeled into sex. That's why I want to ravage big women" (Crumb 2005i, 28). By contrast, for Kafka, the failure often ends in death, or its metaphorical equivalent, as seen for example in *The Metamorphosis* (Boa 1996, 128). In the two parallel images discussed above, Crumb employs the metaphor of nakedness to lay bare entrenched fears and insecurities.

In both Crumb's and Kafka's cases, these insecurities are linked to sexu-ality. As the following examples attest, Kafka also led an anguished exis-tence with regard to his thoughts on sexuality and his relationships with women. About Kafka, who was "unable to integrate his own sexuality into his self-image" and his love life, Reiner Stach describes a constant "oscilla-tion between lust and disappointment [that] had never been interrupted" (2017, 239). This tension can be seen in a quotation from one of his letters to Milena Jesenská, a Czech journalist and translator of some of Kafka's texts who represented, according to Saul Friedländer, the "only passionate attachment of his life" (2013, 69). In the letter, Kafka assesses a rendezvous with a woman in nearly, but not quite, positive terms: "[T]his happiness was only because my ever-grumpy body had given me some peace at last" (cited in Stach 2017, 238). Essentially, Kafka expresses the same level of anxiety and unconcealed tension as Crumb when it comes to describing his relationships, although Crumb is often criticized for misogynistic tendencies. In one of many responses to these allegations, Crumb has admitted that he has a "lot of bitterness against women," but that he has "no desire to shock people for the sake of shocking. These are real things inside of me" (Hanna 2004, 171). Similarly, Kafka's work reflects real things going on inside of him and often, as previously discussed, emphasizes a protagonist thoroughly disgusted with his own sexuality and the topic in general. As his letters, diary entries, and fictional writing attest, Kafka often retreated into his own body, resulting in his heightened attention to internal disease and disorder, which also derived from his failed relationships with women. For Crumb's part, he turns feelings of inadequacy outward, often projecting them onto his sturdy and muscular women, a body type also prominently on display in *Introducing Kafka*. Crumb's robust female cartoon type emerges as a recognizable motif throughout the book and serves as Crumb's visual tool of interpretation for Kafka's disappointing experiences with a variety of women.

While Crumb's and Kafka's mutual thematic indexing initially captures the notion of a tortured, solitary artist, it also expands beyond that singular focus. Specifically, Kafka and Crumb consistently present, as Mairowitz puts it, "supporting female roles" upon whom the central character relies (2007, 127). This results in Kafka's female characters failing to define and own their identities, as a page in *Introducing Kafka* clearly demonstrates. As part of a discussion of Kafka's female literary characters, Mairowitz writes: "[They] are spawned in his imagination in order to distract 'K' or 'Joseph K,' to tempt and ensnare him. Kafka's sexual terror is put to the test time after time" (2007, 128). The corresponding sketch shows a terrified Kafka, eyes hollow and hair unkempt, being nearly torn limb from limb by a series of faceless women who appear in asymmetrical doorways in a crooked room. This rendition presents a visually intense and abstract examination of Kafka's relationships, or the "sexual terror" he senses with women. While not reaching the lewd dimensions that he achieves in his own comics, Crumb applies his techniques and links visual quotations as well as antecedent images, which reveal in blatant terms his "honest" confrontation with "sexual rage or obsessions" (Hanna 2004, 172). In his own body of work, Crumb often draws representations of "perverted" and "twisted" "natural compulsions" (Crumb 2005i, 28). Crumb's sketches in *Introducing Kafka* reveal the same obsessions and compulsions, sometimes in a more tempered way, other times with the bold visual style more characteristic of Crumb's other works. Seemingly uncharacteristic for

Kafka, he often wrote about indecent or even pornographic thoughts as this diary entry from November 1913 reveals: "I intentionally walk through the streets where there are whores. Walking past them excites me, the remote but nevertheless existent possibility of going with one. Is that grossness?" (cited in Friedländer 2013, 74). In his body of work, Crumb also devotes a lot of time to depicting his tendencies of intently observing women, in whom, as this description of Kafka's choices imparts, "[n]o one would have found anything exciting . . . only me" (Friedländer 2013, 74). Despite Kafka's degree of erotic directness, Crumb does not as consistently transfer any obscene elements of his comics style to *Introducing Kafka* as often as might be expected. In this sense, Crumb's milder illustrations mirror Kafka's style of using circumlocution or euphemism when addressing individual acts and confrontations. At other times, Crumb's drawings fill in the gaps with wild interpretations that Kafka, either with stylistic intention or out of shame, leaves unarticulated in his writing.

The broad category of relationships with women boils down to two thematic subthreads that both Crumb and Kafka exhibit in their work: first, women as foils for discovering a disgusting body or embodying a fear of the flesh, and second, women as a positive force offering personal protection. Many Kafka scholars have treated the topic of his repulsion and revulsion to intimacy with the opposite sex, and most discuss the oft-cited example of his describing the first sexual encounter of his life with a shop girl. Mairowitz explains Kafka's approach to the topic: "Kafka's talent would mostly SUGGEST erotic encounter, rather than indulging his characters in that act which he found 'repellent and perfectly useless'" (2007, 133). In the shop girl account, Kafka notes how she made "a tiny repulsive gesture (not worth mentioning)" and "had uttered a trifling obscenity (not worth mentioning), something slightly obscene (not worth mentioning) in the hotel" (Menninghaus 2003, 247). Elusive by design, this meeting marked Kafka's sexual development, his attitude toward sexuality, and the disgust that accompanies it (Menninghaus 2003, 247). This is a case in which Crumb uses his comic to fill in blanks that Kafka deliberately leaves open. The visual accompaniment in *Introducing Kafka* consists of one nearly full-page frame showing Kafka in a bedroom with the shop girl. The viewer sees Kafka from the back, still wearing his shirt, undershorts, and socks. He displays a tentative posture, which has been visually repeated throughout *Introducing Kafka* in a number of scenarios when he feels inferior or uneasy, such as walking to the ocean's edge for swimming lessons with his father (2007, 37) or ascending the stairs of a brothel with a prostitute (38). In this recurring motif, his tentative stance indicates physical weakness. His body bends to one side as if troubled by a slight deformity, and his head leans to one side, with lines and sweat beads indicating exasperation. By contrast, the viewer gets a full frontal view of the shop girl, nude except for thigh-high stockings and ankle-high boots. She authoritatively holds Kafka's wrist, his hand disappearing into her genitals (133). Through this particular interpretation of the thing "not worth mentioning," Crumb emphasizes Kafka's awkwardness and feelings of potential "grossness." Crumb also, however, makes his interpretation of the situation very clear, as the confident and outwardly expressive female is the symbol of the tortured artist's and the reader's objectifying gaze.

A comic antecedent from Crumb's work also shows an "erotic encounter" and exaggerated fears similar to the Kafka sketch. Crumb's strip "Grim Grids" from 1977 is a three-page, twenty-four-panels-per-page comic that encapsulates manic fears and perceptions about sexuality in exaggerated, grotesque, and concentrated form. The small frames allow for a stream-of-consciousness, rapid-fire presentation of Crumb's perceptions and connotations of large, physically overpowering and dominant women. The third page of Crumb's frantic comic features his signature muscular women, who eclipse the protagonist with their size. One particular frame—the comic antecedent for the Kafka shop girl frame discussed above—shows a naked, hulking woman next to whom stands a much smaller male character, his hand vanishing between her thighs. Unlike the Kafka picture, here the reader views both characters head on. The woman does not guide the man's hand. Instead he confidently places it between her thighs, adding, "Well, whatever it is, I wish you'd get busy!! Snicker giggle" in response to the exchange "What will you do?" "Can't tell you . . ." (Crumb 2005c, 369). Comparing the parallel sketches, the visual cues for the Kafka drawing seem to suggest that he would stay at the "What will you do?" stage and not progress to the "I wish you'd get busy" phase. Seemingly contradicting the perceived and even documented version of Kafka as sexually curious and arousable yet fearful to the point of paralysis, Mairowitz writes in the text on the same page that this "repulsive" gesture is "precisely what excited [Kafka]" (2007, 133). Crumb uses his sketches to show his analysis of the slightly less neurotic side of Kafka and his sexuality. An accomplished cartoonist, Crumb has an understanding of comics as a form of storytelling whose carefully selected elements communicate narrative and emotional meaning. In the particular case of the shop girl story, the focus on Kafka's tentative posture and stance, coupled with clearly indicated exasperation, suggests that Kafka's shame about the circumstances outweighs his excitement. Additionally, as with previous examples, Crumb's fantasies of forceful reactions to female desire starkly contrast with the largely passive reactions that Kafka displays.

Crumb's tempered approach to presenting Kafka's sexual encounters indicates that he has not simply "Crumb-ified" Kafka, but has instead presented a multifaceted adaptation of Kafka's life and work.

Many of Crumb's comics consist of very blatant displays of his self-acknowledged nearly uncontrollable lust, yet simultaneous fear of and fascination with women. Personal writings and literary works verify that Kafka held very similar insecurities and obsessions. As mentioned above, in some instances Crumb employs slightly modified, even tempered methods for depicting Kafka's insecurities and obsessions. Consequently, Crumb's interpretations of Kafka's relationships place the topic of blatant sexuality into the background and bring Kafka's general obsessive nature to the foreground. For example, excerpts from Kafka's letters to Milena Jesenská are presented with quite a moderate visual tone. One page in *Introducing Kafka* shows a sweating, anxious-looking Kafka in one bubble and a calm Milena in the other, both writing and receiving letters in the exchange. Kafka explains his feelings about his body: "I'm dirty, Milena, infinitely dirty, that's why I'm obsessed with cleanliness. No song is purer than that sung in the depths of hell" (2007, 105). In a full-page illustration two pages later, a fully clothed Kafka with distant, hollow eyes lies atop Milena, who in turn looks patient. Milena provides an analysis of Kafka's mania: "But ... he will never be healthy as long as he has this fear ... It isn't just about me, about everything which is shamelessly alive, for example, the flesh. Flesh is too open, too naked: he can't bear the sight of it" (107). It is notable that Crumb, who often draws nudes in other contexts, would in this circumstance show a couple, fully clothed, who could just as well be engaging in a couples therapy session. In this instance, he prioritizes through his drawing the theme of intimacy and the complexity of relationships over the simple fear of the flesh.

A pair of parallel images illustrates the second thematic arc: women as a positive supporting force. In this case, the image in *Introducing Kafka* serves as the antecedent for the image that appears in Crumb's "Oh Bear Me Away on Your Snowy White Wings" (1994; Crumb 2005f) (figs. 9.4, 9.5). Other images discussed here so far have been parallel or analogous, but, strikingly, these two images are nearly identical. The sketch in *Introducing Kafka* shows Kafka riding on an angel-like, confident, and capable version of his sister, Ottla, who holds him steady with her strong arms while Kafka simply flies along. Although still displaying a pained and troubled face, he does not emit the level of anxiety or fear that other portraits in the book have shown. In a completely different drawing style, Crumb provides a glimpse of the world above which Ottla whisks her brother away. Mimicking the style of George Grosz (Crumb even inserts an acknowledgment), the artist depicts a collage

Fig. 9.4. R. Crumb, *Introducing Kafka*, Copyright © Robert Crumb, 1993. All rights reserved.

of Grosz-inspired figures in a hectic and frightening world (2007, 135). Mairowitz provides the verbal caption to the picture: "In his personal life, women also provided a REFUGE from his father, the chief bearer of this Herculean task being his younger sister, Ottla" (135). In this fantasy-like drawing, Crumb indeed absorbs and renders the feeling of security that Kafka received from his sister. Elizabeth Boa has noted that Kafka had called his sister "große Mutter," or great mother (1996, 56). Similarly, Saul Friedländer writes that Kafka fostered a "childlike dependency" on his sister (2013, 38). Nonetheless, as his slightly pained expression in the drawing attests, Kafka was well aware of the "loneliness of eternal bachelorhood," which "depressed him" (Unseld 1994, 226). Taken as a whole, the drawing conveys Kafka's overwhelming uncertainties and fear, even in the face of a protective, strong woman close to him.

Crumb's parallel image spans two pages and thus devotes more page time to the preparation for flying away (fig. 9.5). This additional frame allows Crumb to focus on the physical figure of the woman on whom the protagonist will fly. She possesses all the characteristics of his most typical women: sturdy legs, enormous calves, and hulking height. Before flying away, the Crumb-like comic figure says: "I'm ready . . . I've had enough" (Crumb 2005f, 426), to which the woman replies: "Your time has come, Mister! Hop on. I'll take you right out the window" (426). As a parallel to the Grosz-influenced world in the Kafka illustration, this one also shows what they are flying over or even away from: a middle-class house with a fence and sedan (427). The female figure here is Crumb's wife, Aline. The illustration mimics a photo of the two of them, with Crumb on Aline's back as she flexes her right arm (Crumb and Poplaski 2005, 216). A self-proclaimed "Mama's boy," Crumb has stated that he "needed somebody to save [him] from all the life threatening ravages connected with fame" (Crumb and Poplaski 2005, 217). The contradictions of their relationship are played out in "The Crumb Family," a comic that shows Aline alternately dropping back out of the cartoon to let Robert take over and then asserting herself, to both his delight and his chagrin. As emphasized above, this comparison between Crumb's depictions of himself and his representations of Kafka is not to make the overly simplistic argument that Crumb can readily and adeptly "absorb" Kafka's work because of biographical similarities. Instead, the clear similarity between these images—the most analogous of all the ones we have compared here—speaks most definitively for the corresponding index of themes found in Crumb's work, which he then employs as a tool to visually represent Kafka.

In this chapter, I have considered Crumb's interpretation and adaptation of Kafka's life and work in *Introducing Kafka*. I have used parallel or analogous

Fig. 9.5. R. Crumb, "Oh Bear Me Away on Your Snowy White Wings," Copyright © Robert Crumb, 1994.

antecedents from Crumb's work against which to read his interpretation of the primary subject matter: Kafka's life and work. In the presentation of common themes between the two, we see that Crumb's previous work informed the visual styles and themes of *Introducing Kafka*. Analyzing the parallel or analogous images also reveals the common social and political subtexts that the artist and author share. In at times crass, at times tempered terms, Crumb lays bare their shared thematic interest in social satire. Many people associate Kafka's work with seriousness or moroseness, and that is certainly the case in some instances. But Crumb, like Greg Ames, the short story author mentioned at the beginning of this chapter, highlights the humorous aspects of Kafka's work. For Crumb especially, the comics medium amplifies the absurdity that runs throughout Kafka's work. By adapting Kafka into comics form, Crumb blends high and low art as well as literary and comics cultures into a dialogue between the artist Crumb, the author Mairowitz, and the subject Kafka.

WORKS CITED

Alleva, Richard. 2002. "Comic Erudition: R. Crumb Meets Kafka." *Commonweal*, July 12, 18–19, 69.

Ames, Greg. 2017. *Funeral Platter: Stories.* New York: Arcade.

Begley, Louis. 2008. *The Tremendous World I Have Inside My Head: Franz Kafka, a Biographical Essay.* New York: Atlas.

Boa, Elizabeth. 1996. *Kafka: Gender, Class, and Race in the Letters and Fictions.* Oxford: Clarendon Press.

Corngold, Stanley, and Ruth V. Gross, eds. 2011. *Kafka for the Twenty-First Century.* Rochester, NY: Camden House.

Crumb, R. 2005a. "The Adventures of R. Crumb Himself." In *The R. Crumb Handbook,* by R. Crumb and Peter Poplaski, 181–84. London: MQ Publications.

Crumb, R. 2005b. "The Desperate Character." In *The R. Crumb Handbook,* by R. Crumb and Peter Poplaski, 366. London: MQ Publications.

Crumb, R. 2005c. "Grim Grids." In *The R. Crumb Handbook,* by R. Crumb and Peter Poplaski, 367–69. London: MQ Publications.

Crumb, R. 2005d. "The Many Faces of R. Crumb." In *The R. Crumb Handbook,* by R. Crumb and Peter Poplaski, 186–87. London: MQ Publications.

Crumb, R. 2005e. "No Way Out." In *The R. Crumb Handbook,* by R. Crumb and Peter Poplaski, 361. London: MQ Publications.

Crumb, R. 2005f. "Oh Bear Me Away on Your Snowy White Wings." In *The R. Crumb Handbook,* by R. Crumb and Peter Poplaski, 426–27. London: MQ Publications.

Crumb, Robert. 2005g. "The Artist and the Grim Reaper." In *The R. Crumb Handbook,* by R. Crumb and Peter Poplaski, 393–97. London: MQ Publications.

Crumb, Robert. 2005h. "The Litany of Hate." In *The R. Crumb Handbook,* by R. Crumb and Peter Poplaski, 386–87. London: MQ Publications.

Crumb, Robert. 2005i. "Poor Clod." In *The R. Crumb Handbook*, by R. Crumb and Peter Poplaski, 23–67. London: MQ Publications.

Crumb, R., and Peter Poplaski. 2005. *The R. Crumb Handbook*. London: MQ Publications.

Dougan, Michael. 2004. "A Conversation with R. Crumb." In *R. Crumb: Conversations*, edited by D. K. Holm, 164–69. Jackson: University Press of Mississippi.

Friedländer, Saul. 2013. *Franz Kafka: The Poet of Shame and Guilt*. New Haven, CT: Yale University Press.

Hanna, Deirdre. 2004. "R. Crumb Interview." In *R. Crumb: Conversations*, edited by D. K. Holm, 170–74. Jackson: University Press of Mississippi.

Hughes, Robert. 2005. "Time Magazine ART CRITIC." In *The R. Crumb Handbook*, by R. Crumb and Peter Poplaski, 294. London: MQ Publications.

Jones, Jonathan. 2000. "Self-Loathing Comics, Robert Crumb (1994)." *Guardian*, August 19. https://www.theguardian.com/culture/2000/aug/19/art.robertcrumb, accessed August 6, 2018.

Kafka, Franz. 1974. *Letter to His Father*. Translated by Willa and Edwin Muir. New York: Schocken Books.

Mairowitz, David Zane, and Robert Crumb. 1994. *Introducing Kafka*. Northampton, MA: Kitchen Sink Press.

Mairowitz, David Zane, and Robert Crumb. 2007. *Kafka*. Repr. ed. Seattle: Fantagraphics.

McKenna, Kristine. 2004. "Moving Day: A Visit with R. Crumb." In *R. Crumb: Conversations*, edited by D. K. Holm, 158–63. Jackson: University Press of Mississippi.

Menninghaus, Winfried. 2003. *Disgust: Theory and History of a Strong Sensation*. Translated by Howard Eiland and Joel Golb. Albany: State University of New York Press.

Mercier, Jean-Pierre. 2004. "Who's Afraid of R. Crumb?" In *R. Crumb: Conversations*, edited by D. K. Holm, 191–222. Jackson: University Press of Mississippi.

Nelson, Brandon. 2017. "'Sick Humor Which Serves No Purpose': Whiteman, Angelfood and the Aesthetics of Obscenity in the Comix of R. Crumb." *Journal of Graphic Novels and Comics* 8, no. 2: 139–55.

Stach, Reiner. 2017. *Kafka: The Early Years*. Translated by Shelley Frisch. Princeton, NJ: Princeton University Press.

Stein, Daniel, and Jan-Noël Thon. 2013. *From Comic Strips to Graphic Novels: Contributions to the Theory and History of Graphic Narrative*. Berlin: De Gruyter.

Strich, Fritz. 1949. *Goethe and World Literature*. London: Routledge.

Unseld, Joachim. 1994. *Franz Kafka: A Writer's Life*. Translated by Paul F. Dvorak. Riverside, CA: Ariadne Press.

Wallace, David Foster. 1998. "Laughing with Kafka." *Harper's*, July, 23–27.

Part IV

THE FINE ART OF COMICS

Chapter 10

ROBERT CRUMB AND THE ART OF COMICS

DAVID HUXLEY

A distinctive feature of Robert Crumb's career has been the early, and continuing, interest in his work from art historians. He was featured in the journal *Art and Artists* as early as 1969. In 1972, art critic Robert Hughes described him as "a kind of American Hogarth," and in Terry Zwigoff's 1995 documentary *Crumb*, Hughes describes him as "the Bruegel of the last half of the twentieth century." The list of respected art historians queuing up to praise Crumb is quite impressive, and this has generated a great deal of critical material. As early as 1981, Don Fiene's *R. Crumb Checklist* compiled 170 pages listing works by, and writings on, Crumb. Subsequent years have done nothing to dampen critical interest in his work, and for a man who has a reputation as a recluse, he has given a large number of interviews throughout his career.

ART AND GRAPHICS: A VIEW FROM THE 1960S

The idea of discussing Crumb in relation to art is hampered by the massive problem of defining "art" itself. There are also many various ways of defining practitioners—they might be described as artists, fine artists, illustrators, graphic artists, or indeed comic artists. Each term carries a different connotation in relation to the perceived status of the person described. In practical terms, it is impossible to resolve these problems in the space available here. In the field of the visual arts, everything from a "readymade" to a Pollock drip painting to a Leonardo anatomical drawing could be included. Thus, indeed, it might not be possible to provide an adequate definition even with much more space available—the *Stanford Encyclopedia of Philosophy* takes nineteen pages and over ten thousand words in an attempt at a definition and includes a disclaimer that the exercise may in the end be fruitless: "[T]he phenomena of art are, by their nature, too diverse to admit of the unification that a satisfactory definition strives for, or that a definition of art, were there to be such a thing, would exert a stifling influence on artistic creativity" (Adajian 2018).

When asked about the status of his "readymades" as art, the iconoclast artist Marcel Duchamp explained:

> Can we try to define art? We have tried. Everybody has tried. In every century there is a new definition of art, meaning that there is no one essential that is good for all centuries. So if we accept the idea of trying not to define art, which is a very legitimate conception, then the readymade comes in as a sort of irony, because it says, "Here is a thing that I call art, but I didn't even make it myself." As we know, "art," etymologically speaking, means "to hand make." (Hamilton 2018)

The rest of this chapter will be, in effect, a discussion that leads to an implied definition of art, one that can account for the comics of R. Crumb and the potential view of him as a "fine artist." Toward this end, I will analyze the nature and quality of Crumb's drawings and the influences on his style. One facet of Crumb's comics art is that, despite the fact that it is largely mechanically reproduced through printing, it nonetheless bears intentional marks of the "handmade," a notion that connects Crumb to people like Duchamp and also figures prominently in Crumb's own understanding of his work as art.

Yet Crumb's attitude to fine art is made crystal clear on the back cover of a 1969 issue of *Plunge into the Depths of Despair* comics. Under the headline "Drawing Cartoons Is Fun!," a simple stick-figure version of Crumb indicates a bearded, haloed figure on a pedestal in a traditional artist's smock. The figure is labeled "Faker" in large letters, and the text explains: "ART is just a racket. A HOAX perpetrated on the public by so-called 'Artists' who set themselves up on a pedestal and promoted by panty waste [*sic*] ivory-tower intellectuals and sob-sister 'critics' who think the world owes them a living!" Over a photograph of a woman fondling a shoe, the text continues: "It doesn't take a 'genius' to transform the photo on the left into the cartoon below! A sense of humor is all that's needed!" Unfortunately, Crumb's drawing is a skillful cartoon that owes little to the photographic source, which rather undermines the claim next to the drawing that "[t]here is no such thing as 'inborn talent.'" Nevertheless, Crumb's distaste for the art world is palpable, if somewhat ironic in relation to his current standing in the art world.

The difficulty of drawing like Crumb is demonstrated in a parody of his work that appeared in the January 1972 issue of *National Lampoon*, a publication that is characterized by its extreme irreverence. This issue, titled "Is Nothing Sacred?," features an image on the cover of Che Guevara being hit in the face by a large egg. The Crumb parody, "Fritz the Star," was written by Michael O'Donoghue, and the first two pages are essentially an attack on Crumb's Fritz the Cat through film director Ralph Bakshi's animation of the character, which Crumb hated unreservedly. The strip in *National Lampoon* was drawn by the perfectly capable and often dynamic cartoonist Randall Enos, and although he is able to catch something of the early look of Fritz in some panels, his crosshatching carries none of the conviction and control found in Crumb's work. The third page shows "Crumbland," a kind of underground Disneyland, but there is none of the strong design and clear composition so often found in Crumb. On the final page, there is a version of Crumb (which does not catch his style at all) who is described as "America's best-paid underground cartoonist," and who exclaims: "Honest, kids, I haven't sold out! My staff and I are gonna keep dishin' up those swell commix about '51 Hudsons and big lipped spades that say 'Yowsuh!' and 'Sho 'nuff!' and 'Lawzy me!' and cakewalking ketchup bottles and gandy goose and chubby squab-job teenyboppers with shiny boots and wow hooters ..." (O'Donoghue 1972, 61). The parody in fact largely misses the point, as Crumb, often struggling for money, prided himself in not "selling out."

In an issue of *The People's Comics* from 1972, in "The Confessions of R. Crumb," the author sits at his desk with a note saying, "Notice: R. Crumb does not sell out." Next to this is a trash basket with crumpled paper showing offers from "big time publishers" and agencies, which Crumb occasionally did receive. *National Lampoon* is also somewhat hypocritical in criticizing the potentially racist and sexist content of Crumb's work, as the same issue features another item by O'Donoghue, "The Vietnamese Baby Book," which today still retains the ability to shock. (Indeed, it is probably more shocking now than it was in the climate of 1972.) While a publication like *National Lampoon* parodies Crumb's success while making visible Crumb's distinction from mainstream cartooning, some of the first interest in Crumb from the traditional art world came even earlier, in 1969, when an edition of the august British art journal *Art and Artists* featured an article on American underground comics. In fact, the main focus of the article is Crumb's compatriot, the equally controversial S. Clay Wilson, and the cover features a violent, blood-soaked, full-color image of Wilson's pirate characters, with the journal's title stylized as *Art 'n' Artists*. The six-page article has more illustrations of Wilson's work, as well as works by other *Zap Comix* collective members

Victor Moscoso, Gilbert Shelton, and Rick Griffin. Crumb's importance is acknowledged in the text, where his sex comics are seen as a liberating force. The author, David Zack, comments: "If the matter comes to a fair trial, it would be easy to show *Zap*, *Snatch* and *Jiz* have all sorts of aesthetic value" (1969, 14). He quotes extensively from Crumb's comics and admires his style, writing, "*Zap* and *Snatch* do more than take pop images as high art material, a la Warhol, Indiana, Lichtenstein, Ramos, Thibaud. They extend the scope of popular art" (15). As we will see in due course, some later critics would see them in a different light. Although many fine art critics have continued to value Crumb's work, some comic historians, fellow cartoonists, and cultural historians have been highly critical of him.

On the other hand, there is little written about Crumb's way with words. His "Keep on Truckin'" image, its history and influence, are well known, but his work is littered with memorable text from "It's only lines on paper, folks!" to "More sick humor which serves no purpose." All of this is delineated in Crumb's distinctive lettering, a painstaking style with small serif marks on capital letters. The back pages of early issues of *Zap Comix* display his flair for design, with his lettering playing an important part. The back page of *Zap* #6 has "Cliffy the Clown" explaining: "You can help to solve the overpopulation problem this quick, easy way! This year, why not COMMIT SUICIDE!?" Below a leering clown face, that last line is executed in large, rounded letters, picked out in red. With a red explosion carrying the message "Too many people!" and several different lettering styles and sizes, the page is both attention grabbing and classically designed. Indeed, Crumb's comic pages are similar in that he nearly always uses a simple layout of six to eight pages, delineated in a shaky, hand-drawn line. The page designs he creates are made up of positive use of white space, solid blacks, and his usual crosshatching. The overall effect is to allow the drawings to breathe, at the same time creating a satisfying and balanced pattern design across the whole page.

In the early part of his career, Crumb's influence was felt outside the field of comics—it extended to the whole field of graphics. In 1971, *Print* magazine published an article titled "The Critique of Pure Funk" by Patricia Dreyfus, with a classic image of Fritz the Cat fondling his girlfriend above the title. Dreyfus describes "Funk" as "the kind of layout, drawing or photograph that makes the viewer gasp, with delight or disgust, 'They can't be serious!'" (1971, 13). Dreyfus interviewed a series of designers, who attributed this new aesthetic to the influence of underground comics and Crumb in particular. Peter Bramley of Cloud Studio commented: "Comix tell you about how people really feel. R. Crumb is into the mundane—you know, garbage and gas stations—but it's still about people living together and relating to each other"

(Dreyfus 1971, 62). Michael Gross, art director for *National Lampoon*, added: "We like to shake people up—it's a kind of Lenny Bruce attitude; the shock makes it even funnier" (Dreyfus 1971, 63). Other advertising images in the article show a range of influences. Even if advertisements or humor occasionally water down the shocking content of some underground comics, the impact of Crumb (in particular) and his peers is evident. Marks have meaning, and Crumb's drawing style amounts to a "statement" even before the content of his work is examined in more detail; advertisers can claim countercultural connections just by appropriating an underground drawing style.

ART AND COMICS IN THE TWENTY-FIRST CENTURY

After the underground boom died away, only a handful of artists were able to remain in the public eye. Crumb, perhaps along with Art Spiegelman, are rare examples of comic-book artists who achieved a wider cultural and artistic significance in the late twentieth century than is normal in the field. Bart Beaty and Benjamin Woo have pointed out that Crumb holds a unique position for a comic book artist, writing: "On the basis of specifically art-world prestige, Crumb is an elite cartoonist" (2016, 39). Beaty and Woo further argue that, although Crumb has this status in the art world, he is less studied in academic terms by comics scholars than some other artists, in particular Art Spiegelman and Alison Bechdel. The reasons for this, they believe, are twofold: "First, . . . Crumb works almost exclusively in shorter forms. Second, the interpretive strategies that are dominant in humanistic studies of culture are confounded by the deeply troubling content of much of Crumb's work" (30).

Beaty and Woo summarize their argument thus: "Unlike his friend Art Spiegelman, who is celebrated for a few great works (well, really one), Crumb is celebrated as a total artist. . . . Spiegelman may be known for producing *Maus*, but Robert Crumb is known for producing R. Crumb, and in the art world that makes all the difference" (41). They establish that figures who have produced one well-regarded graphic novel are the most written-about artists from a comics scholars' point of view (mainly artists, but with the addition of one writer, Alan Moore). Crumb's status, however, depends on both the catalogue raisonné–like publishing of his entire oeuvre by Fantagraphics Books, and the high prices achieved by his original artwork. The art world appears to be more forgiving of Crumb's sometimes controversial subject matter, and in Europe, in particular, he has been well regarded for some time. Part of this is due to how Crumb's work has been placed in fine arts traditions.

Brandon Nelson, although he recounts some problems with Crumb's imagery, sees elements in Crumb's work that relate to surrealism: "[T]he fetishized female bodies that so preoccupy Crumb . . . are turned over and around, folded and twisted and bent. . . . Salvador Dali is a highly visible precursor to Crumb's use of the female form, as seen in such works as *Le Rêve*" (2017, 152). For Ian Buruma, "his graffiti-like caricatures of animal greed and cruel lust in twentieth century America are closer to George Grosz than any artist I can think of. Like Grosz, Crumb is a born satirist, who brandishes his pencil like a stiletto. But he is funnier than the German artist, and wackier" (2006, 26).

However Crumb's later work has not always been to the liking of scholars and critics. Despite Crumb's pride in not selling out, he was again accused of this because of his 2009 *Book of Genesis*. In an interview, comics historian Paul Gravett pointed out to Crumb that "[a]mong the reviews of your *Book of Genesis*, Michel Faber in the *Guardian* wrote that it comes across as the fruits of indentured drudgery" (Gravett 2012). Crumb responded: "It sure felt like indentured drudgery when I was working on it," and in another interview he explained, "Well, the truth is kind of dumb, actually. I did it for the money and I quickly began to regret it" (Widmer 2010).

Yet Crumb's status in the art world is underlined by the number of exhibitions of his work that have appeared in traditional art galleries. He has appeared in many group and one-person exhibitions, particularly since the 1980s—on their website, the art gallery Sprüth Magers lists seventy-one exhibitions that include work by Crumb between 1983 and 2006. What is clear is that these exhibitions have gradually moved to more prestigious venues, particularly in the twenty-first century. In 2002, New York's Paul Morris Gallery held the exhibition *Who's Afraid of Robert Crumb? Cartoons and Drawings*. In 2003, the Daniel Weinberg Gallery in Los Angeles held the one-person exhibition, *Robert Crumb, On Paper: Drawings from the 1960s to the Present*.

In 2005, the exhibition *Robert Crumb: A Chronicle of Modern Times* was held at the Whitechapel Gallery in London. In a review of the exhibition in the *Guardian*, Laura Cumming commented:

> In the long fanfare to this present exhibition, Crumb has been favourably compared to Bruegel, Bosch and Gillray, Hogarth, Goya and even Monet (two souls turning themselves inside out for the sake of their art, it seems). And no praise appears without that blank word "genius." . . . But is it art? The time is long past when cartoons were thought too low to be high; even in his day, Gillray was compared with Michelangelo. (2005, 10)

It is a sign of the prestige that museum and gallery exhibitions can grant to a cartoonist that in a major left-leaning newspaper, the exhibition is singled out for such praise, with no real acknowledgment of Crumb's controversial status. Instead, the exhibit is an occasion to confirm the high-art status of the comics medium. Part of the fine art world's acceptance of Crumb's more outré sexual content may be due to the long-standing tradition of fine artists engagement with explicit sexual imagery. Although sometimes relegated to separate, discreet volumes, it is not difficult to find extreme sexual images produced by Thomas Rowlandson or Aubrey Beardsley. The list of major artists whose work includes or is centered around sexual imagery—equally shocking in their day—is vast, for instance Gustave Courbet, Pablo Picasso, Paul Gauguin, Egon Schiele, and Henri de Toulouse-Lautrec. The passing of history has lent a veneer of respectability to some of these works, but if there is a tacit agreement that the nature of certain artists (perhaps due to their perceived "genius") places them above and beyond the normal rules of propriety and behavior, then some of this license may have attached itself to Crumb's persona.

DRAWING STYLE AND MEANING

Crumb's influences have been widely chronicled. For instance, Mark Estren argues that Crumb was certainly influenced by Walt Disney and EC Comics as well as by many earlier American comic-strip artists. Crumb's drawing style developed through his early influences, artists such as Rube Goldberg, undergoing a series of stylistic changes in the subsequent forty-year period. Crumb has noted that one of his earliest inspirations was Walt Kelly's *Pogo*: "[Kelly's] characters inhabited a little world that attracted me. I didn't copy him directly, but I imitated his drawing style closely" (Crumb and Poplaski 1998, 23).

Crumb's *Big Yum Yum Book*, originally published in 1975 but drawn in 1963, is very linear and shows various influences, from Disney animation to the illustrator Maurice Sendak, and particularly in a large planet with a face that echoes Winsor McCay and Georges Méliès. However, Crumb's established drawing style as he became a major figure in underground comics is full of stylistic elements taken from early newspaper comic-strip artists. Cityscapes in his backgrounds are rendered with a strong outline of tall buildings, suggesting many windows to emphasize their bulk. The buildings are left quite plain, and the sky above them is accentuated with many swift horizontal lines. This design, which makes a clear but elegant backdrop to a

Fig. 10.1. R. Crumb, "Mr. Natural," Copyright © Robert Crumb, 1970. All rights reserved.

given frame, can be found in almost the same exact form in the backgrounds of early strips by Jack Farr and Rube Goldberg.[1] Crumb's characters, and the way they are drawn, also owe a debt to many classic newspaper-strip artists. The protruding noses, loose hatching in background, and also hatching to help delineate figures can be found in work by most humor artists in American newspaper strips in the early part of the twentieth century. Thus, figures who ironically look a little as if they had escaped from a Crumb comic can be found in the work of George Herriman, Bud Fisher, E. C. Segar, Rudolph Dirks, Fred Opper, Cliff Sterrett, and many others. Crumb is absolutely clear that he admires these artists and owes them a debt. In a discussion of Segar, Crumb praises the grounded nature of these cartoonists: "In the old days, those cartoonists just came out of the soup. It shows in their work, they couldn't escape it. They were part of that world" (George 2004, 57). The difference in Crumb's mature style is the density and weight of some of his lines, which make his figures seem more grounded and solid. Even character design shows Crumb's debt to early newspaper strips. Mr. Natural from 1970 (fig. 10.1) and Segar's character Professor O. G. Wotasnozzle from a 1934 *Sappo* strip (a companion strip to *Popeye*) (fig. 10.2) are remarkably similar in both design and drawing style.

Fig. 10.2. E. C. Segar, *Sappo*, 1934.

The change in Crumb's style from juvenilia to "classic" underground is evident in *The Complete Fritz the Cat*, published by Belier Press in 1978 and currently kept in print by Fantagraphics Books. The first story, in pencil, from 1959, clearly shows the influence of rounded, cute Disney characters. There are then several strips, including the story that became the basis for the 1972 animated version of the character, in which Crumb uses a thin, often eccentric line. Although there is quite a lot of hatching, this is mainly used to make certain areas stand out, and the whole feeling is quite open and airy. "Fritz the No-Good," from 1968, is a transitional strip. The main lines vary in thickness, and there are more passages with denser crosshatching and solid black areas. Finally, "Fritz the Cat: Superstar" from 1972, in which Crumb kills off the character, consistently uses heavier lines and more extensive crosshatching, the latter often emphasizing the shape and weight of different characters. This kind of crosshatching, if effective, can indicate how light is falling across an object, thus giving it weight and solidity. This technique is difficult to achieve with any degree of subtlety, as evidenced by *The Simpsons* creator Matt Groening. Remembering his time as a teenager trying to learn from existing comics, Groening comments: "We tried to figure out how to crosshatch like R. Crumb, but man, did our stuff look lame" (qtd. in

Beauchamp 1998, 2). Donald Ault points out the tension between these flat drawings ("it's only lines on paper, folks") and their presence as a "reality": "Crumb thus insists on the flatness and cartoony qualities of his drawings and yet draws them as if they are genuine, rounded beings whose ongoing worlds we are periodically glimpsing" (Ault 2004, 5). Yet it also true that even with a simple line drawing, Crumb has the ability to conjure up the illusion of objects in space, as in the drawing of the *Three Graces*, published in the *East Village Other*'s special cartoon issue in 1969 and later used as the cover image for *Cozmix Comics* #1 (1972). The preface to the book on Crumb's exhibition at the Museum Ludwig in Cologne comments on his early portraits: "Extraordinary in these works, but even clearer in the pen drawing of the *Three Graces* executed in 1968, is not only the precision of the drawn line, but also the extraordinary lightness with which Crumb suggests the figures' volume solely by means of contours" (Museum Ludwig 2004, 30).

Crumb's early style was created using a 0.0 Koh-I-Noor Rapidograph, which tends to produce a consistent, and in that size, very thin line. His more mature work benefits from the use of a crow quill pen. This is a modern version of a traditional quill pen and allows an artist to produce much more flexible and fluid marks that can be manipulated to produce an even more dynamic line. Interestingly, although much of Crumb's work seems spontaneous, he also admits to using Wite-Out, a correctional fluid that allows corrections to be made to a pen-and-ink drawing. These details are all brought out in an interview with Crumb by British political cartoonist Steve Bell in which Crumb, in a rare positive comment on his own artwork, adds: "I can crosshatch like a motherfucker" (Bell 2005). Crumb certainly seems, at times, to be identifying with well-established graphic artists such as William Hogarth and Thomas Rowlandson. In the 1987 BBC film *The Confessions of Robert Crumb*, he is seen poring over a James Gillray print with a magnifying glass, examining the artist's crosshatching. He voices his admiration for Pieter Bruegel and George Cruickshank as well as Gillray as he does so. There is a further complication here, in that certain artists who worked largely in print media, such as Gillray, Gustave Doré, and Honoré Daumier, are seen by some as "graphic artists" and therefore inferior in some way to "fine artists." Some of this criticism can be seen as simplistic, and unconvincing, boundary creation based on mediums—for instance, fine artists use oil paint, graphic artists use a pen. Work for pay is also inadequate as any true indication of status—fine artists are tied to agents and dealers in monetary pacts that are as restricting (although more lucrative) as contracts entered by jobbing, "for hire" illustrators. The only possible comparative judgments must be based on quality, despite the obviously subjective nature of such deliberations. What is certainly true is that Crumb's drawing style is outside the mainstream of American comic-book art styles.

Some of the classic artists of American comics, as varied as Kurt Schaffenberger and Jim Steranko, have a definitive drawing style that delineates every object and face in clear detail. Others, more commonly in newspaper strips, such as George Herriman, have a much looser, gestural style. Crumb lies somewhere between the two. The ability to render 3D objects from the "real world" in lines of pen and ink is a specific skill that Crumb has in common with earlier artists he admires, in particular Gillray and Hogarth.

The other key element in the success of a drawing is the actual quality of the line, the sense of the gesture and movement as the artist's hand moves across the paper. It is easy for a labored drawing to look flat and dead. Chris Ware's *The Acme Novelty Date Book, 1986–1995*, is a reproduction of his sketchbook, much of which is very similar in content and even style to Crumb's sketchbooks. In one pen-and-ink life drawing, Ware places a word balloon coming out of the sitter's mouth, saying "overdrawn" (2003, 97). With drawing, it is often the case that the key is knowing what to leave out, and when to stop. Walt Disney would complain to his artists that as their work was transferred to celluloid it would lose the vitality of their original sketches (although, as anyone who has tried to ink an animation cel will know, this is virtually inevitable). In *The Acme Novelty Date Book*, Ware describes Crumb as "the world's greatest living artist" on the verso title page.

Jed Perl, in a rather harsh review of a 2013 exhibition of Art Spiegelman's work, argues:

> Even the movie critic J. Hoberman, in his introduction to the catalogue of "Co-Mix," confesses that Spiegelman is only a "workmanlike draftsman" and that his "drawing may lack Crumb's virtuoso fluency or the charmingly stilted primitivism of a Kim Deitch. Spiegelman's draftsmanship is dead on arrival, an embarrassment when measured against the work of R. Crumb, the founder of the trippy comic, whose drawings, love 'em or hate 'em, can never be denied their rococo-grunge velocity. (Perl 2013)

"Rococo-grunge velocity" is a florid but not inaccurate description of Crumb's drawing style, but this is a very unfavorable review, and it is rather unfair to compare Crumb with any of his underground contemporaries, as he is widely acknowledged as the outstanding draftsman of the period. Interestingly, Crumb himself disagrees with this assessment. In a 1988 interview, he was confronted with the fact that Gil Kane (a hugely experienced comic book artist responsible for DC Comics' *Green Lantern* in the 1960s, and much more) had said that Crumb was one of the most natural, gifted draftsmen who had ever worked in comics. Crumb's response was, "Really? He must be blind. Talking through his hat. Good draftsman, my ass" (George 2004, 58). Whether this is simple perversity or genuine modesty is not clear. It is entirely possible, of course, for a talented artist to be unsatisfied with their work. Striving for better quality keeps many artists working for their whole lives. Crumb might accept the high quality of his crosshatching, but he may see this as only a bright spot in a catalog of other, wider failures.

There were further developments in Crumb's style—some of his sketch-book work became even looser, and some strips much darker, the latter variation due largely to his increased use of a brush. This gave Crumb's figures even more density and at times made them look a little more like some mainstream American comics styles. In the first issue of *Hup* (1987), both the front cover and inside front cover display a brash, bold version of Crumb's hatching technique, produced with brushwork rather than pen. The figure of graphic novel marketing man Stan Schnooter, both his face and his sharp suit, are portrayed as if dramatically lit and hewn from some solid, tangible material. The self-congratulatory Stan, who ironically promises the audience "more than just . . . spectacular inking!," is thus portrayed in the most gro-tesque manner, appearing almost as repulsive as Crumb's most unflattering portraits of himself. It is also clearly a heartfelt attack on mainstream comics management figures Stan Lee and Jim Shooter, distinguishing the work of an artist like Crumb from the corporate comics industry.

Although Crumb's most famous and arguably most outstanding work is in black and white, he has produced many works in color as well, but these are generally not as highly regarded. Award-winning photorealist painter Marc Trujillo comments, "Crumb's color work doesn't live up to his line work. It just sits on top of the drawing, like part of separate, less interesting conversation. The color doesn't integrate with the drawing, tonally" (qtd. in Beauchamp 1998, 156).

However, I would argue that there is some variation in Crumb's color work. Examples in his sketchbooks, and some painted covers that use water-colors to supplement his line drawings, work very well. Although some of his fully painted works are very striking, they tend not to show the consummate skill in handling the medium when compared to his pen-and-ink work. A book like *R. Crumb's Heroes of Blues, Jazz, and Country* provides a direct comparison between fully painted subjects and the ink-and-color renditions of the same subject matter. The former, though just as effective a likeness of the subject, does not have the dynamism, the 3D illusion, or the impact of the ink-and-color versions. Crumb's paintings are often dynamically designed and never less than highly competent. His line work, however, whether colored or not, is remarkable and marks him out as one of the outstanding draftsmen of his day.

CONTENT AND CONTROVERSY

In looking at how Crumb drew his comics and what qualities they display in terms of draftsmanship and design, the content of his work is arguably secondary. Yet such is the controversy surrounding the content of some of his work that it cannot be ignored, particularly as his drawing style directly impacts the way his content is perceived. It is worth pointing out that a huge amount of Crumb's output is comparatively inoffensive. Some strips featuring Mr. Natural, the revisiting of childhood characters with Fuzzy the Bunny, many of his observational sketches, and much more are not calculated to or likely to offend. But it is his forays into sexual imagery and his portrayal of ethnic characters that have caused problems. People are never going to agree about these aspects of Crumb's work—he is simply too divisive—but I will rehearse some of the key arguments.

A central argument in defense of Crumb draws from his cultural context in mid-twentieth-century America. It is difficult, perhaps, for those who didn't live through the 1950s and early 1960s to realize just how liberating the attitudes of the counterculture were in the later 1960s. This is reflected in the David Zack article mentioned earlier (1969). There seemed a possibility that young people could help sweep away the hypocrisy and dull conformity of the immediate postwar period. To an extent, it can be argued that this did happen, but of course in reality the changes were more complex and contradictory.

Particularly troubling for many were the stories that portrayed violence toward women, even if, for Crumb, they were couched in comedic terms. There were other defenses of Crumb during the time he was producing his early work. In 1970, Harvey Pekar wrote: "In addition to the stuff about sex and dope there's also some good healthy violence in Crumb's work—Bertrand Russell getting hit with a meatball (nothing is sacred to Crumb), a kid smashing his head against a wall, a sadist biting a girl's toes . . . all kinds of violence" (1970, 684). Pekar concludes: "There is a mean, cynical side to Crumb's work" (684).

For some, what had begun as a new freedom in addressing sexual matters then became license, and abuse of that freedom for others. Roger Sabin

comments: "To say he was slow to recognize the aims of the Women's Liberation would be an understatement: his strips are crowded with misogynist
images, often involving violence. His excuse was that he was expressing his
innermost feeling, as every artist has a duty to do; but this did not satisfy
feminists" (1996, 95–96). This is something of an understatement in itself,
and it should also be pointed out that the offense Crumb caused was not
just to feminists. Fellow underground cartoonist Trina Robbins describes her
reaction to his work: "I was horrified! It was very hostile to women. Now, I
hadn't even heard of the term 'women's liberation' yet . . . but I knew anti-
woman hostility when I saw it" (qtd. in Beauchamp 1998, 41). Susan Goodrick,
interviewing Crumb, told him: "Some of your stories make me angry. Except
for Lenore Goldberg [a character in Crumb's *Motor City Comics* (1969–1970)]
you don't show women that are warm, compassionate, intelligent, or independent" (Donahue and Goodrick 1974, 14). In the first standard history
of underground comics, Mark Estren laments: "What is upsetting about
Crumb's attitude to women is that he seems unable to escape chauvinism
even when he really wants to" (1987, 130). In an interview from 1974, Crumb
seems fairly relaxed about the controversy, claiming: "You can't criticize the
idea of complete freedom or artistic freedom, of course. Some people are
going to take advantage of that" (Green 1974, 22). For many, Crumb was the
one taking advantage. In the same interview, he also claims: "I'm a has-been.
You should be interviewing Aline [an underground cartoonist staying at
Crumb's farm]. You'd get a much more dynamic story—all about the new
women's movement in comics. It'd definitely be more interesting than doing
me" (Green 1974, 20). It is interesting that at this point Aline Kominsky (later
Kominsky-Crumb) is relatively unknown, and also that Crumb is genuinely
championing women's comics. Yet there is no doubt that his portrayal of
women did alienate readers both within and outside the counterculture.
However, Art Spiegelman's defense of 1930s small-format pornographic comics, referred to as "Tijuana bibles," could be equally be applied to Crumb's
sexual content: "There are bound to be those who will loudly declaim that
the Tijuana Bibles demean women. I think it's important to note that they
demean everyone, regardless of gender, ethnic origin, or even species. It's
what cartoons do best, in fact" (Spiegelman 2004, 9).

Equally troubling for many readers was Crumb's perceived racism, particularly in his character Angelfood McSpade, who first appeared in 1967.
When I first wrote about this, I saw him as patently satirical, but it is clearly
a more complex issue than that (Huxley 2002). As a man who has had two
Jewish wives and labored at great length to produce portraits of Black blues
singers, it is unlikely that Crumb should be labeled as an overt racist, but

using outdated racist imagery with satirical intentions is clearly fraught with danger. As Gerald Early writes: "It would be fair to him and his art to suggest that he might be dramatizing his own racism in some way, or collective white fantasies" (Early 2004, 76).

Crumb eventually did admit that he could, in retrospect, see some of these problems: "Irrespective of its satirical content, McSpade became simply too hot to handle. . . . It got so damn touchy," he said of the matter in an interview with the *Guardian* in 2005. "I was naïve when I was young, I thought everybody would see the satire, this making fun of racist images. . . . But I can understand it, I can see it can be hurtful. Yes" (Lowey and Prince 2014, 94). Estren comments: "[O]ne can perhaps find some understanding for S. Clay Wilson, whose drawings are equally debasing to everyone and everything and who is therefore less a chauvinist and more an out-and-out misanthrope" (1987, 129). This might be applied to Crumb as well, although his use of racist tropes from cartooning history add a historical sweep to his work that tempers the expressive meaning one may infer from his comics.

Crumb has cited artists such as Rowlandson and Hogarth as influences on his style, and the content of the work of all three artists contains imagery that their respective contemporaries found to be offensive on either sexual or political grounds. According to Frederick Antal, Hogarth's contemporary and friend, artist and writer George Vertue

> reports that the artist painted a certain prostitute getting out of bed *en dishabille* and, when the picture proved a success, followed it up with a companion piece; later on the idea of a moralising cycle based on these occurred to him. . . . Hogarth was no prude; his own small collection of engravings included the mezzotints of John Smith after the cartoons of *The Loves of the Gods*, attributed to Titian and belonging to the Duke of Marlborough, a series with very obvious erotic appeal. (Antal 1962, 17)

Martin Barker has pointed out the difficulties of providing a definitive reading of any given comics text. In a discussion of Carl Barks (another artist admired by Crumb) and Scrooge McDuck, he examines four different approaches to this work. The stories are seen as an endorsement of American capitalism, a parody of wealth, a critique of capitalism, and a dialogic text in which different characters embody various attitudes to life as a whole (Barker 1989, 279–99). Barker sums up: "The same information, interpretable in four different ways . . . these disagreements seem to turn on the role of humour in the stories" (287). Crumb's work varies hugely, and the majority of his work that has been accused of being racist, if taken as humorous, can be seen as ironic and broad satire. His work that deals with sex is also problematic. Some can again be seen as satire, but the more personal and confessional strips are frequently misogynistic and sexist.

In the end, Crumb's artwork has an impact on the way all these issues are debated. The bold, rounded, "in your face" nature of his drawings means that when he deals with sexually explicit imagery, the viewer is spared no detail, and the images are startling in their impact. If he is compared to another controversial artist of the underground comics field, S. Clay Wilson, a contrast can be seen. In Wilson's chaotic drawing style there is sexual violence aplenty, but the images are flat and cartoony compared to Crumb's figures. In some cases, in order to see genital mutilations, decapitations (and much more), the viewer almost has to search them out, particularly in his larger, dense panels. Crumb's work is, in contrast, lucid and therefore more shocking. With Crumb, it is as if a talented but rogue Walt Disney or Max Fleischer from the 1930s had delineated sexual themes in great clarity and without any censorship mechanism in place.

CONCLUSION

It is interesting to look at how various guides and sources have tried to summarize Crumb since he came to prominence. Maurice Horn's *The World Encyclopedia of Comics* acknowledges Crumb's difficult content but concludes: "In short, Crumb, a living anachronism in personal life . . . completely changed the mores in the 1960s and early 1970s" (Horn 1976, 189). Lambiek Comiclopedia describes him as "the creator of unforgettable characters" (2020). Wikipedia's "Robert Crumb" entry opens with the following summary: "His work displays a nostalgia for American folk culture of the late 19th and early 20th centuries, and satire of contemporary American culture." Not until the ninth line is the "scatological" and "pornographic" nature of some of his work mentioned, and overall the criticism of his work is neglected. It seems as if Crumb's historical importance and influence outweigh his controversial status. This is due, in part, to the fact that he has been canonized by art museums and galleries.

It could be argued that the art world is populated by many people with a great deal of money but little idea of what actually constitutes a good painting. Thus they rely on "experts" to tell them what is "good art," and reputation becomes paramount. A Rembrandt drawing that does not have recognized attribution may still be a Rembrandt drawing, but worth only a fraction of a fully attributed one. In 2017, Crumb's *Fritz the Cat* cover of 1969 sold for $717,000 in New York. The prices of Crumb's artwork may wax and wane, as prices do with any artist, but his name alone connotes value in the art world. On the one hand, collectors can rely more on the provenance of works from a living artist, and Crumb's fame (or notoriety), the films made about him, and other factors underscore his status and thus his market value. His eccentricity and personal fame are, in fine art terms, virtually "normal" for the traditional notion of the artist as "genius."

Crumb has appeared in numerous group exhibitions, and perhaps the most telling in terms of his increasing status in the art world is the 2016 exhibition at the Seattle Art Museum, *Graphic Masters: Dürer, Rembrandt, Hogarth, Goya, Picasso, R. Crumb*. He appears, unapologetically, with five of the most prestigious graphic artists in the history of art, all of whom, due to the immense variety of their output, are clearly recognized as important "fine artists." It appears that the only reason his name comes last in this august company is that the artists are listed in chronological order. The 2004 Museum Ludwig book mentioned earlier asked the question, "Yeah, but is it art?" On page 10, the book's authors answer the question: "Yeah, of course."

NOTE

1. An example of this kind of background in Jack Farr's *Bringing Up Bill* can be found in Holtz 2005. A 1911 drawing by Goldberg with a similar background is compared to Crumb's work in Huxley 2002, 18.

WORKS CITED

Adajian, Thomas. 2018. "The Definition of Art." *Stanford Dictionary of Philosophy*, rev. August 14, 2018. First posted, October 23, 2007. https://plato.stanford.edu/entries/art-definition/#HisDef.

Antal, Frederick. 1962. *Hogarth and His Place in European Art*. London: Routledge and Kegan Paul.

Ault, Donald. 2004. "Preludium: Crumb, Barks, and Noomin; Re-Considering the Aesthetics of Underground Comics." *ImageTexT* 1, no. 2. http://www.english.ufl.edu/imagetext/archives/v1_2/intro.shtml, accessed September 13, 2018.

Barker, Martin. 1989. *Comics: Ideology, Power, and the Critics*. Manchester: Manchester University Press.

Beaty, Bart, and Benjamin Woo. 2016. *The Greatest Comic Book of All Time: Symbolic Capital and the Field of American Comic Books*. New York: Palgrave Macmillan.

Beauchamp, Monte, ed. 1998. *The Life and Times of R. Crumb*. New York: St. Martin's Press.

Bell, Steve. 2005. "Robert Crumb." *Guardian*, March 18. https://www.theguardian.com/film/2005/mar/18/robertcrumb.comics.

Buruma, Ian. 2006. "Mr. Natural." *New York Review of Books*, April 6, 26–31.

Crumb, R. 1978. *The Complete Fritz the Cat*. New York: Belier Press.

Crumb, R. 2006. *R. Crumb's Heroes of Blues, Jazz, and Country*. New York: Harry N. Abrams.

Crumb, R., and Peter Poplaski. 1998. *The R. Crumb Coffee Table Book Art Book*. London: Bloomsbury.

Cumming, Laura. 2005. "The Artist Who Ain't Brougil." *Guardian*, April 3, 10. https://www.theguardian.com/artanddesign/2005/apr/03/art.robertcrumb.

Donahue, Don, and Susan Goodrick, eds. 1974. *The Apex Treasury of Underground Comics*. New York: Links Books.

Dreyfus, Patricia. 1971. "The Critique of Pure Funk." *Print* (November–December): 13–21, 62–65.

Early, Gerald. 2004. "The 1960s, African Americans, and the American Comic Book." In *Strips, Toons, and Bluesies: Essays in Comics and Culture*, edited by D. B. Dowd and Todd Hignite, 60–81. New York: Princeton Architectural Press.

Estren, Mark James. 1987. *A History of Underground Comics*. Berkeley, CA: Ronin Publishing.

Fiene, Don. 1981. *R. Crumb Checklist*. Cambridge, MA: Boatner Norton.

George, Milo, ed. 2004. *The Comics Journal Library*. Vol. 3, *R. Crumb*. Seattle: Fantagraphics.

Gravett, Paul. 2012. "Robert Crumb: Interview." http://www.paulgravett.com/articles/article/r._crumb1/.

Green, Keith. 1974. "What's a Nice Counter-Culture Visionary Like Robert Crumb Doing on a Secluded Farm in California?" *Inside Comics* 1, no. 1 (Spring): 18–25.

Hamilton, George Heard. 2018. "A 1959 Interview with Marcel Duchamp: The Fallacy of Art History and the Death of Art." Artspace, February 21. https://www.artspace.com/magazine/art_101/qa/a-1959-interview-with-marcel-duchamp-the-fallacy-of-art-history-and-the-death-of-art-55274.

Holtz, Allan. 2005. "Perennial Reprint Comic Strips." Stripper's Guide, November 1. http://strippersguide.blogspot.com/2005/11/perennial-reprint-comic-strips.html.

Horn, Maurice, ed. 1976. *The World Encyclopedia of Comics*. London: New English Library.

Huxley, David. 2002. *Nasty Tales: Sex and Drugs and Rock 'n' Roll in the British Underground*. Manchester: Headpress.

Lambiek Comiclopedia. 2020. "Robert Crumb." https://www.lambiek.net/artists/c/crumb.htm.

Lowey, Ian, and Suzy Prince. 2014. *The Graphic Art of the Underground: A Countercultural History*. London: Bloomsbury.

Museum Ludwig. 2004. *Yeah, But Is It Art? R. Crumb Drawings and Comics*. Cologne: Museum Ludwig and Walter König.

Nelson, Brandon. 2017. "'Sick Humor Which Serves No Purpose': Whiteman, Angelfood and the Aesthetics of Obscenity in the Comix of R. Crumb." *Journal of Graphic Novels and Comics* 8, no. 2: 139–55.

O'Donoghue, Michael. 1972. "Fritz the Star." *National Lampoon*, January, 58–61.

Pekar, Harvey. 1970. "Rapping about Cartoonists, Particularly Robert Crumb." *Journal of Popular Culture* 3, no. 4 (Spring): 677–88.

Perl, Jed. 2013. "Art Spiegelman Is Comics' Most Pretentious Faux-Artist." *New Republic*, November 19. https://newrepublic.com/article/115649/art-spiegelman-retrospective-jewish-museum.

Sabin, Roger. 1996. *Comics, Comix and Graphic Novels: A History of Comic Art*. London: Phaidon.

Spiegelman, Art. 2004. "Those Dirty Little Comics." In *Tijuana Bibles: Art and Wit in America's Forbidden Funnies, 1930s–1950s*, by Bob Adelman, 4–10. New York: Simon and Schuster.

Ware, Chris. 2003. *The Acme Novelty Date Book*. Vol. 1, *1986–1995*. Amsterdam: Oog and Blik.

Widmer, Ted. 2010. "R. Crumb, the Art of Comics No. 1." *Paris Review*, no. 193 (Summer): 19–57.

Zack, David. 1969. "Smut for Love, Art, Society." *Art and Artists* 4, no. 9 (April): 12–17.

ⓋⒾⒺⓌⒾⓃⒼ Ⓡ. ⒸⓇⓊⓂⒷ

Chapter 11

Circles of Influence in Fine Art Museums

KIM A. MUNSON

In 2010, when it was still surprising to see the work of a comics artist featured in an exhibition at a major fine arts museum, I happened to wander into *Compass in Hand: Selections from the Judith Rothschild Foundation Contemporary Drawings Collection. Compass in Hand* surveyed contemporary works on paper then recently acquired by the Museum of Modern Art in New York (MoMA). I was pleased to find a pair of excellent examples of R. Crumb's work, *God Wants Me to Draw* (2003), a group of quick sketches of people and complicated vehicles on a placemat, and *The Complete Fritz the Cat* (1976), a drawing of Fritz lying under a tree dreaming of women. Surrounding the two Crumb drawings were works that had arguably been influenced by either Crumb himself or underground comics in general, by artists such as Jim Shaw, Mike Kelley, Rosemarie Trocket, Kai Althoff, Karen Kilimnik, and H. C. Westermann.

The focal point of the gallery was Paul McCarthy's 2001 mural-sized drawing *Penis Hat*, which depicts a pirate with a penis and testicles draped over his head, a cannon for his nose, and jokes about "penis sausages." McCarthy's work clearly draws influence from the randy pirate comics drawn by S. Clay Wilson, like *Zap Comix* #2's "Head First" (1968). Although it was obvious to me that underground comics and their sexual themes were a common thread among most of the works that were hung there, curator Christian Rattemeyer makes no reference to comics in either the show's wall panels or in its substantial catalog. Indeed, the Crumb and McCarthy works are reproduced without comment in *Compass in Hand*'s exhibition catalog (Rattemeyer 2010, 283, 292).

MoMA has minimized the importance of comics before, most notably in the controversial 1990 show *High & Low: Modern Art, Popular Culture,* curated by the museum's then-new director Kirk Varnedoe and *New Yorker* art critic Adam Gopnik. *High & Low* set out to celebrate the links between comics, caricature, advertising, and graffiti. Although Gopnik writes of the interaction between fine art and comics with great insight and detail in the enormous show catalog, the exhibit design in the museum left comics fans and advocates feeling that the curators were still showing works by respected cartoonists like Winsor McCay, George Herriman, and Crumb only as source material for renowned works in MoMA's permanent collection by Jasper Johns, Andy Warhol, Roy Lichtenstein, and Philip Guston.[1] MoMA's *Compass in Hand* and *High & Low* exhibits were both inclusive and dismissive, two landmark moments in comics art's contentious incorporation into museums and the larger art world.

In comics' uneven acceptance into the museum and art world, R. Crumb has been a reluctant but essential figure. From his first show at the Art Museum of Peoria (Illinois) in 1966 to the present, Crumb has become one of the few cartoonists to be so accepted by the fine art and museum establishment in the United States. He had a solo, multicity touring exhibit, *R. Crumb's Underground* (2009–2010), and is represented by a major New York City–based gallery, David Zwirner. Most recently, Crumb's *Book of Genesis Illustrated* has been shown in the United States and Europe, and he was the subject of a career-spanning retrospective at the Musée d'Art Moderne de la Ville de Paris in 2012. Crumb has set sales records for original comic art with Heritage Auctions' 2018 sale of his 1969 *Fritz the Cat* cover art for $717,000.[2] Curators like Gopnik in the *High & Low* exhibition catalog often praise Crumb as one of "the most singular and original comic artists since Herriman" (Varnedoe and Gopnik 1990, 213).

Such celebrations of originality are often accompanied by controversy. Some of Crumb's challenging comics from the 1960s and 1970s, for example, have been criticized for their depictions of rape, violence, misogyny, and racism by both contemporaries like Trina Robbins and those who have encountered his work in the wake of the #MeToo and #TimesUp movements. Later in this chapter, I will briefly examine these controversies and some of the broad generalizations surrounding them, as well as comments by three prominent artists—Trina Robbins, Margaret Harrison, and Rebecca Warren—whose responses to Crumb's extremes shaped their own work.

Before getting into that, I will discuss some of the reasons why Crumb's work is exhibited with the kind of attention and publicity usually extended to fine art superstars, such as his career longevity, his central place in the history of comics, his distinctive art style, the breakthrough of his uncensored personal content, his artistic forebears, and the multitude of artists who cite him as an influence, just a few of the many factors that attract curators to his work. MoMA may have silently included Crumb with his peers and followers in the *Compass in Hand* exhibit, but many other shows, such as *Underground Classics*, *Masters of American Comics*, and *Graphic Masters* are much more direct when they place Crumb among different peer groups and movements. The last third of this chapter will look at the curatorial strategies behind these and other shows in some detail, focusing on how Crumb has been positioned within the fine arts.

WHY CRUMB?

For decades, comics artists have had an ambivalent relationship with the fine art world. In the 1950s and 1960s, abstraction was dominant in US museums, galleries, college art classes, and art publications, supported by the ever expanding, lucrative art market that grew up around modernism. Comics art as well as most representational and commercial art was generally considered to be "low art" by the art world, and comic book publishers themselves endured a decade of repressive censorship in the United States because comic books were deemed a threat to literacy and a cause of juvenile delinquency. Even the artists working in comics often looked at themselves as craftspeople and entertainers, believing that their original drawings were nothing but artifacts of the production process.

Following the distribution chain of psychedelic rock posters into head shops, record stores, and college bookstores, the underground comics movement of the late 1960s was independent and definitely for adults, expounding on counterculture politics and the drug culture. R. Crumb was one of the first successes in underground comics, famously selling copies of *Zap #1* out of a baby buggy in San Francisco's Haight-Ashbury district in 1967 and rapidly finding himself in the center of the movement.

So how, given the resistance the art world had to "kitschy" genres like comics, did the artist known for "Keep on Truckin'" become one of the breakthrough comics artists, headlining high-profile museum and gallery exhibits? The following list captures what made Crumb viable as a comics artist in the art world:

- Film: Crumb and his creations have been featured in several films, notably Ralph Bakshi's animated version of *Fritz the Cat* (1972) and Terry Zwigoff's documentary *Crumb* (1995), which exposed his work to a wider audience.

- The Counterculture: Museumgoers have shown an affectionate fascination with the 1960s counterculture in general and the Haight-Ashbury "Summer of Love" scene in particular. In Crumb's case, museums can point to him as a pioneer, one of the founders of the underground movement that was born with the memorable *Zap* baby carriage story. His art also became associated with 1960s music icons like Janis Joplin and the Grateful Dead.

- Timing: The peak and fizzle of the underground era coincides with the rediscovery of comics by university art galleries in the early 1970s. College students were also an audience deeply interested in underground comics.

- Independence: Underground comics were perceived as personal, independent works not driven by newspaper syndicates or the major comic book publishers, and as such the cartoonists were always considered creators in their own right. Many intellectuals came to celebrate the undergrounds as a breakthrough for the comics medium.

- Content: Related to the underground's independence from mainstream publishers and the censorship of the Comics Code Authority, the undergrounds featured autobiographical, political, and social content. Topics ranged from sex, violence, and fantasy to real-life problems and gender issues. They are a record of their era, distinctly depicting the clothes, customs, and attitudes of the counterculture.

- Art style: Crumb is a skilled draftsman drawing in a detailed, anxious, throwback style, influenced by old masters like Rembrandt, Bruegel, and Goya, comics predecessors like Herriman, Ahearn, Capp, Segar, and Wolverton, and cartoonists like Nast, Gillray, and Cruikshank. Because he was also an important influence on the generations of artists following him, Crumb is attractive to curators who wish to show his work as a hub in the wheel of art history.

- Variety: Crumb's work spans decades. As his projects and interests have changed and his style has evolved, curators have a wide variety of work to choose from.

While many of the items above have to do with Crumb's historical context, he is often celebrated by critics and curators alike as a singular genius. In the opening pages of his 2006 book *In the Studio*, critic and curator Todd Hignite offers this summary of Crumb's cultural legacy:

> Robert Crumb stands as the foremost artist of the past forty years to work in the comic medium. Two generations of cartoonists have looked to him as an ideological role model, both in terms of the expertly crafted realization of his aesthetic and, if not specific subject matter, then certainly his complete freedom of content, markedly lacking in concession or self-censorship. Nobody has been more significant to the move away from genre restrictions or commercial imperatives of any kind toward a personal vision than Crumb: his example of dogged introspection and total rejection of the medium's most egregious pandering to a juvenile market has provided encouragement to a generation of inventively autobiographical, socially engaged, and artistically committed cartoonists. (Hignite 2006, 6)

In agreement with those ideas, John Carlin, curator of the 2005 blockbuster exhibition *Masters of American Comics* (shown jointly at the Hammer Museum and the Museum of Contemporary Art in Los Angeles), points out how Crumb's line work reveals his psychological state, giving future artists permission to express themselves freely: "One can see this [Crumb's mental state] in Crumb's line work as well as in what his lines depict. He deliberately draws lines that seem out of place and about to drift across the page to convey a sense of the emotional impact of what he is looking at and drawing. Herriman's line work also defied convention, but Crumb took the approach further, giving future cartoonists not just the freedom to express themselves but also the tools with which to do so" (Carlin 2005, 125). Carlin goes on to discuss Crumb's interest in 1920s music and old cartoons in the context of older folk styles appropriated by counterculture musicians like Bob Dylan, Arlo Guthrie, and the Grateful Dead. Contrasting this rediscovery of folk styles to the conceptual art filling the art museums of the 1960s, Carlin says: "At a time when abstract and conceptual art dominated American culture, Crumb's comics stubbornly remained based on skillful realistic drawing. At first this made his work seem old-fashioned and out of touch. But Crumb's work was able to represent significant aspects of modern life that were almost completely missing in mass media. He showed how it felt to be alive in the middle of the twentieth century as well as how it really looked" (125).

While Hignite and Carlin celebrate Crumb for returning autobiography, recognizable figures, and the things of everyday life to art, many people have objected to the fantasies of misogyny, explicit violence, and open racism in some of Crumb's cartoons. Crumb may dismiss this by claiming that "it's only lines on paper, folks," but by 2018, problematic racial and sexual representations could no longer be so cavalierly brushed aside. At the Ignatz Awards ceremony at the 2018 Small Press Expo, mentions of Crumb's name were twice met with boos from the audience. In a blog post at Medium.com, writer and cartoonist Thor K. Jensen notes the skill in Crumb's drawings and recognizes the incentives the art establishment has in keeping Crumb visible. Then Jensen signals his own ambivalence about Crumb's work in a discussion of transgression in art:

> Who benefits when "transgressive" art ultimately bolsters the power structures that it claims to transgress against? . . . The Crumb work at the center of these objections—stories like *Angelfood McSpade* and *When The Niggers Take Over America*, stories like *Memories Are Made of This*—unpack a mindset where the American male is sexually and racially obsessed and prepared to dehumanize the "other" as a figure of lust, fear or both. . . . Would I have booed the name of Robert Crumb were I in that audience? Probably not; as I've made clear, I'm pretty torn on his value and his legacy. But when an audience that used to look like the dehumanizers in his work is looking more and more like the dehumanized, you can't fault them for standing up for themselves. (Jensen 2018)

Curators have to rethink how to exhibit Crumb's more challenging works when activists are willing to carry their protests into the museum, as they did when the Whitney Biennial in New York displayed *Open Casket*, a controversial portrait of lynching victim Emmett Till by Dana Schutz (Kennedy 2017). As I spoke with museum professionals around the country while researching my book *Comic Art in Museums*, several people in smaller institutions told me off the record that they were offered the loan of substantial collections of Crumb's older work, and they turned it down because their board felt it was too controversial. I wonder how larger museums that have a substantial investment in Crumb's work, like the Lucas Museum of Narrative Art in Los Angeles, which has added Crumb's entire two-hundred-page *Book of Genesis* to its collection, will respond.

Millennials and the generations that have followed them, who are encountering Crumb's work all at once for the first time through the internet and collected editions, seem to have little patience for his early jabs at racism, sexism, and other eccentricities, wondering why an artist celebrating such ugly ideas is still so idolized in comics history. Yet other exhibits, like the

2016 *Graphic Masters: Dürer, Rembrandt, Hogarth, Goya, Picasso, R. Crumb*
exhibit at the Seattle Art Museum, successfully challenged this trend, count-
ing on Crumb's celebrity to bring a young audience into a show of old master
drawings and prints, as I will detail in this chapter's conclusion.

Comics readers who experienced the turmoil of the cultural and sexual
revolutions of the 1960s and 1970s concurrently with Crumb have situated
the different phases of Crumb's evolving work within their own experience
of cultural shifts from decade to decade. For many feminist artists of that
generation, an important component of that experience was fighting for
women's rights and struggling to break through male dominance in politics,
arts, and culture. It seems like a strange twist, then, that Crumb's uncensored
1960s and 1970s comics became a catalyst in the careers of three influential
artists: Trina Robbins, Margaret Harrison, and Rebecca Warren.

In the next section, I will examine how Robbins, underground cartoonist
and herstorian, developed erotic comics for women in response to the sexism
and exclusionary attitude of Crumb and his circle in San Francisco, while two
British artists, painter Margaret Harrison and sculptor Rebecca Warren, took
Crumb's 1960s work as permission to break sexual and cultural boundaries.

DOING IT FOR THEMSELVES: THE FEMINIST RESPONSE TO CRUMB

When James Brown sang "It's a Man's World" in 1966, he could have been
singing about the underground comics scene in 1960s San Francisco. Crumb
and the male artists at the center of the comics movement, such as S. Clay
Wilson, Spain Rodriguez, and Robert Williams, attracted strong criticism
for the aggressive sexuality shown in their cartoons. In his essay "Theorizing Sexuality in Comics," comics scholar Joe Sutliff Sanders points out that
Crumb's circle of peers "embodied a movement, an alternative press whose
explicit sexuality was the opposite of the sublimated sexuality of the mainstream press. In their collaborations, Crumb and the men who surrounded
him struck out against the discourse of sexuality whose limits were defined
by the Comics Code" (2010, 156).

In a separate universe from what DC and Marvel Comics published to
comply with the Comics Code Authority, the undergrounds often depicted
violence and the subjugation of women, including rape, dismemberment,
and incest. For example, in one 1969 comic, "Nuts Boy," originally published
in *Bogeyman* #2, a deranged man attacks and brutally dismembers a random
woman whom he stalks on the street simply because he is bored with what's
on TV (fig. 11.1). After he chops her in half and gleefully chops her body into

small pieces, he holds a detached breast in his hand and says "I feel better now ... got rid of all my pent-up hostilities and repressions! An' it's only a comic book, so I can do anything I want" (reproduced in Crumb 2012, 88).

"In this new vision of sexuality in comics," Sanders notes, "Crumb and his colleagues felt a vital liberation." In an interview, Crumb talks about the influence Wilson and Williams had on his ability to release all those pent-up hostilities and repressions:

> I cast off the last vestiges of the pernicious influence of my years in the greeting card business. I let it all hang out on the page. Seeing what Wilson and Williams had done just gave me the last little push I needed to let open the floodgates. Blatant sexual images became a big thing, still happy and positive at first—a celebration of sex. But the very sight of all those sweaty, bulbous cartoon characters fucking and sucking immediately drove away most of the female readers. As Trina says, I "ruined" underground comics by encouraging all the younger boy artists to be bad and do comics about their own horrible sex fantasies. Ha ha! (Rosenkranz 2008, 88–89)

Women cartoonists trying to break into the male-dominated San Francisco scene, especially those who were vocal about their objections to these misogynic comics, were excluded from their social circle and prime publishing opportunities. As Robbins explained to Mark James Estren, author of *A History of Underground Comics*: "What does concern me is the hostility towards women I see in this work, especially by Crumb. It's hard to relate to him as a person when you see what he does to women in his strips.... Crumb's porn upsets me, as does the work of a whole lot of the other guys who think underground comix means Porn. Rape is NOT FUNNY!" (qtd. in Lopes 2009, 82). In response to this situation, Robbins and other female cartoonists developed erotic comics that were more appealing to women, such as *Wimmin's Comix, All Girl Thrills, Tits & Clits*, and *Wet Satin*.

About the same time Robbins was dealing with male exclusion and misogyny in San Francisco, a young painter named Margaret Harrison was graduating from the Royal Academy in London. Harrison was eager to do work that communicated her views on the political and social issues of the era—women's rights, the Vietnam War, and questions of class and gender—but struggled to find her way into it. Trained in a curriculum focused chiefly on traditional figure drawing that seemed unchanged since Sir Joshua Reynolds established the Royal Academy in 1768, she needed some modern inspiration. She found it in Marvel Comics and in the uncensored comics of

R. Crumb and Eric Stanton, whose styles she felt she could layer with other meanings. In a 2010 interview, she told me:

> Yes, in comics, bodies are in motion. Around 1968, 1969, when all that stuff was bubbling ... the Paris riots ... Here was Captain America, who was supposed to do good in the world and he represented the USA at that point, for me and for other people. Actually, they were doing bad in the world. ... At the same time, the women's movement was coming in. We were meeting and had just formed the women's workshop of the artist's union, and we were talking about gender and stuff. The notions of fixed gender identity just seemed kind of ridiculous. I will try and just change a few body parts around. I will dress this guy in a corset basically, but he's going to be Captain America ... Let's see what happens. (Munson 2011, 374)

Her first exhibit, at the Motifs Editions Gallery in London in 1971, featured her cross-dressing Captain America. The most controversial work in the show was *He's Only a Bunny Boy but He's Quite Nice Really*, a full-body drawing of Playboy publisher Hugh Hefner in a corset with a pipe, protruding nipples, and a bunny penis (fig. 11.2). A second Hefner drawing depicted his head on a bearskin rug, accompanied by lingerie-clad women posing with food. Reflections and opposites are a common theme throughout Harrison's work, and in *Bunny Boy*, Hefner, a man who built his brand on the subjugation of women's bodies, became a passive sexual object himself.

Much to Harrison's shock and dismay, the London police closed the exhibit for indecency after the first day. Harrison has since had a successful, award-winning career, but traces of Crumb's influence still appear in her continuing relationship with her cross-dressed Captain America in the paintings *What's That Long Red Limp Thing You Are Pulling On?* (2010) and *Getting Very Close to My Masculinity* (2014), as well as *You Talking to Me?*, a 2013 diptych portraying pinup girl Bettie Page.

Following in the footsteps of the generation of artists that includes Harrison, 2006 Turner Prize–nominated sculptor Rebecca Warren also saw Crumb's eccentric sexual comix as a springboard for her own explorations of women's power and sexual dynamics.[3] Her series of sturdy, thick-legged, headless, hand-built clay women bear titles like *Helmut Crumb* (1998), *Homage to R. Crumb, My Father* (2003), *Come Helga* (2006), and *SHE*, a group of seven sculptures created in 2003 (fig. 11.3). In a 2017 interview with Laura Smith of the Tate, Warren explained her thought process and Crumb's influence on her work:

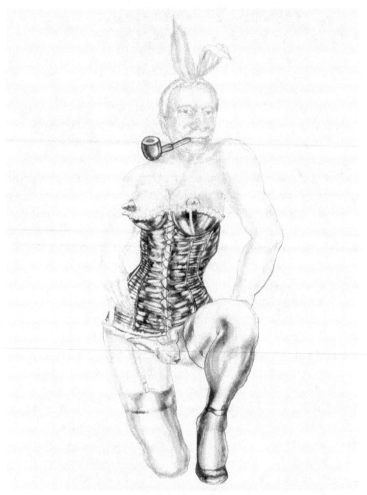

Fig. 11.2. Margaret Harrison, *He's Only a Bunny Boy but He's Quite Nice Really*, 2011.
Courtesy of the artist.

I like to mix things up, turn things on their heads. I'm not a stickler for thinking there is or isn't a categorical difference between high and low, so I mess around in there too. In the end, you like the things you like, and, if you like the whole of something, that's noticeable. . . . When I was drawn to clay, I was also drawn to Crumb and his way of getting to his own desirable forms without worrying about disapproval. Cartoons boil everything down to essential curves. It was a useful—and risky—place to start when I was trying to get an understanding of my own ideas. I used to worry a lot about meaning and where it should come from. Initially I wanted my work to be robustly female, to

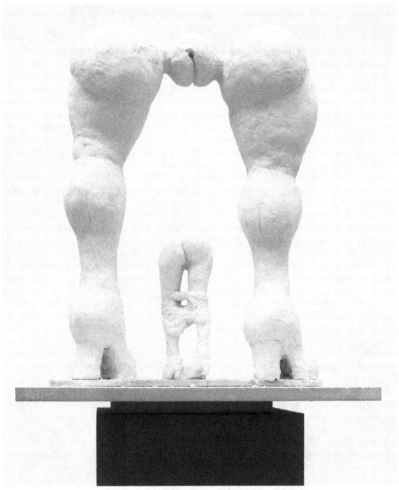

Fig. 11.3. Rebecca Warren, *Helmut Crumb*, 1998, Copyright © Rebecca Warren. Courtesy of Matthew Marks Gallery.

push that side of things, and this helped in that it allowed me to make anything at all! Starting out, I was holding onto the idea that I needed these anchors to make things. That's pretty much cured now and I've gone on without any need for these qualifiers. (Smith 2017)

Like Harrison, Warren found a way to take Crumb's uninhibited sexual images and make something of her own from them. In the case of her sculpture *Helmut Crumb* (1998), she used an image from the highly sexualized fashion photography of Helmut Newton, putting it under the arch made by the much larger legs derived from Crumb's cartoon *Girls, Girls, Girls* (1972).[4] Warren's motivations and outcomes are complicated here as she slides together the work of these two men. As she says, these images, rendered in fragile, unfired clay, seemed to both repel and attract, to be reverential and iconoclastic, never achieving a stability of meaning.

CRUMB AND HIS PEERS MOVE INTO THE GALLERY

In the late 1960s and early 1970s, just as underground comics gained their widest reach, museums and university art galleries were rediscovering comics art. At the forefront of these shows was the 1967 exhibition *Bande Dessinée et Figuration Narrative* at the Musée des Arts Décoratifs (Paris), organized by the French intellectuals Claude Moliterni and Pierre Couperie, which displayed photographic blowups of American comic-strip panels in response to Pop art and Roy Lichtenstein. The widely read English translation of the exhibition's catalog, *A History of the Comic Strip* by Couperie and Maurice Horn (1968), and *The Great Comic Book Heroes* by Jules Feiffer (1965) provided both a historical canon and an intellectual framework that could be expanded into new exhibitions.

For these and other reasons, a wave of large comics survey shows were produced, such as *The Spirit of the Comics* (1969, University of Pennsylvania); *Aaargh! A Celebration of Comics* (1970, Institute of Contemporary Art, London); *Comics as an Art Form* (1970, University of Nevada, Las Vegas); *The Art of the Comic Strip* (1971, University of Maryland), *75 Years of the Comics* (1971, New York Cultural Center); and several others. Except for *The Spirit of the Comics*, a fine art show exploring the influence of comics, all these exhibits were comics history survey shows that selected one or two examples of original artwork from Richard Outcault's *Yellow Kid* and Winsor McCay's *Little Nemo* to William Moulton Marston and Harry G. Peters's *Wonder Woman* and Charles Schulz's *Peanuts*. Curators often included an assortment of underground comics in these shows in recognition of the new intellectual energy they brought to comics, and because of the college-aged audience they attracted. In an interview with Lesley Oelsner of the *New York Times* promoting his 1971 show *75 Years of the Comics*, historian Maurice Horn emphasized the importance of the undergrounds, explaining that "comics were experiencing a rebirth in the form of underground comics ... and more and more critics and intellectuals should be concerning themselves with them" (Oelsner 1971, 54). The artists most commonly chosen to represent this "rebirth" were Vaughn Bodē, Spain Rodriguez, Gilbert Shelton, Art Spiegelman, Skip Williamson, and Crumb.[5]

At this point in his career, Crumb had the best public name recognition outside of his circle of underground peers, known not only for such projects as *Zap Comix* and his comic strips in the *East Village Other* and Harvey Kurtzman's *Help!*, but also for his often-reproduced creations "Keep on Truckin'," Fritz the Cat, Mr. Natural, and Big Brother and the Holding Company's *Cheap Thrills* album cover. Because of *Zap*, he was commonly thought of as the founder of the underground comics movement (although technically he was preceded by at least three underground cartoonists: Frank Stack (Foolbert Sturgeon), Joel Beck, and Jack Jaxon), and the *Zap*/baby carriage story had taken on the aura of urban mythology. Accordingly, every exhibit focused on underground comics themselves included Crumb as a core contributor.

The first show dedicated exclusively to underground artists, *The Phonus Balonus Show of Really Heavy Stuff*, was organized in 1969 by the cartoonist/writer/filmmaker Bhob Stewart at the Corcoran Gallery of Art's Dupont Circle location in Washington, DC. It was a celebration of the underground comics community showcasing the best-known artists in the movement at the time, such as Vaughn Bodē, Crumb, Kim Deitch, Larry Hama, Jay Lynch, Spain Rodriguez, Gilbert Shelton, Art Spiegelman, John Thompson, and Skip Williamson, as well as Stewart himself, without privileging one over the other. Critics were both intrigued and disgusted by the works of Crumb and his contemporaries. One reviewer, Paul Richard of the *Washington Post*, opined that Crumb was "the best of all" and then went on to say:

> They're revolting, true, but I use the word in the sense of revolution. It's worth remembering that formal institutions, the police, the military, the administrations of universities, are not the only things the radical young attack. They've set their sights as well on "accepted moral standards," on the rules—social, sexual, and otherwise—by which we've all been told to live. Imagine an artist or a mass of artists powerful enough to reach the many in addition to the few . . . accessible to everyone at once because it's topical, urgent, varied, inexpensive, and available everywhere. . . . Suppose the artist who assumes this power is not a writer selling paperbacks or a musician making records but a man who reaches people's minds because of the way he draws. (Richard 1969)

Like Carlin, Richard contrasts the emotional rawness and inclusive nature of the comics with the exclusive and cerebral conceptual work championed by museums like MoMA. Perhaps this easy accessibility provides a gateway to one of the key powers of Crumb's art, to make us participants in his anxious, twitchy life; or, as the *New Yorker*'s Françoise Mouly says, "Crumb is matchless in that he succeeds at making you see through his eyes and know what it feels like to be R. Crumb. Sometimes the experience is so magical that you forget you do not actually want to be R. Crumb, an anxiety ridden perpetual loser, any more than he does" (2005, 278).

Far from being portrayed as perpetual loser, Crumb was shown as one of the most influential figures of the underground movement in the 2009 show *Underground Classics: The Transformation of Comics into Comix*, organized by cartoonist/publisher/collector Denis Kitchen and scholar James Danky at the Chazen Museum of Art in Madison, Wisconsin. This show of the work of more than sixty artists identified with the undergrounds was assembled from the massive collections of Kitchen and Eric Sack. The exhibit included a wide selection of Crumb's work, showing self-portraits, album covers, his 1993 serigraph *A Short History of America*, several of his portraits of blues musicians, and even products featuring his character Mr. Natural. His starring role is made plain in the lavishly illustrated catalog, as Crumb's drawing for the cover of *Snarf* #6 (1975) dominates the book cover, and two ratty artists drawn by Will Eisner ponder the question "after Crumb what is there left to say?" on the back cover.

The show included many rare examples of comics "jam" pages that show Crumb as a collaborator within a larger community. *Miracle Rabbis: A Doctor Gesundheit Story*, a 1992 collaboration with Crumb's old friend Harvey Pekar, is one example. *Let's Be Realistic Comics* (1971) is a good example of the collaborative comics artists would create by passing a page around at parties, each adding a panel in their own style to advance the story. On the whole, *Underground Classics* did a good job of representing the entire far-flung underground community that either worked with Crumb or was influenced by him, not only in San Francisco but in Wisconsin (where Kitchen Sink Press was based), Texas, New York, and other outposts of the counterculture. *Underground Classics* was presented again in 2013 by the Kunstmuseum in Lucerne, Switzerland, where it was renamed *R. Crumb and the Underground*. In a 2017 essay "Comic Art in Museums: An Overview," Kitchen reflects on his selection strategy for these shows and Crumb's place in them:

> In curating theme shows around underground cartoonists, the generation immediately following Kurtzman, Eisner, and their colleagues, I've tried to stress the deep diversity of talent and content. In *R. Crumb and the Underground*, at the Kunstmuseum in Lucerne, Switzerland, in 2013, the Crumb name headlined the show to draw crowds but it

was important for cocurator James Danky and myself to show that Crumb was part of a larger art movement, not a singular figure working in a vacuum. We put the collective works in the context of a counterculture and anti-war movement in America, a convulsive period in which the freewheeling and creator-owned undergrounds separated themselves in every way from traditional newsstand comic books, a schism that permanently influenced the aesthetic direction and economics of the larger medium. (Kitchen 2020, 20)

The exhibit's original title, *Underground Classics: The Transformation of Comics into Comix*, emphasizes the movement and not the individual, while the title *R. Crumb and the Underground* places Crumb directly in the spotlight. In both venues, Kitchen and Danky recognized the strong name recognition of and audience interest in Crumb, and they created a show-in-a-show displaying a wide selection of work from different points in his career, in contrast with the usual one or two pieces by the majority of the other artists. But Kitchen and Danky were able to successfully show Crumb not as a lone genius but as part of a larger art movement by stressing the importance of group collaborations in small works like the comics jams and in larger projects like the continued publication of *Zap Comix* as a collective enterprise.

CRUMB IN CONTEMPORARY ART

As noted at the beginning of this chapter, MoMA's 1990 *High & Low: Modern Art, Popular Culture* exhibit largely neglected comics as a unique art form and instead seemed to treat the medium as raw material that inspired fine artists working in traditional media like painting. In this section, I will look more particularly at how curators have contextualized Crumb's work and his influence on contemporary art, from *High & Low* and beyond.

High & Low was a controversial show that seemed to make no one happy. It was an attempt by Kirk Varnedoe, the new director of MoMA, to break the museum's adherence to connoisseurship and modernist dogma. Opinion on all sides was harshly critical, feeling that the show either went too far (such as the modernist critic Hilton Kramer) or not far enough (such as the *Nation's* critic, Arthur Danto). Crumb was included not only because of his groundbreaking style and content but also because the curators wanted to show his work in dialogue with the paintings of Philip Guston.

Crumb has frequently told the story of how the designs of many of his best-known characters came to him during an intense LSD trip that inspired

him to leave Cleveland and his job with American Greetings behind to begin
a new life as a cartoonist in San Francisco. Around the same time, Guston
had a similar epiphany, abandoning abstract art for representational paintings of things he thought of as symbols of real life, like light bulbs, shoes,
and pipes. In the early 1980s, Crumb saw Guston's work and appropriated
his bean-shaped cyclops character on the front and back covers of *Weirdo* #7
(1983). In the back-cover cartoon, "A Fine Art Piece of Business," the cyclops
says, "Oh, what a fool I've been, and will continue to be" (Varnedoe and
Gopnik 1990, 227). The *High & Low* exhibit included *Weirdo* in a display case
of Crumb comics along with two or three framed pages of Crumb's cover
art, but they were completely overwhelmed by the monumental paintings
of Guston, some of which were as long as one hundred inches. In the eyes
of comics fans and advocates, this problem of scale accentuated the feeling
that comics were secondary to the paintings on display.

The 2005 *Masters of American Comics* exhibit solved this problem of
scale by containing the work of each of the fifteen chosen comic artists in
a dedicated minigallery of their own (fig. 11.4). *Masters* generated a huge
amount of attention and media coverage, mainly because of the choice by
the curatorial team (John Carlin and Art Spiegelman, with Brian Walker as
cocurator) to select fourteen white male cartoonists and African American
George Herriman in an effort to create a traditional "lone genius" art historical canon, which largely excluded women and people of color (other than
Herriman). In Los Angeles, artists representing the evolution of the comic
strip were shown at the Hammer Museum in the Westwood area near UCLA.
Representing the evolution of the comic book downtown at the Museum of
Contemporary Art were Will Eisner, Jack Kirby, Harvey Kurtzman, Crumb,
Art Spiegelman, Gary Panter, and Chris Ware.

In the context of the show, Crumb's work represented the importance
of the independent underground comics movement as well as the idea that
his personal and uncensored content opened up new topics for exploration
in comics. In her *Masters* essay, Françoise Mouly notes that every artist she
reviewed for *RAW* in the 1970s had a "Crumb period before they found their
own voice," and she continues with a discussion of how Crumb's form of
visual expression pushed comics into postmodernism:

> It's arguable whether comics ever had a modern period (maybe
> Herriman was its Picasso and its Matisse?), but, in incorporating the
> discarded past in the present (Crumb's work of the sixties, a mix of
> E. C. Segar's *Popeye*, the Marx Brothers, Walt Kelly's *Pogo*, Carl Barks,
> Disney Comics, and early *MAD* comics, was jarring and totally out

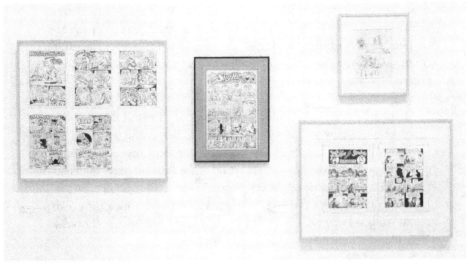

Fig. 11.4. Installation view of *Masters of American Comics*, November 20, 2005–March 12, 2006, MOCA Grand Avenue. Courtesy of the Museum of Contemporary Art, Los Angeles. Photo by Brian Forrest.

of tune with the spare approach of a Charles Schulz or with the then-nascent Art Nouveau–inspired psychedelic graphics), by embracing paradoxes rather than attempting to resolve them, by using the popular form of comics as a means for artistic self-expression, Crumb undoubtedly propelled comics to their place as a fundamental postmodern art form, central to the culture of the twentieth century. (Mouly 2005, 282)

Shifting from the postmodern back to the classic masters of the art history canon, Crumb found himself in the midst of an august group of peers in the Seattle Art Museum's 2016 exhibit *Graphic Masters: Dürer, Rembrandt, Hogarth, Goya, Picasso, R. Crumb. Graphic Masters* displayed around four hundred works on paper, including woodblocks, engravings, etchings, and aquatints, and concluded with the two hundred original pen-and-ink drawings that make up Crumb's *Book of Genesis Illustrated*. Except for Rembrandt, who was represented by a handful of mythological prints, each artist had a sequential series of works in the show: Dürer's *Large Passion* (1497–1511), Hogarth's *A Harlot's Progress* (1732) and *A Rake's Progress* (1735), Goya's *Los Caprichos* (1799), and Picasso's *Vollard Suite* (1930–1937). The museum was able to obtain high-quality early-edition prints, and it was a feast for the eyes. Crumb was a natural fit with these artists, as his *Genesis* looks very much like the style of these masters as filtered through Basil Wolverton and Hollywood.

Seattle-based cultural journalist Rob Salkowitz found it "hard to suppress a cheer" when he saw Crumb included in this august company at the *Graphic Masters* exhibit (2018, 138). Quoting Chiyo Ishikawa, the exhibit's curator, Salkowitz details how Crumb works in a space like the Seattle Art Museum today:

> Attendance was strong, and because the quantity and detail of the works on display was so overwhelming, it drove a higher-than-average number of people to buy museum memberships so they could come back and see it again and spend more time on parts they had missed. . . . It also helped the art museum reach a younger generation. "They've heard of Crumb," says Ishikawa, "so presenting a show like this is a good way to demonstrate the continued relevance of the older artists who they may not have heard of." (145)

Crumb was not only considered a descendent of traditionally revered artists, but he was the star of the show. The Seattle Art Museum embraced Crumb and even counted on the accessibility of comics and specifically the popularity of Crumb to bring people into the museum who might not have found a show of old master drawings and prints compelling. As Crumb, and comics and graphic novels in general, continue to grow in importance, I suspect this trend will continue.

NOTES

1. For an extended analysis of Gopnik's *High & Low* exhibition text, see Beaty 2012, 198–208. In general, MoMA has had a strange history with comics art. The museum included two frames from Disney shorts in its 1936 exhibit *Fantastic Art, Dada* at the urging of gallerist Julian Levy. It has exhibited Art Spiegelman's *Maus* as a Project Show curated by Robert Storr in 1992, *Comics Abstraction* (abstract painters working with comics elements, no comic art) in 2010, and the *Art of Pixar* (a small show of concept art outside the museum's screening room) in 2016, among others.

2. According to an article on the Bleeding Cool website, the previous record was set at another Heritage Auction in 2014, where a page from *The Incredible Hulk* #180 (Marvel, 1974), penciled by Herb Trimpe and inked by Jack Abel, sold for $657,250 (Seifert 2017). It was the first appearance of the fan-favorite character Wolverine. As Rob Salkowitz (2018) points out, comics collectors are unique among art collectors because they often collect for personal reasons, such as the debut of a famous character, instead of more common reasons, such as who the artist is or the valuation of the work in the art market.

3. I thank Paul Gravett for pointing Warren's work out to me.

4. The Helmut Newton photograph on which Warren modeled *Helmut Crumb* is *In My Apartment*, 1975 (sometimes also titled *Jenny in My Apartment*). The photograph was published in Newton's 1976 photobook *White Women*.

5. I have dedicated an entire section of my book *Comic Art in Museums* to this interesting period in exhibition history, not only for the sudden rediscovery of comics art but also because of the birth of dedicated institutions like the Museum of Cartoon Art and the Cartoon Art Museum around that time.

WORKS CITED

Beaty, Bart. 2012. *Comics Versus Art*. Toronto: University of Toronto Press.

Carlin, John. 2005. "Masters of American Comics: An Art History of Twentieth-Century American Comic Strips and Books." In *Masters of American Comics*, edited by John Carlin, Paul Karasik, and Brian Walker, 25–175. New Haven, CT: Yale University Press.

Crumb, R., et al. 2012. *R. Crumb: De l'underground à la genèse (From Underground to Genesis)*. Paris: Musée d'Art Moderne de la Ville de Paris.

Danky, James, and Denis Kitchen. 2009. *Underground Classics: The Transformation of Comics into Comix*. New York: Harry N. Abrams.

Flock, T. S. 2016. "SAM's Enormous, Century-Spanning Printmaking Exhibit Brims with the Grotesque and the Divine." *Seattle Weekly*, July 6. https://www.seattleweekly.com/arts/sams-enormous-century-spanning-printmaking-exhibit-brims-with-the-grotesque-and-the-divine/.

Green, Diana. 2013. "Crumb, Robert." In *Icons of the American Comic Book from Captain America to Wonder Woman*, edited by Randy Duncan and Matthew J. Smith, 158–68. Santa Barbara, CA: Greenwood Press.

Herdeg, Walter, and David Pascal, eds. 1972. *The Art of the Comic Strip*. Zurich: Graphis Press.

Hignite, Todd. 2006. "Robert Crumb." In *In the Studio: Visits with Contemporary Cartoonists*, 6–39. New Haven, CT: Yale University Press.

Jensen, Thor K. 2018. "Some Crumbs." Medium, September 17. https://medium.com/@kthorjensen/some-crumbs-88478c4e3b6d, accessed January 4, 2019.

Kennedy, Randy. 2017. "White Artist's Painting of Emmett Till at Whitney Biennial Draws Protests." *New York Times*, May 21. https://www.nytimes.com/2017/03/21/arts/design/painting-of-emmett-till-at-whitney-biennial-draws-protests.html, accessed January 14, 2019.

Kitchen, Denis. 2020. "Comic Art in Museums: An Overview." In *Comic Art in Museums*, edited by Kim Munson, 14–22. Jackson: University Press of Mississippi.

Lopes, Paul. 2009. *Demanding Respect: The Evolution of the American Comic Book*. Philadelphia: Temple University Press.

Mouly, Françoise. 2005. "It's Only Lines on Paper." In *Masters of American Comics*, edited by John Carlin, Paul Karasik, and Brian Walker, 278–89. New Haven, CT: Yale University Press.

Munson, Kim. 2011. "Censorship and Super Bodies: The Creative Odyssey of Margaret Harrison." *International Journal of Comic Art* 13, no. 2 (Fall): 369–92.

Oelsner, Lesley. 1971. "A Retrospective on the Comics Opens (Pow!)." *New York Times*, September 8, 54.

Rattemeyer, Christian. 2010. *Compass in Hand: Selections from the Judith Rothschild Foundation Contemporary Drawings Collection*. New York: Museum of Modern Art.

Richard, Paul. 1969. "Revolting, in the Sense of Revolution." *Washington Post*, June 1.

Rosenkranz, Patrick. 2008. *Rebel Visions: The Underground Comix Revolution, 1963–1975*. Seattle: Fantagraphics.

Salkowitz, Rob. 2018. "Splashing Ink on Museum Walls: How Comic Art Is Conquering Galleries, Museums, and Public Spaces." *Full Bleed: The Comics and Culture Quarterly*, no. 2: 138–46.

Sanders, Joe Sutliff. 2010. "Theorizing Sexuality in Comics." In *The Rise of the American Comics Artist: Creators and Contexts*, edited by Paul Williams and James Lyons, 150–63. Jackson: University Press of Mississippi.

Seifert, Mark. 2017. "Robert Crumb 1969 Fritz the Cat Cover Art Sells for Record $717,000 at Auction." Bleeding Cool, May 18. https://bleedingcool.com/comics/robert-crumb -1969-fritz-cat-cover-art-sells-record-717000-auction/, accessed January 5, 2019.

Smith, Laura. 2017. "Interview: Rebecca Warren: From the Mess of Experience." *Tate Etc.*, no. 41, October 6. https://www.tate.org.uk/tate-etc/issue-41-autumn-2017/rebecca-warren -interview-from-the-mess-of-experience, accessed January 6, 2019.

Varnedoe, Kirk, and Adam Gopnik. 1990. *High & Low: Modern Art, Popular Culture*. New York: Abrams.

Chapter 12

ROBERT CRUMB AND ÖYVIND FAHLSTRÖM

The Marriage of Social Satire and Ideological Critique

CLARENCE BURTON SHEFFIELD JR.

In 1969, the Brazilian-born, New York–based Swedish artist Öyvind Fahlström surveyed the American art scene: "One of the few truly major American artists today is a barely thirty-year old American cartoonist. Really. His name is Robert Crumb. You could say that he makes Pop Art in the true sense of the word: art for the people, popular art" (Fahlström 2001, 236). Fahlström's comments demonstrate a prescient awareness of Robert Crumb's importance in modern American culture, and his complex and quirky relationship to the Pop art movement. Crumb is a touchstone for Fahlström and provides a key critical lens by which to understand Fahlström's art. Conversely, there is a reciprocity to this relationship, since a critical analysis of Fahlström reveals important new insights into Crumb. Fahlström is generally labeled a Pop artist. He resists such pigeonholing in much the same way that Crumb has continuously worked across the borders of different media, celebrating hybridity, experimentation, and the subversion of most formal rules. Neither ever avoids offending his audience. Both share an unrelenting concern for politics and international events, fusing high and low culture as well as the marginal, banal, and disenfranchised while maintaining a steadfast belief that art can stimulate social change by criticizing authority and challenging established norms.

Fahlström and Crumb question the myth of American exceptionalism as well as its puritanical prejudices, jingoism, and conservatism. Both decry the hubris, hypocrisy, and pretense implied by such naïve ideals. Institutions of power and figures of authority are unrelenting targets in their work. They often allude to the anxiety caused by the threat of nuclear annihilation, the

perils of advanced industrial technology, the risks of environmental degradation, and unbridled global capitalism.

Underground culture as well as the marginal, wacky, freakish, and dys-
functional aspects of contemporary society are mainstays of their art, which
embraces the lewd, irreverent, and vulgar. Fact and fiction are blurred in their
respective artistic worlds, which include celebrities and ordinary citizens,
the powerful and the disenfranchised, wealthy and poor, eccentrics and the
plebeian. Tabloid media, in particular, with its often prurient, sensational
headlines, are a favorite source for Fahlström. While Crumb seems not to
use such tabloid sources directly, the absurd and often fantastical aspects of
his narratives certainly refer to them. Fahlström, who incorporates political
facts and economic and statistical data into his compositions, is more overtly
engaged in an ideological critique. He also wrote manifestos explaining
his basic precepts.[1] Crumb, on the other hand, appears to have been more
ambivalent and less explicit about his politics and ideology, at least initially,
while still sharing Fahlström's sense of irony, cynicism, and paranoia. Both
are unapologetic about any shock their work might provoke.

Like Crumb, Fahlström took LSD and acknowledged that his initial experiments with acid were a decisive turning point in his artistic career and
creative process. Timothy Leary, the 1960s countercultural icon, is mentioned often in Fahlström's texts and notebooks, and Crumb also acknowledges Leary's importance. One of Fahlström's best-known works is a pair
of commercial signs. The first is the logo of the oil company Esso, which is
juxtaposed to a second sign identical in every way, but with the letters LSD
(1967). Fahlström scribbled these abbreviations, along with several variations,
in subsequent drawings and studies for his installations, including *Study
for Meatball Curtain* (1970), which shows his lifelong interest in anagrams,
puns, onomatopoeia, and poetic wordplay.[2] *ESSO-LSD* (1967) is Fahlström's
last concrete poem.

Fahlström's strong kinship with Crumb culminates in one of his most
important and ambitious works, *Meatball Curtain (for R. Crumb)* (1969),
commissioned for Maurice Tuchman's famous *Art and Technology* exhibition at the Los Angeles County Museum of Art (fig. 12.1). A large variable
sculpture, it consists of a series of flat silhouettes made of enameled sheet
metal that stand upright and are arranged in a constellation across the gallery
floor. Small Plexiglas cutouts are attached to the flat silhouettes by magnets
or inserted into slots cut into them. The work's title comes from Crumb's
story "Meatball," first published in *Zap Comix* #0 (1968), about a supernatural
event when meatballs rain down from the sky, sporadically at first and then
in a steady torrent over central Los Angeles. They transform everyone they

Fig. 12.1. Öyvind Fahlström, *Meatball Curtain (for R. Crumb)*, 1969.
Courtesy of the Öyvind Fahlström Foundation.

hit—celebrities like the philosopher Bertrand Russell and the actress Kim Novak, and ordinary citizens—into a state of ecstatic bliss.

In an interview with Jane Livingston, Fahlström acknowledged Crumb's importance for this composition:

> I've been looking a lot at the underground cartoon makers. They have a sort of exuberance and precision, and that extreme expressiveness of their outlines. . . . I would say that sixty, seventy per cent of the images in this piece are direct outlines from Robert Crumb. I think it should be said that this work is an homage to Robert Crumb, to a great American artist. (Livingston 1971, 109)

Meatball Curtain (for R. Crumb) epitomizes Fahlström's unique formal aesthetic, which emphasizes a dynamic, playful, interactive relationship between the viewer and the work of art. He coined the term "variable painting" for these eclectic compositions, which consist of installations, mixed media assemblages, and shaped metal panels. Their individual elements could be manipulated by a viewer, like the pieces of a board game or a jigsaw puzzle. Theoretically, the audience could participate in determining their shape, structure, and meaning, which was never fixed. With each subsequent exhibition and installation, the order and position of the individual elements could change. Fahlström hoped that serial editions, like board games, could be made and distributed, a goal both progressive and nonelitist. Chance, randomness, and the element of surprise, in addition to the possibility of endless permutations and combinations, characterize his extremely conceptual method, which recalls the aleatory aspects of Dada and neo-Dadaism, especially as practiced by John Cage, Fluxus, and Happenings. Fahlström's work was deliberately theatrical; it sought to blur the line between the private and public spheres, the audience and the work of art.[3] He wrote that "the finished picture stands somewhere in the intersection of paintings, games ... and puppet theater" (Fahlström 1964, 226).

Variable painting is one of Fahlström's greatest contributions to modern art. It challenges the traditional notion of a painting as a static entity. By attaching magnets to the separate parts, as well as using grooves and slits, he solved the problem of their installation and display while also transforming the staid relationship between the gallery wall, ceiling, and floor. On a formal level, they resemble a children's pop-up book. Their installation and display pose difficult challenges for any gallery or museum. Fahlström's painstaking instructions demonstrate that variability and interaction did not imply a "willy-nilly" or "anything goes" solution. An inevitable tension exists between his original intentions and careful calculation of where each and every element is to be placed, and the notion that they can be randomly arranged. Above all, he wanted to create a meaningful visual experience as well as protect the works from damage or theft. Fahlström addressed this dilemma in a text written shortly before his death. He considered the possibility of high-quality editions, affordable and collected by the general public, who could arrange them as they wished, as a practical alternative to the large, expensive originals installed according to his instructions in a public gallery or museum, where access was tightly controlled and restricted:

Most of my paintings are variable, that is, the cut-out elements can be arranged in any number of ways. Thus, in principle, the spectator may participate in organizing the images. Nevertheless, if the public is encouraged to do so—within the limitations of a gallery or museum display—the result tends to be a mixture of partial and unrelated changes plus remaining features of my original arrangements. As an artist, I want to present the spectators, most of whom only want to look at the objects, with a worthwhile visual experience. The variable quality of my paintings will remain mainly conceptual until high quality multiples are made. Only then will the spectator feel at ease to participate and assemble the images in any way he chooses.[4]

In many respects, the variable paintings share striking formal similarities with Robert Rauschenberg's "combines," which incorporate found elements and three-dimensional objects into the flat, two-dimensional canvas (Schimmel 2005). These hybrid, radically "impure" paintings, with their richly textured, heterogenous parts, subsequently were construed by the art historian Leo Steinberg as proto-postmodern (Steinberg 2007).[5] It is not surprising that Rauschenberg and Fahlström were very close friends, even before Fahlström's arrival in New York City in October 1961.[6] In fact, Fahlström and his wife lived in Rauschenberg's recently vacated studio at 128 Front Street. Both became important participants in avant-garde happenings, performances, and dance events associated with the Judson Memorial Church. They were also deeply involved in E.A.T. (Experiments in Art and Technology), which was a historical precursor to the 1969 Los Angeles exhibition. E.A.T. sought to forge an alliance between artists and engineers while also strengthening their ties to industry (Schultz Lundestam 2004). One of its best-known events was the performance series 9 *Evenings: Theater and Engineering*, which was held at the Sixty-Ninth Regimental Armory in New York City in October 1966. The organization owed its existence to Rauschenberg and Billy Klüver (1927–2004), a Swedish electrical engineer who worked at Bell Telephone Laboratories in Murray Hill, New Jersey. They subsequently enlisted the support of the Swedish art historian and curator K. G. Pontus Hultén (1924–2006), who organized the landmark 1968 MoMA exhibition *The Machine*, which featured a separate section devoted to E.A.T. (Hultén 1968). The inclusion of Fahlström and Rauschenberg in the 1969 *Art and Technology* exhibition in Los Angeles is therefore not surprising.

For the fabrication of *Meatball Curtain (for R. Crumb)*, Fahlström collaborated with Heath and Company, a commercial sign company based in Los Angeles whose clients included the fast food franchise Kentucky Fried Chicken. His initial visit to Heath and Company was arranged by Jane Livingston. She recalled that Hal Glicksman, another well-known figure in the California art scene, had shown Crumb's work to Fahlström during his first trip to Los Angeles in the spring of 1969.

Livingston recognized that Fahlström's individual figures are "bold and uncluttered," as well as immediately intelligible due to his deliberate elimination of any unnecessary details. Fahlström explained his intentions to her:

What I wanted to do here was to avoid working in a great deal of detail as I have usually done in the past, with complicated outlines— black outlines indicating creases, and elaborate clothing details, etc. I wanted rather to simplify. In order to do this I had to choose pieces

Fig. 12.2. R. Crumb, "Keep on Truckin'," Copyright © Robert Crumb, 1967. All rights reserved.

that were either single figures, or combinations of figures and objects that were expressive plus being understandable immediately or, if not, at least ambiguous in an interesting way. (Livingston 1971, 112)

Fahlström's preparatory drawings and sketches for this variable sculpture distinguish between standing, inverted, and magnetic elements. The complexity of its individual parts, as well as the many possible variations in their arrangement, make it a challenge just to describe the final work. Two drawings in particular document the process by which he refined the individual figures and shapes, eliminating certain elements, as well as his conceptualization of the finished work. *Study for Meatball Curtain* (1970) includes written instructions regarding the fabrication and installation of the pieces, which are identified by numbers. He circled in pencil the figures chosen for the final ensemble, and the remaining figures then are omitted from *Elements for Meatball Curtain* (1970). Some of the figures that he chose to include in this second drawing, however, are multiplied, combined with one another, or altered in color. Instead of a single blue police car with siren, there are three. Likewise, instead of a single rat riding atop an AK-47 rifle, there are three; two are orange, one is yellow. Text and ordinals are also used to identify the figures. For instance, beside the single red hand with six fingers Fahlström has written "6!" Likewise, he has written "meatball" and "bullet" beside the shape containing a meatball in a thought bubble that is pierced by a bullet.

Among the largest and most significant standing figures in the final installation are an orange panther, and an orange rocket with a red star on its fuselage that rises vertically from the gallery floor and that leaves behind a bright yellow plume of contrail. A large green wave, to which an ornamental band of light green foam is attached, is another major component, adapted from an image by Crumb, who had, in turn, appropriated it from Hokusai. Crumb's *Yarrowstalks* #3 (1967) is the source.

Another large standing shape is a dancing pinhead figure, which is repeated four times in a linked sequence. As it moves closer to the viewer, the heads are reduced in size, while the shoes of each grow larger. Their gestures, pose, and sequential relationship are based on Crumb's "Keep on Truckin'" (1967) (fig. 12.2).

A large blue figure with spiky hair holds a lightbulb shape adorned with a heart. It is based on Mr. Goodbar, a character who appears in Crumb's "Jive Comics" from *Gothic Blimp Works* #1 (1969). In Crumb's original drawing there are three lightbulbs, each with a heart, that encircle his head.

A large silhouetted figure sticks its head into a toilet (it is based on Crumb's "Glorifying the American Girl," from the *East Village Other* #4/13, March 1, 1969). The figure is blue, and the toilet and toilet seat are different shades of green.

Smaller figures and Plexiglas shapes are held in place by magnets throughout the entire installation. Slots are also used to insert several of them into the larger silhouettes. Some of the smaller figures are attached by magnets to the blue metal trajectories of bounce lines that are bolted to the floor and stabilized by microfilament fishing line tied to eye hooks in the ceiling.[7] They include a lightning bolt, police cars with sirens, a figure carrying a cross on its back (derived from Crumb's "Head Comix," from *Yarrowstalks* #2 [1967]), a junkie shooting up with a syringe (based on Crumb's "Stoned," from *Cavalier Magazine* [1967]), stacks of dollar signs, flying rats on AK-47 rifles, a mountain landscape with setting sun, a pipe with a mushroom cloud of smoke rising from its bowl, Band-Aids, the wingspread of an eagle with a banana attached, a single hand with six fingers, a pair of hands each holding a gun aimed at a head that is clad in a military-type helmet, a gorilla, a beatnik running exuberantly with raised arms (appropriated from Crumb's "Ol' Uncle Uh Uh and His Garbage Truck," from *Zap* #1 [1968]), and a policeman running with a raised nightstick (based on Crumb's "Those Cute Little Bearzy Wearzies," from the *East Village Other* [1969]), as well as a standing man with a large nose who is masturbating, a disembodied hand jerking off a penis, and another hand that is touching a breast (all of which are based on Crumb's "You Gotta . . .," from *Gothic Blimp Works* #1 [1969]).

There is also a small bottle shape with hands and feet that has a question mark protruding from its neck. Crumb's "Hamburger Hijinx" from *Zap* #2 (1968) is its source. The figures of small penises with legs are taken from Crumb's "Tales from the Land of Genitalia" (*The Pricksters*, 1969). Another small figure with the head and wings of a bird, but whose lower extremity is in the shape of a phallus, was taken from an image by the Swedish photographer Christer Strömholm (*Tokyo*, 1963).

Another large silhouetted figure is a woman who squats with legs splayed, her arms extended back behind her head and down to the floor for support. She was appropriated from an image in a Danish pornographic magazine. She wears knee-high blue boots. Her body is brown, and the nipples of her breasts are orange.

In what seems to be a rape, a silhouetted male figure with a very large nose has dropped his pants around his ankles. He holds a young girl with a ribbon in her hair from behind, suspended in his arms, above the floor, at his waist height. She appears to be screaming and waving her limbs helplessly, struggling to break free from his clutch. This image is taken from Crumb's "ShooShoo Baby," originally printed in *Gothic Blimp Works* #1 (1969). Scattered throughout the entire ensemble are eight brown meatballs made from vacuum-formed plastic mounted on metal spring wire. Fahlström explained the overall impression that he hoped to convey with these figures and why he had found Crumb's work so compelling: "I wanted my figures to have a sort of quality of exuberance and the energy of American life and the fatality and rawness of it and the sort of dumbness about it too and the animal-like quality which is very well depicted in Crumb's drawings, as well as the aspect of madness, the ecstatic factor" (Livingston 1971, 109).

It is not surprising that Crumb's story of meatballs randomly falling from the sky would have had such enormous appeal for Fahlström. After all, his sensibility had been shaped by his parents, a Norwegian father and Swedish mother, who had emigrated separately to Brazil at different times. They married in 1927, and he was born in 1928. Fahlström, who had been sent alone to visit his aunt and grandfather in Stockholm for six months in July 1939, was forced to remain there in exile for a decade, when World War II was declared a month and a half after his arrival. He adopted Swedish citizenship in 1948 and remained there for university and the start of his career. For many, there is nothing more Swedish than meatballs, and they remain one of the most popular items on the menu at IKEA showrooms worldwide. A recent article in the *Guardian* on the possible Turkish origins of the Swedish meatball characterized the Swedish response as equivalent to a loss of national identity (Henley 2018). When queried by Livingston, however, as to whether there was any deeper symbolic or scatological significance to the meatballs, Fahlström responded: "No. They're just meatballs. A meatball is very plain and down to earth. It represents food—plain everyday sort of food" (Livingston 1971, 112).

Considering the ubiquity of the meatball as the quintessential Swedish comfort food, his remark emphasizing their banality is noteworthy. It also happens that food was a ubiquitous subject for Pop artists, especially among Fahlström's contemporaries such as Claes Oldenburg, Wayne Thiebaud, Tom Wesselmann, and Andy Warhol. Oldenburg in particular crafted food sculptures in canvas, vinyl, plaster, and papier-mâché. Thiebaud's paintings consistently feature candy and desserts. Canned vegetables, fruits, cereals, and condiments are recurring themes in Wesselmann's paintings. Warhol appropriated his imagery from such common consumer staples as Campbell's soup, Coca-Cola, and Del Monte green beans. Indeed, Warhol played himself in the brief 1982 film by Jørgen Leth, *Andy Warhol Eats a Hamburger*. Not to be overlooked are the many screen prints by Sister Corita Kent inspired by advertising slogans and commercial jingles for supermarkets that underscore "pop art's food fixation" (qtd. in Dackerman 2015, 163).

For Fahlström, the "cultural politics of pop" took on an almost baroque excess that approached the zany, a concept that further reinforces his connection to Crumb.[8] As an aesthetic category, zaniness suggests a frantic, frenetic, precarious, and ambiguous state of activity, as well as a special character type. Simply put, the zany is a recurring character in Fahlström's art.

Likewise, Crumb's quirky characters, his utter disregard for political correctness, and his tendency to shock and offend his audience, to push the borders of decency, and to celebrate the "polymorphous perversity" of human nature, bear a striking affinity to the aesthetic sensibility known as camp. Susan Sontag's classic 1964 essay "Notes on 'Camp'" characterized this notion as "a good taste of bad taste," a "success in failure," and a tendency to be "serious about the frivolous, frivolous about the serious," while she underscored its playfulness, theatricality, and vulgarity (Sontag 1964). Sontag posited a strong connection between camp and Pop art while also recognizing their subtle differences. As she wrote:

> Here, one may compare Camp with much of Pop Art, which—when it is not just Camp—embodies an attitude that is related, but still very different. Pop Art is more flat and more dry, more serious, more detached, ultimately nihilistic. (Sontag 1964, 292)

Camp and the zany are not synonymous, although they do share important characteristics. Sianne Ngai has astutely analyzed their complex and tendentious relationship. She argues:

> [W]hile camp thus converts the pain of failure and loss into victory and enjoyment, zaniness highlights its own inability to do this; indeed, the desperation and frenzy of its besieged performers, due to the precarious situations into which they are constantly thrust, point to a laborious involvement from which ironic detachment is not an option. It is in this sense that the zany marks a set of conditions under which even camp's way of revaluing failure fails. (Ngai 2012, 12)

Throughout her analysis Ngai differentiates the zany from the closely related aesthetic categories "the cute" and "the interesting" while underscoring their importance for late capitalist consumer culture. Zaniness, she writes, ultimately suggests an "erosion of the distinction between playing and working" (188). She further contends:

> The zany thus has a stressed-out, even desperate quality that immediately sets it apart from its more lighthearted comedic cousins, the goofy or silly. Although zaniness is playful in all its manifestations across genres, media, and cultural strata, it is an aesthetic of action pushed to strenuous and even precarious extremes. (Ngai 2012, 188)

In short, the zany is a misfit, a virtuoso failure, anxious about his own anxiety and flummoxed by his own sincerity and earnestness. According to Ngai, the zany is a "social loser" and the "utter antithesis of ironic cool." He frets and perspires in the course of his almost always futile, manic labor: "Far from being 'divinely untroubled,' zaniness projects the 'personality pattern' of the subject wanting too much and trying too hard: the unhappily striving wannabe, poser, or arriviste" (189). In my opinion, Crumb and Fahlström embrace the zany and zaniness as a fundamental aesthetic sensibility. It provides an important insight into the many social outcasts and oddballs, along with the garish and outlandish events, that recur throughout their work.

Fahlström's vast knowledge of comics is also demonstrated by his many publications as an art critic and journalist, in addition to his frequent remarks about the medium in radio and television interviews. First and foremost, he understood the distinct, formal possibilities of comics and the medium's richness and complexity: its ability to suggest movement and serial action in a condensed space, its potential for nonlinear narrative and peripeteia, the possibilities it holds for different points of view such as close-ups and panoramas, and its use of the nuances of color, frame, dialogue, signs, and varied light effects. In one of his earliest newspaper articles from 1954, Fahlström recognized that "the comic simultaneously has the omniscient narrator's versatility, the depth composition of film and the graphic qualities of drawing" (Fahlström 1954, 115). He also emphasized their mass appeal and entertainment value. Fahlström's fascination with comics was clearly not limited to Crumb. In 1955, he wrote about Will Elder's *Mad* magazine cartoons for the same Swedish newspaper, *Expressen*. In 1956, he published a two-part article there on Al Capp. One of the first comic artists to inspire his art was George Herriman. Similarly, Fahlström's drawing *Feast on MAD* (1957–1959) incorporates graphic imagery taken directly from the popular satirical magazine founded by William M. Gaines, rearranged in a rich collage in his own manner. There are also at least three early paintings by Fahlström based on the theme of *Krazy Kat*.[9] Furthermore, he appropriated and repeated with slight variations the shape of Batman's cape in his seminal painting *Sitting* (1962).

Fahlström's article "The Invasion of the Underground Comics" ("De underjordiska serierna breder ut sig") demonstrates his keen insights into Crumb and his contemporaries. First published in Swedish in *Dagens Nyheter* in 1969, it warrants careful reading. He writes almost exclusively on Crumb's stylistic development and his many eccentric characters, while praising his immense talent and future promise. Fahlström lauds Crumb's raw, "uncompromising" drawing style and suggests that its likely inspiration derives from the earlier generation of comic artists, especially notable work from the 1930s such as Donald Duck, Popeye, the Katzenjammer Kids, and Barney Google and Snuffy Smith. Underlying Crumb's "chubby lines," Fahlström says, is a "tight precision that cannot be separated from the devastating characterizations" (Fahlström 2001, 236). The most enigmatic and appealing aspect of Crumb's imagery, according to Fahlström, is his ability to combine "a safe, cozy, childish style" as a means to examine shocking, taboo, racy, and pornographic subjects. Fahlström writes:

> The coarse folksiness of Crumb's comics may at first seem sensational or derogatory. But without lecturing, it actually communicates much of the howling brutality—sometimes good-natured, sometimes wild, but always bovine—of the worn-out, brainwashed and over-exploited people of the American inner cities. (237)

What at first appears to be innocent in Crumb's work is often deeply troubling and offensive. Fahlström contends that, for most Americans, instead of the disclaimer "Adults Only," Crumb's imagery probably falls more appropriately into the category "Not Even Adults." One of Crumb's unique strengths, Fahlström contends, is his ability to portray "myth as concrete reality" (Fahlström 2001, 237). According to him, "Crumb's stories are always true comics, where word and image work together as inseparably as sound and image in film" (237). Fahlström also found Crumb's treatment of inner liberation, spiritual enlightenment, and psychedelic experience greatly appealing, and he mentions the parable of the meatballs as a prime example. Fahlström writes that he remains uncertain whether Crumb intends his work to trigger radical social change or if his aim is more modest, simply social satire and criticism. Nevertheless, Fahlström argues that "Crumb is a formidable source of inspiration, strewing thumbtacks under the paws of the colossus" (237).

In addition, Fahlström frequently used his personal collection of EC Comics from the 1950s as an important source for his art. He began to appropriate body fragments (heads, upper and lower torsos, arms, and legs) and other shapes that appealed to him, especially figure/ground relationships and unique architectural patterns and spatial forms from individual panels, gluing these into notebooks, which then served as templates for subsequent work. He cut out portions of clothing from figures and then reused them in *The Planetarium* (1963) and *Dr. Schweitzer's Last Mission* (1964–1966). Many of the figures from *Meatball Curtain (for R. Crumb)* recur in subsequent work (e.g., the walking penis appears in *Pentagon Puzzle* [1970], the figure with its head in a toilet returns in *Blue House* [1970], and the rat riding an AK-47 recurs in *Pentagon Diptych (for Saul Gottlieb)* [1970]). In *Notes 3 (Mass Elements)* (1970), Fahlström wrote "R. Crumb" in the lower right-hand corner along with arrows pointing to the walking penis figures (fig. 12.3).

Crumb claims that he has no personal recollection of any direct contact with Fahlström, but he also repeatedly acknowledges that if anyone recalls anything clearly from that turbulent, drug-induced era, then one must not really have been there. It is noteworthy, however, to find in Fahlström's personal Swedish address book, among the "namn och address" entries, Crumb's name, phone number and address, "17551 van Arsdale Rd., Potter Valley, Calif.," as well as that of his girlfriend in San Francisco. This is written just above an entry for the artist Christo.[10]

The American artist Mike Kelley (1954–2012) greatly admired Crumb and Fahlström, and wrote very perceptively about their critical connections.[11] Kelley's work, which is exceptionally varied and diverse, demonstrates a strong anti-authoritarian tendency, an ironic and ludic component, and bold theatricality, as well as an impulse to shock and frequently offend his audience. In short, subversion, abjection, and transgression are mainstays of his art. Kelley's great love for punk music and punk subculture, and his collaborations with groups such as Sonic Youth, are just another important aspect of this impulse.

Kelley's 1995 essay "Myth Science," commissioned for an exhibition of Fahlström's installations organized in Bremen, Germany, contains many valuable insights.[12] Above all, he considers Fahlström's complex relationship to Pop art, agitprop, and politics in addition to his strong connections to Crumb. Kelley writes: "Fahlström's tactics have more in common with the ambitions of the Conceptualists than with those of the Pop artists" (2003, 161).[13] He suggests that Fahlström's approach was far more complex and idiosyncratic than a desire to elevate or displace "low" cultural material to the

Fig. 12.3. Öyvind Fahlström, *Notes 3 (Mass Elements)*, 1970. Inv. Nr. C. 1971/2107; Feder in Schwarz; Gouache; 42.2 x 35.3 cm., Staatsgalerie Stuttgart, Graphische Sammlung with photo ©Staatsgalerie Stuttgart.

status of "high" art. Kelley regards the high/low distinction as meaningless, and he recognizes that Fahlström's use of comics suggests an exceptional and distinct formal deconstructive strategy. He maintains that for Fahlström this deconstruction "is predicated on the construction of an artistic world—in the form of a model" (Kelley 2003, 161). Fahlström, he writes, constantly subverts or undermines the viewer's ability to clearly separate the "political" from the "formal."

> With a dizzying and conflicted array of "factual" material presented using this language, and by presenting cartoons in an unnatural way, Fahlström works against the implication that a popular lexicon represents a homogenous audience. The cartoon's "naturalism" lies in its air of anonymity, in its invisibility, which is why cartoons lend themselves so well to use in agitational propaganda. They have an air of truth about them; they appear as given, pre-existing, unconstructed. Fahlström's busy, unstable compositions and information overloads throw this naturalism into question. The only true "political" image is the unnatural one, the one that challenges preordained and unquestioned pictures of reality. This "unnaturalism," however, does not necessarily imply a desire to escape the pictorial; it can be understood as a dissection of the "pictorial." (Kelley 2003, 168)

It is now widely recognized that Pop art was a much more complex global phenomenon than most standard art historical narratives admit.[14] Fahlström appears to have been much more radical and progressive than Crumb. While Fahlström was decidedly more cosmopolitan, a polyglot and a polymath, with a noteworthy transnational trajectory, he nonetheless possessed an extensive knowledge of comics. It was Crumb who became his touchstone, and who provides such an important critical lens by which to understand his art.[15] *Meatball Curtain (for R. Crumb)* thereby assumes a privileged place in Fahlström's oeuvre. Likewise, Robert Crumb's importance and centrality within an expanded context for modern American art, as noted prophetically by Öyvind Fahlström fifty years ago, now appears to be a certainty.[16]

NOTES

1. One of the best examples of such manifestos is Fahlström's text "S.O.M.B.A. (Some of My Basic Assumptions)," 1972–1973, published in English in *Wedge*, no. 1 (Summer 1982): 60–63 (reprinted in Chevrier 2001, 280–84). It was also the subject of one of his variable paintings with the same title.

2. For an analysis of Fahlström's interest in language and experimental poetics, see Bäckström (2017; 2019), Bessa (2008), Lilja (2016), and Olsson (2005; 2017).

3. The provocative sexual and political content of Fahlström's work, as well as the tableau format, closely resemble the work of his contemporary Edward Kienholz (1927–1994).

4. This statement on the limits of variability was written by Fahlström and posted on the wall of the Sidney Janis Gallery for the artist's last show in New York City in March 1976. Thanks to Sharon Avery-Fahlström for bringing it to my attention, discussing its importance, and furnishing me with a copy as well as granting permission to use it here.

5. Steinberg posited the "flat bed picture plane" as a distinct formal device used by Rauschenberg, and he was one of the first to characterize this work as signaling the postmodern.

6. See Fahlström's essay on Rauschenberg published in Swedish in 1961, "En gata full av presenter." Rauschenberg wrote a brief essay on Fahlström in October 1961 (published in 1964). His personal collection included works by Fahlström: *Ade-Ledic-Nander 1* (1955) and *Performing K. K. #3* (1965), as well as works he dedicated to Fahlström, most notably *N.Y. Bird Calls for Öyvind Fahlström* (1965) and *For a Friend and Krazy Kat (Spread)* (1976). Furthermore, Fahlström's *Study for Sitting* (1961–1962), a complex collage of shapes and texts inspired by comics imagery, is in the personal collection of Jasper Johns.

7. Sharon Avery-Fahlström has suggested Berenice Abbott's photograph *A Bouncing Ball in Diminishing Arcs* (1958–1961) as the source for this shape.

8. See Huyssen 1986; and see Kelley 2003 for Kelley's notation of the "baroque aspect" of Fahlström's aesthetic.

9. These paintings are *Performing KK* (1963), *Performing KK, no. 2* (1963–1964), and *Performing KK, no. 3* (1965).

10. I am grateful to Sharon Avery-Fahlström for bringing this detail to my attention and for providing me with a copy of the address book entries.

11. The exhibition *Eye Infection*, at Amsterdam's Stedelijk Museum in 2001–2002, paired Crumb and Mike Kelley with Jim Nutt, Peter Saul, and H. C. Westermann.

12. In a postscript, Kelley recounted his first meeting with Fahlström in New York in 1975 and a subsequent invitation he made for Fahlström to lecture at the School of Art at the University of Michigan on April 7, 1976. Kelley bore sole responsibility for hosting his visit to Ann Arbor and, in retrospect, regarded it as a disaster. Kelley slightly revised "Myth Science" when it was published in 2003. Sharon Avery-Fahlström, who commissioned his original 1995 essay for the Bremen exhibition of the installations, alerted me to these changes. She suggests that it shows the great importance he placed on his writing.

13. While I agree with Kelley's remark about Fahlström's links with conceptualism, there are also important connections, in my opinion, to West Coast Funk, Junk, and Beat artists, especially Bruce Conner (1933–2008). Conner's bomb-head figure, his frequent use of burlesque striptease and pornography, and his ironic and playful work in film and assemblage suggest this relationship. John F. Kennedy's assassination inspired Connor's seminal film *Report* (1963–1967) as well as a series of Fahlström's literary texts (*Oswald Returns*, 1967) and artistic works (*Parkland Memorial* [1967] and *Lifecurve, no. 2 (Snowfield Oswald)* [1967]).

14. Fahlström's obsession with Richard Nixon has striking affinities to Philip Guston's *Nixon Series* (1971) as well as Kjartan Slettemark's *Nixon Visions* images and his *Nixon Passport* (1974). Moreover, Fahlström's close ties to Brazil, Italy, France, Sweden, and the

United States underscore his cultural fluidity and complex national identity. In addition, the specific Scandinavian context of Pop art and Fahlström's relationship to his Nordic contemporaries such as Erró, Slettemark, Per Kleiva, Per Olof Ultvedt, and Claes Oldenburg warrant further study.

15. The exhibition *Öyvind Fahlström/R. Crumb*, at Espace Gustave Fayet in Sérignan, France (June 17–September 3, 2000), provided further evidence for their important relationship.

16. I am very grateful to Sharon Avery-Fahlström for her enthusiastic support and invaluable feedback on earlier drafts of this chapter, as well as her detailed replies to my queries. Her extraordinary insights and kind assistance with permissions and image rights, exhibition checklists, and other documentation have been crucial. Likewise, Robert Crumb and the Lora Fountain Literary Agency generously granted permission to use his work. Thanks as well to Aurel Scheibler, the Aurel Scheibler Gallery in Berlin, Margitta Heinlein, Staatsgalerie Stuttgart, Núria Montclùs, the Öyvind Fahlström Foundation and Archives, and the Museu d'Art Contemporani de Barcelona.

WORKS CITED

Avery-Fahlström, Sharon, ed., with Eva Schmidt and Udo Kittelmann. 1995. *Öyvind Fahlström: The Installations*. Ostfildern, Germany: Cantz Verlag.

Bäckström, Per. 2017. "The Trumpet in the Bottom: Öyvind Fahlström and the Uncanny." *Edda* 104, no. 2: 176–98.

Bäckström, Per. 2019. "Fahlström stannade i Stockholm." *Edda* 106, no. 1: 39–53.

Bessa, Antonio Sergio. 2008. *Öyvind Fahlström: The Art of Writing*. Evanston, IL: Northwestern University Press.

Braun, Christiaan, ed. 2001. *Eye Infection*. Amsterdam: Stedelijk Museum.

Chevrier, Jean-François, ed. 2001. *Öyvind Fahlström: Another Space for Painting*. Barcelona: Museu d'Art Contemporani de Barcelona.

Chute, Hillary. 2017. *Why Comics? From Underground to Everywhere*. New York: HarperCollins.

Dackerman, Susan, ed. 2015. *Corita Kent and the Language of Pop*. New Haven, CT: Yale University Press.

Fahlström, Öyvind. 1954. "The Comics as an Art." *Expressen*, August 27, 115.

Fahlström, Öyvind. 1961. "En gata full av presenter." *Konstrevy* 37, nos. 5–6: 176–81.

Fahlström, Öyvind. 1964. "Manipulating the World." *Art and Literature*, no. 3: 225–26.

Fahlström, Öyvind. 2001. "The Invasion of the Underground Comics." In *Öyvind Fahlström: Another Space for Painting*, edited and translated by Jean-François Chevrier, 236–37. Barcelona: Museu d'Art Contemporani de Barcelona.

Henley, Jon. 2018. "My Whole Life Has Been a Lie: Sweden Admits Meatballs Are Turkish." *Guardian*, May 3. https://www.theguardian.com/world/2018/may/03/my-whole-life-has -been-a-lie-sweden-admits-meatballs-are-turkish, accessed May 28, 2019.

Hultén, K. G. Pontus. 1968. *The Machine as Seen at the End of the Mechanical Age*. New York: Museum of Modern Art.

Huyssen, Andreas. 1986. *After the Great Divide: Modernism, Mass Culture, Postmodernism*. Bloomington: Indiana University Press.

Kelley, Mike. 2003. "Myth Science (on Öyvind Fahlström)." In *Foul Perfection: Essays and Criticism*. Edited by John C. Welchman, 158–77. Cambridge, MA: MIT Press.

Lee, Pamela M. 2017. *Öyvind Fahlström: Monopoly*. Stockholm: Moderna Museet.

Lilja, Eva. 2016. "Öyvind Fahlström's Bord: Visual Devices in Poetry." *Studia Metrica et Poetica* 3, no. 2: 7–31.

Livingston, Jane. 1971. "Thoughts on Art and Technology." In *A Report on the Art and Technology Program of the Los Angeles County Museum of Art, 1967–1971*, edited by Maurice Tuchman, 102–13. Los Angeles: Los Angeles County Museum of Art.

Ngai, Sianne. 2012. *Our Aesthetic Categories: Zany, Cute, Interesting*. Cambridge, MA: Harvard University Press.

Olsson, Jesper. 2005. *Alfabetets användning: Konkret poesi och poetisk artefaction i svensk 1960-tal*. Stockholm: OEI Editör.

Olsson, Jesper. 2017. *Öyvind Fahlström: Ade-Ledic-Nander*. Stockholm: Moderna Museet.

Rauschenberg, Robert. 1964. "Öyvind Fahlström." *Art and Literature*, no. 3: 219.

Schimmel, Paul, ed. 2005. *Robert Rauschenberg Combines*. Los Angeles: Museum of Contemporary Art.

Schultz Lundestam, Barbro, ed. 2004. *Teknologi för livet / Om Experiments in Art and Technology*. Paris: Schultz Förlag.

Sontag, Susan. 1964. "Notes on Camp." In *Against Interpretation*. New York: Farrar, Straus and Giroux.

Steinberg, Leo. 2007. *Other Criteria: Confrontations with Twentieth-Century Art*. Chicago: University of Chicago Press.

Tuchman, Maurice, ed. 1971. *A Report on the Art and Technology Program of the Los Angeles County Museum of Art*. Los Angeles: Los Angeles County Museum of Art.

Chapter 13

CRUMB AND ABSTRACTION

PAUL FISHER DAVIES

s Thierry Groensteen has observed, abstraction presents an interesting test for the study and theorization of comics (Groensteen 2013, 9). Without representational content—the specifics of story, setting, or character—all that remains is the sheer form of comics. One useful way to put this is that abstract comics omit or attenuate the *ideational* function of comics. The ideational is the function whereby comics, like other rich forms of communication such as language, seek to represent human experiences: to "construe" them and bring them into being as they reflect them. This ideational function is not the only one comics enact, although it is often the representational function on which critics focus. As with language, the drawing and reading of comics is also a social exchange, embodying an interaction between human beings. Crumb's early experience of writing with his siblings exemplifies this social bonding performed through the creation and consumption of comics (Crumb 1998, 3). This second function we may call the *interpersonal* function of comics. It comprises not only the interactions performed through the medium but also the way that personal judgments and values are inscribed into any attempt to construe experience. Underlying these two major "metafunctions" is a third: a *textual* function. Comics, like languages, have means to indicate where texts begin and end, how one part of a text relates to another, and how texts connect to the world. When we consider the abstract features of comics, especially where they abstract ideational content away for us, the interpersonal exchange, the personal evaluation, and the textual ties of the medium are exposed more clearly. In this consideration of Robert Crumb's work, I look at the way abstractions in his comics, and abstract elements within his comics, serve to enact these functions.

ABSTRACT COMICS?

Crumb's work appears in the opening pages of Andrei Molotiu's *Abstract Comics: The Anthology* (2009). Crumb's "Abstract Expressionist Ultra Super Modernistic Comics" (1968), first appearing in *Zap Comix* #1, represents one of two types of "abstract comics" Molotiu identifies in his foundational collection. Although it contains representational features, the work is "abstract," according to Molotiu, in the sense that it does not communicate a narrative: it doesn't signify or tell a story.[1]

Abstraction tends to be opposed to mimetic, representational storytelling, and because of that, many may think that comics simply can't be abstract—or that, in a sense, abstract comics are not really comics.[2] But abstraction demands definition in order to assess this possibility. There are many ways in which comics may be said to be "abstract," and I will explore a range of them in this chapter. Most of the comics in Molotiu's collection are abstract in a way different from Crumb's. The figures in most abstract comics aren't mimetic; they do not represent persons and places by resemblance. They may act, they may certainly be perceived by the comics reader to move and transform, but they do not represent specific characters.[3]

Crumb doesn't quite use this kind of abstraction in his storytelling, but he does explore a range of features of the abstract. Meaningful words in "Abstract Expressionist Ultra Super Modernistic Comics" are limited to the title and "The End." On page 1, the nonsense utterances "spa" and "fon" allude to Al Feldstein's "Panic," published in EC's *Weird Science* #15 (fig. 13.1). They are the now legendary words uttered by invading Jupiterians, whose carnage is conveniently ignored by those inured to the radio scare by a parallel of Orson Welles's notorious *War of the Worlds* broadcast. But the words in Crumb don't carry any meaning other than this intertextual connotation. There are no recurring characters to carry meaning or intention. The image of the disembodied eye recurs in the first three panels; the protuberance or pointing finger for the next loose tier of panels; and a rounded female nude for two panels. But these figures resemble each other only loosely. There is a sequence of humanoid shapes along the bottom tier of page 1 apparently exchanging conversation, but they change from panel to panel in color and size. One of the basic tenets of comics readership—that recognizable characters recur—is absent from "Abstract Expressionist Ultra Super Modernistic Comics."

The comic does trade in the abstract, non-mimetic machinery of comics in another sense. What Groensteen calls the "formal apparatus" of comics is present here (2013, 11). Crumb divides the story into panels, which can be read in tiers as I have done above, although the angles and curves in the panel

Fig. 13.1. R. Crumb, "Abstract Expressionist Ultra Super Modernistic Comics,"

shapes challenge reading order somewhat. "Spa" and "fon" are marked as utterances by the conventional word balloon, although the balloons emerge from nondescript protuberances in a sparse landscape. Speech balloons appear throughout the comic even though there is no meaningful wording to fill them. In the place of verbiage, Crumb draws such elements as a loose maze, an image of an eyeball, inkblots, "asemic writing" (script-like marks that only resemble language and are uncoded), and at times nothing at all. Although these balloons are abstract in the sense that they are not taken to be a material part of the diegesis, Crumb shades them at the edges, lending a degree of concreteness to them. The formal conventions of comics—panels, word balloons, page layout—are made visible as formal devices, not as containers of narrative content.

A further notational device appears on page 2. Musical notes appear in balloons, in text boxes, spoken by machines, by substituted dots, from unknown spaces (between teeth, up a skirt). Arrows, pointers, and flashes of explosions join this abstract iconography, guiding the reader's eye around the page and imbuing the images with bursts of motion and direction, not bound to supporting a particular narrative. Readers may find themselves on the hunt for the repeated characters they expect but of which they find themselves deprived: seeking to identify continuity between the curves repeated through tier 2 of page 2, for example; or the dot singing a note in panel 4 growing into the tusk emerging from the ground in panel 5. But the comic sustains none of them, moving fluently to the next invention. The reader resists the non sequiturs, seeking connection in the textual hooks of recurring shape, exchange of utterance, or continuity of the notes from image to image.

On page 3, the concretized curves of the word balloons in panel 1 are reflected in the legged creatures with their tail-heads below: the abstract made concrete, and the concrete abstract. Reading order is problematized, and perhaps even reversed for tier 2, as the whirl of paper leaves depicted in panel 3 enacts a curve around, leading to the note sung by the vagina represented below. The sexual content lurking below the surface becomes more concrete here with this disembodied vagina and the circle of disembodied breasts in tier 2; sweat beads and sperm-like explosions continue this theme through tier 3. "The End" is reached arbitrarily, spoken from a concentric array of diamonds in the final panel.

In describing "Abstract Expressionist Ultra Super Modernistic Comics," I have found myself drawing on a number of ways to understand the notion "abstract." In the next section, I will explore what this term might be taken to mean and lead to a conceptualization that will structure the remainder of the chapter.

THE NATURE OF ABSTRACTION

As a verb, "abstract" means "to remove, to draw away from." In *Visual Thinking*, Rudolf Arnheim argues that degrees of abstraction and the definition of abstraction are central to the meaning-making work of drawing. Diverging from Charles Sanders Peirce's three-part division of signs into symbol, icon, and index but approaching similar distinctions, Arnheim notes three functions of images, which he defines by the degree and type of abstraction the images engage in. First, for Arnheim, an image is a sign "to the extent to which it stands for a particular content without reflecting its characteristics visually" (2004, 136). This maps to Peirce's "symbol." Second, an image is a picture if it portrays things "located at a lower level of abstractness" than itself. That is to say, it renders something concrete using abstracted means—rendering some relevant qualities: "pictures are not mere replicas" (137). For Arnheim, this is an act of interpretation and thereby an engagement by the creator with the thing portrayed through means of the image. The image-maker passes some judgment on the qualities of the image's object. He argues against the notion that a reader must "complete" an image to understand it. This idea lies at the heart of Scott McCloud's thinking about comics, both in the sense of a "masking effect" of simplified images and of "closure," which for Arnheim would efface the abstractness of the image, its judgments, by replacing it with remembered or conceived detail. For Arnheim, "[a] cartoon is seen at exactly the level at which it is drawn" (138). This function of the image maps well to Peirce's "icon." Third, for Arnheim an image is a "symbol" in the opposite way to that which makes it a "picture": it portrays something at a higher level of abstractness than itself. So, in other words, a symbol makes concrete a more abstract concept (138).

Arnheim stresses that abstraction occurs on a continuum, not as a binary opposition. Images are abstract by degrees and are pictures and symbols in degrees also, allowing for the possibility that a given image may serve the function of both. There are two scales of abstraction presented on this model: one operating in the qualities of the image, the other in the object of experience represented. To recruit Peirce once more, we may translate this as abstraction in the signifier (the image) and the signified (the object of experience). Crumb's "Abstract Expressionist Ultra Super Modernistic Comics" need not then be placed in a binary position as one type of abstract comic as opposed to another, but its many elements may be explored as placing it along a continuum of abstraction, with its stylized objects representing forces or ideas. While Arnheim calls attention to the replica as a representation of particular objects at the bottom of his abstraction diagram, at the top the ability of non-mimetic forms to render concepts and energy is likewise proposed in this system of thinking.

THINKING ABOUT ABSTRACTION

There are a number of interesting ideas here that we can take forward into a model of abstraction in comics drawing and then apply in an exploration of Crumb's work. One is the argument that any degree of abstraction represents the engagement and intervention of a person in the act of representation. A second is the notion that abstract drawing is suited for rendering generalities, notions, motions, and emotions. A third is the idea that abstraction is a matter of degree, of what we will call "clines," not binaries. And a fourth is that degrees of abstraction occur along a number of dimensions, not just one.

Arnheim has separated image and experience as two vectors of abstraction. But if we look at how abstraction is spoken of, including by Arnheim himself, we may find that there are more to account for. Arnheim titles two of his chapters "What Abstraction Is" and "What Abstraction Is Not" (173, 153). That second idea is especially fruitful: if abstraction (Latin *abstrahere*) is "movement away from," then to ask "away from what?" can help us define our terms.

If we turn to the Oxford English Dictionary for guidance, definitions 1a and 1b of "abstract" explicitly oppose it to "concrete." Definitions 1c, 1d, and 1e make reference to the particular and specific. (Definition 2 notes its use as implying "difficulty"; 3 is an obscure heraldic use, related to 4 and 5, which returns to its verbal definition as distancing.) Definition 6a focuses on the art object: not an attempt to represent external reality, in 6b especially dispensing with narrative. Definition 6b calls attention to music as abstract in this sense. Mimesis is not mentioned specifically, but in 6a the use "purely" of shape, color, and texture is identified: so one might separate not representing by mimesis from not representing at all. This leads us to the following dimensions along which to explore abstraction:

In what is signified:
　1. Non-specific
　2. Non-concrete

In the "signifier":
　3. Non-mimetic
　4. Non-signifying

According to Arnheim's schema in *Visual Thinking*, the closer one approaches non-signification, the less a signifier may be either mimetic or non-mimetic. This mimesis–non-mimesis cline masks a further distinction to be made between the Peircean *symbolic* and *indexical*, but since both may be considered abstract, this may be considered a complexity one may place aside for now. As we approach indexicality as mere trace of the artist, we can perhaps move on this diagram of clines toward the "non-signifying," whereas the deliberate use of a sign as part of a coded set of symbols adheres to the signifying edge by definition.

How might this array of types of abstraction, and clines between them, help us think about abstraction in Crumb? We do not have to limit ourselves to declared works of abstraction such as "Abstract Expressionist Ultra Super Modernistic Comics," for one. We can see Crumb's explorations in caricature as taking positions along the clines of abstraction, and treat those along with Arnheim as having interpersonal value: expressing Crumb's emotions, ideas, and judgments through the "modalization" of the line (that is to say, the degree of concretization of the abstract, and abstraction of what is represented mimetically). I use the word "cline" here to cohere with Michael Halliday's use of the word to indicate the way in which language may by degrees mark arbitrarily fine levels of reality, desirability, possibility, and other personal judgments through resources for marking *modalization* (Halliday and Matthiessen 2014, 172). "Modalization" in language is the function by which speakers express their evaluations of the content of their speech, both in terms of its reality status and its moral force, as well as their judgments of its quality. I propose here (and elsewhere) that degrees of abstraction may be read as serving comparable purposes in the drawing of comics (Davies 2017). Further, we can treat abstraction as a "non-signifying" feature of Crumb's work, serving if anything a "textual" function, binding his work together as a cohesive whole at the same time as it affords a reader the pleasure of lines on paper to inscribe as well as read.

NON-MIMETIC ABSTRACTION

To explore these dimensions of abstraction, we will start with the non-mimetic, since that is the starting point for much of Molotiu's collection *Abstract Comics* as well as a central characteristic of abstraction in fine art discourse more broadly. We will then move from the signifier to the aspects of abstraction in what is signified, and return to abstraction as non-signification toward the end of this chapter.

"Abstract Expressionist Ultra Super Modernistic Comics" is not Crumb's only experiment with this sort of consciously abstract work. The title speaks to his typical stance toward abstraction and modern art, particularly, abstract expressionism:

> The "fine" art after World War II doesn't do it for me. It just seems life-less, a posture, a pose. Jackson Pollock, Willem DeKooning [*sic*], on down to pop art, performance art, minimalism, whatever. . . . I don't get what it's about. You're supposed to express yourself, but you're not supposed to say anything? If your statement is too straightforward, easily grasped, then it's not "fine art," or what? (Crumb and Poplaski 2005, 298)

Crumb expresses frustration with the rejection of mimesis and the "ide-ational" aspect of the work: it seems hidden, obtuse deliberately. In *Weirdo* #2 in 1981, he published "Weirdo Art Section: It's Art for Art's Sake" with the caption "Whatsit all mean?," and the subtitle "Cubism for the masses" (reproduced in Crumb 2013, 30–31). More than a decade after "Abstract Expressionist Ultra Super Modernistic Comics," these pages feature only partially paneled sections, though they share the motif of the eye-on-a-stalk and distorted, transforming shapes, only partly mimetic. There are more recognizable human figures here, though rendered with the angularity that speaks to the allusion to cubism, rendered with Crumb's late geometric crosshatching style, which I will discuss below. More meaningful verbal utterances appear here than in the earlier work, though they also comment on the lack of narrative signification: "express yo'self," "It's deep!," and "It is fascinating is it not" accompany the ironic captions. Onomatopoeia expresses unmusical noises "plut," "splup," "honk," and others. While there is mimesis in the elements, as with "Abstract Expressionist Ultra Super Modernistic Comics," the wholes do not connect and the panels do not follow to imply action between each. Here, there is no recognizable continuity or identity between the images in sequence. The effect in both works is trippy, but what it communicates just as much as an LSD experience is the playfulness of creative line work, unguided by the elements of narrative. Crumb's presence is revealed in the stylized hatching work, the crazed expressions, the startle-marks in the emanata (lines, stars, sweat beads emanating from faces and objects), and their significations of motion, explosion, glowing, and pain. These lines, some symbolic, some expressive, communicate the energy and focused decoration around the page.

Sketchbooks in the early 1980s explore this semi-mimetic and non-mimetic space, sometimes with allusion to specific exercises. In *The R. Crumb Sketchbook*, vol. 3, "Problems in Composition" features the eye, the drip, and a cubist fragmented guitar, with explorations in crosshatching and the comment "It's too tight!" (Crumb 2018, 321). An untitled page dated September 8, 1980, depicts a fragmented figure at the heart of a jagged, crosshatched composition reminiscent of cubism, surrounded by features of the modern world that pressure the figure in a way Arnheim would count as "symbolic": containers for "booze" and "dope," a TV labeled "media," cars, spacecraft, disembodied erogenous zones. The aim here seems to be to capture experience along a cline of abstraction: some mimesis, but partial, combined with images used for their own expressive value, and not at all times aiming to represent concrete experience. The verbal expressions of frustration signal Crumb's attitude to these experiments: "WHUTIZZIT?" in relation to the purely abstract shapes (349); and "Hey, this art stuff is fun, huh?" on the purely abstract patterning alongside the caption "drawing as Therapy for TV overloaded eyes" (426). There is some delight in these images. "A Meditation on Sophie's Scribbling" appears to reproduce or decorate with hatching textures the free lines of his daughter's marks (Crumb 2018, 421), and "MUTATE NOW" seems more proudly to recognize the expressiveness of abstract shape in another sketchbook page from the 1980s (Crumb 1998, 217). Some of the cubist experiments of the early 1980s Crumb finds worth developing into full-color paintings—"Oy Oy Oydle-Oil Painting #1 or Blue-Green Man" and "The Green Aline," for instance—although the doubts about "art" still persist, revealed in the title "Aline in a Cubist Nightmare" (Crumb 1998, 221, 222, 218). Although Crumb disdains art from the second half of the twentieth century, cubists take a place in the list of "Fine Art!" creators Crumb admires, presented as part of a summary of influences in "R. Crumb's Universe of Art" (Crumb and Poplaski 2005, 432).

"Cubist BeBop Comics" from the 1970s combines this play with cubist abstraction along the mimetic scale with the abstraction presented by music as a non-mimetic, non-signifying form (Crumb and Poplaski 2005, 307–14). Although the images in the panels are largely mimetic, representing the places and people creating and enjoying the jazz music that inspired the piece, the angled panel shapes and disruption of linearity reflect Crumb's work in "Abstract Expressionist Ultra Super Modernistic Comics," as does the composition of the title. The symbolic representation of musical notes—abstract in the sense of non-concrete as well as non-meaningful—does much of the work, although other emanata and commentary accompany the drawings.

By page 2, the motif of the disembodied eye emerges as Crumb seems to be seeking metaphorical representation of his experience of the music: the "stream of consciousness" labeled in the style of political newspaper cartoons, and the eye's thought "gettin' down" as it floats down the stream in panel 2. In the second tier, a naked listener asks (in a cry repeated throughout many of these experiments in abstraction), "What DOES it all mean?" The dancing bodies of hippies dominate tier 3, and on page 3, the bodies creating and responding to the music are represented with abstract motion lines and Wassily Kandinsky–style patterns emerging from a saxophone in the central panel. Music is linked to motion and abstraction in the dance of bodies, the pattern of the notes, and the angled and curved structuration of the panels. The abstract elements of comics such as these motif lines and musical notes take on concrete qualities: reflective on page 1, patterned on page 4, drawn shakily to express the quivering of a voice. Elements of cubism appear in the figures on pages 5 and 6; the eye recurs; Crumb's sexual interests creep into the imagery by page 7; and the final page returns to elements of pure abstraction, with just the hint of sound in onomatopoeic "zt-zt." The final, typically self-derogatory comment, is: "Oh it's absurd—Yeah, but is it art?"

In the context of abstract comics, Thierry Groensteen quotes semiotics thinkers Groupe Mu on visual art:

> A work of visual art can be examined from the point of forms, from the point of view of colours, from the point of view of textures, and from that of the whole formed by all these together. It should also be noted that these visual data are co-present, so that the image is, from the outset, always potentially tabular. A comparison may be made with temporal arts (poetry, music . . .), where tabularity can only be achieved by a process of construction. (qtd. in Groensteen 2013, 12)

Later in *Comics and Narration,* Groensteen devotes a whole chapter to the notion of "rhythm" in comics and the metaphor of comics as musical in their structure. He notes that most reviewers have "pointed to the musical dimension of the formal dynamic at work on the page, whether this is a matter of harmony, dissonance, or progressive transformation." After Charles Hatfield, he affirms that the whole book might be seen as a musical piece (Groensteen 2013, 134). To illustrate the musicality of comics, Groensteen uses "Mr. Natural's 719th Meditation" by Crumb (in French translation), in which Mr. Natural begins by whistling a note as he sits down in a "the barren wastes" to meditate. There he stays silently as the world around him develops and changes, implicitly over large amounts of time as a town, then a city, grows into being. He begins to hum, projected in a word balloon as a growing, lengthening, enlarging sequence of "MMM"s, which rises then falls through pages 2–3—and which precipitates the destruction of the civilization around him, leaving him to return to consciousness with a note reflecting the start in an empty desert landscape (original in Crumb et al. 2017, 65–67).

This is not in itself an abstract comic, but its operative elements—the structure and sequence of regularly sized panels, the musical note, the meaningless syllable of Mr. Natural's om chant—all connote the abstract in the sense of non-mimetic, or even non-signifying. Mr. Natural seems oblivious to what has happened. "That wuz a pretty good session, boy," he remarks, as he packs up to leave in the final panel, disregarding the mimetic events of the story and referring instead to the abstract structure of rising and falling events that marks his experience.

Crumb's musical notes, while non-mimetic, quite often take on concrete qualities. In *Weirdo*'s "I Remember the Sixties," the music of the period is given textured, distressed physical form in the representation of sound and notes (Crumb 2013, 63). On page 2, tier 2, the shaky notes of rock music pursue the represented Crumb out of a concert, pressing at his back, and trail a hippie girl dancing in the fields in tier 3. On the final page, notes are represented as visible to the acid-taking Crumb in the first panel. In "The Old Songs Are the Best Songs" (Crumb 2013, 68–75), Crumb mainly represents the ideational content of the lyrics, visualizing the people brought to mind by the content. But emanata represent the singing, accompanied by semimaterial sweat beads or saliva, which likewise emerge from the trumpets in "My Guy" (Crumb 2013, 70). The trumpets themselves intrude from outside the panel at key moments in the narrative of the lyric recounted in this segment. Jimi Hendrix's "Purple Haze" is made concrete around his head, rendered as inhabited with symbology: paisley, dollar signs, stars. He and his hippie dancing partner appear physically blown around with a wind that reflects this "haze," and Hendrix's hair is represented full of abstract shapes reflecting Crumb's experiments in cubism in the penultimate panel of this segment. The music is moved along a cline of abstraction: made a physical presence in the narrative conjured up by the ideational content in the lyric, and carrying some of that energy of sheer motion explored in the abstraction of "Abstract Expressionist Ultra Super Modernistic Comics" and "Cubist BeBop Comics." There is a similar connection between music and cubist abstraction in Crumb's reverie at the center of "Uncle Bob's Mid-Life Crisis" (Crumb 2013, 86–87). In "Where Has It Gone, the Beautiful Music of Our Grandparents?," electric blues music is initially abstract and pleasant, yet ultimately becomes so loud as to punch the narrating Crumb explosively in the side of the head (Crumb 2013, 137–41).

This operation of the cline between concrete and abstract, mimetic and non-mimetic, is frequently used to represent states of mind in Crumb, especially extreme states of mind. As well as the attribution of images to emotional states projected by represented figures in the experimental "cubist" work, abstraction emerges in thought and speech balloons to represent confusion, dream, and exhilaration in Crumb's other works. Abstract emanata appearing as concrete presences haunt his backgrounds and reach into some foregrounds. For example, in the brushwork of "The Religious Experience of Philip K. Dick," concretized emanata invade or emanate from Dick's mind (Crumb 2013, 181–88). Elsewhere, the image of the brain as a maze is represented as mimetic though metaphorical in 1967's "Head" (Crumb et al. 2017, 55) and is used in more abstract form for instance in "Puzzle Page" (Crumb and Poplaski 2005, 391), inviting readers to interact with a cutaway head and follow the maze paths through the mind of the "brilliant young fellow" seeking "spiritual enlightenment," as well as in the visually similar patterns making up a face in "When I Was Young I Took a Lot of LSD" (Crumb and Poplaski 2005, 125).

Abstract inscriptions are also used to represent unknown or unknowable speech. Crumb uses what Tim Gaze calls "asemic writing" (Gaze and Jacobson 2013) to indicate utterances without meaning, not only in the deliberately abstract comics as observed above but also in other representational comics. *Weirdo*'s "TV Blues with Etoain Shrdlu" represents the blaring of a "foreign-language show" with asemic writing alongside musical notes (Crumb 2013, 5–13). By page 3, these are filling word balloons, with their concretized edges, overlapping and occupying the physical space around Etoain. The events in the TV become concretized; on page 4, the erotically charged leg of the dancer he is viewing emerges from the TV (and transgresses the panel borders for the reader, too), and Etoain, grabbing the physicalized leg, is drawn into the TV. The hosts engage him in physical manipulations, shoving and dancing; while musical notes mark the sound in the background, this asemic writing continues to dominate the word balloons, against Etoain's protests: "I can't follow gibberish!" Underlying this is the likewise human, emotional, but otherwise non-representational accompaniment of onomatopoeia for applause and laughter, running along the bottom section of the panels as the music runs along the top. Etoain is surrounded by the embodied meaninglessness of the television show, as captured by Crumb's use of abstraction to signify the semantically empty.

NON-CONCRETE ABSTRACTION

Crumb revels in what Mort Walker has playfully called the "lexicon of comicana" (2000), the abstract motion lines, containers, and emanata that express material, verbal, and mental action. The earliest sketchbook images published tend not to feature these, being largely composed of mimetic observational sketches of concrete subjects. As Crumb develops Fritz the Cat and uses the sketchbooks more frequently for comics images and drafts of comics, the classic enclosures of word balloons, thought balloons, and panels emerge. His drawing becomes more expressive and more from the imagination as these abstract elements appear, and even mimetic sketches take on abstract elements.[4] Crumb explores the possibilities of emanata in "I'm a Ding Dong Daddy," featuring a big-footed central character leaping and dancing around a space with little materiality (Crumb and Poplaski 2005, 134–35). When a brick wall is introduced in the last panel of the first page for him to bang his head against, the motion lines, startle lines, and puffs of smoke from his footsteps become a physical presence. The character performs with such material energy that he explodes on the second page into a puff of emanata stars, which then are shown to exist within a shaded, concretized cloud. The cloud trails off as a thought balloon, emanating from the head of the very character introduced in panel 1. The recursive possibilities of the idea-projecting function of the thought balloon are brought to light by the meeting of the material and immaterial in comics iconology.

As well as the making-material of the musical notes discussed above, word and thought balloons tend to be hatched and shaded as if they were physical elements in the diegetic space of the narrative, perhaps especially in splash pages and covers. Crumb does his own lettering, of course, so there is an engagement by the text with the page, a shared space between the abstract elements that are non-concrete and the represented diegesis of the narratives. His line work engages with the page at all levels; the shadows, too, seem worked and crafted, and I will discuss the development and reception of Crumb's hatching below.

Drop shadows in the text panels and captions likewise lend a materiality to the verbal commentary in Crumb's work. The playful mode in "Drawing Cartoons is Fun!," emulating promotional pages in the comics of Crumb's youth, make the cartoonist line-like as a stick figure (Crumb and Poplaski 2005, endpapers). The startle-lines appear almost as bold as his arms, and arrow elements are made three-dimensional with shadows like the caption boxes to the lower left. Lettering is made fat and marked with reflective highlights and outlines, and a range of styles imitate type and handwriting.

Lettering is a central component of Crumb's world, not only in the beloved record covers and comics covers he explores and replicates[5] but also in text-only or text-dominated sketchbook pages.[6] In an image in *The R. Crumb Handbook*, the self-reflective text appears as emerging from a hole in a head—a concretized word balloon—with the increasing shakiness of the line enacting a decaying state of mind indexically, as the wording devolves into asemic writing and the non-signifying symbolic (Crumb and Poplaski 2005, 384). Again, this play with the cline between the abstract (non-concrete writing) and the concrete is expressive of emotional states and the engagement of the self in what is drawn.

Crumb no doubt would hate this sort of talk. As he points out in "Drawing Cartoons Is Fun!," "It's only lines on paper, folks!!" (Crumb and Poplaski 2005, endpapers). But lines on paper are never only lines on paper. They make material what is felt, and give feeling and judgment to what is material. Crumb is perhaps resisting in advance any criticisms readers might make of the evaluation his abstract choices might seem to imply of the figures he draws. This is perhaps especially significant when he generalizes social groups and the human body, especially the female body, as the next section will explore.

NON-SPECIFIC ABSTRACTION

Abstraction as generalization is likewise something Crumb would be likely to distance himself from. Proclamations like those in "Drawing Cartoons Is Fun!" tend to be playfully self-effacing, and the work is surrounded by denials of meaning or questioning of the authority with which proclamations are made. However, characters appear in Crumb who are named as types, and the abstraction of the body and typification of persons have led Crumb into some dubious territory.

Crumb's characters often take deliberately nondescript names such as Etoain Shrdlu mentioned above, or perhaps most obviously Shuman the Human. Other punning names include Eggs Ackley, John Q. Public, and Ed Everyman (Crumb and Poplaski 2005, 257). They are "narrated" doing nothing much, although the extreme case of this is Bo Bo Bolinsky, "The No. 1 Human Zero," drawn doing absolutely nothing from nine angles in *Uneeda*, 1970. These playful generalizations emphasizing the mundanity of the average American cause controversy when Crumb depicts certain behaviors, and readers take Crumb's depiction to attach a positive evaluation to what he shows or to indicate a moral personal stance or attitude toward the content. Joe Blow from *Zap* #5 looks like just one of these harmless everyman figures, but he is shown engaged in smilingly incestuous relationships with his 1950s domestic-bliss family. Recurring character Angelfood McSpade caricatures African American womanhood in a way that blends Crumb's erotic fixations with the endemic racism of the day. The tension between what is specific to Crumb, and therefore blameworthy, and what is general to the period in which he was and is creating, is a further way in which degrees of abstraction are reflected in his work.

ABSTRACTING THE FIGURE

Perhaps most controversial is Crumb's abstraction of the female figures represented in his artwork. Notoriously, the Mr. Natural and Flakey Foont story "A Bitchin' Bod" features "(sort of) Devil Girl" taken to Flakey Foont under the control of Mr. Natural, without a head (*Hup* #4, 1992, reproduced in Crumb 1998, 231–43). "The head was always a big problem . . . she had such an irritating set of sensibilities!" explains Mr. Natural on page 2. By pages 5–6, Flakey is using this decapitated body as a sex object—although he is haunted by concretized visions of the disembodied head at the moment of orgasm. This is followed by declarations of shame and an attempt to compensate for the missing fake head, which had kept the body acceptable in public. Toward the end of the tale, it is revealed that Devil Girl was not decapitated after all but that her head was concealed inside her body. When her head reappears, Devil Girl reports her subjective experience: "That was so-o-o WE-E-EIRD!"; "It was pure sensation . . . it's like, I wasn't there or something . . . stuff was happening to me . . . I could feel it, but it was very . . . impersonal!" When she discovers that she has been given to Foont for his sexual gratification, she ends the strip enraged, only to have her anger dismissed and minimized by Mr. Natural.

This is standard narrative rather than abstraction in the senses we have discussed so far. But it embodies abstraction in the sense of *removal*—the removal of the head as well as the removal of experience and lived sensation in Devil Girl's report. The abstracting away of the head has recurred in Crumb's sketchbooks over the years, leading up to this story. In Crumb's sketchbooks in the mid-1960s, Mr. Natural's first appearance shares a page with the big-foot figures that led to Crumb's first taste of fame with "Keep on Truckin'," their legs and shoes emphasized and the heads radically attenuated (Crumb 2016, 210). *The R. Crumb Coffee Table Art Book* reproduces a sketch where this reaches an extreme, the heads just a line (74–75).[7] These are male figures, but the truncation of female figures appears as early as "Twot," with Crumb's

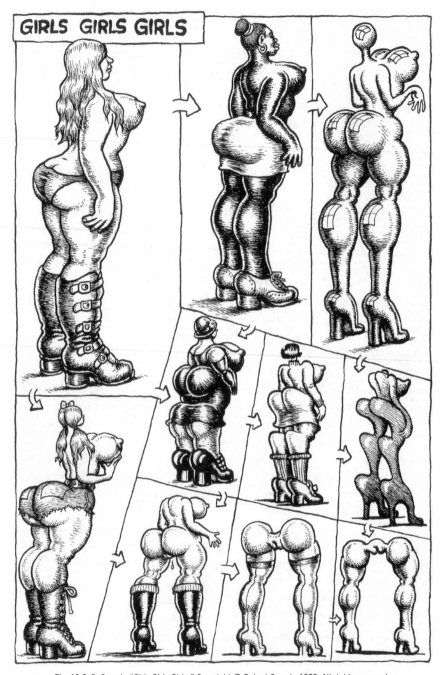

Fig. 13.2. R. Crumb, "Girls Girls Girls," Copyright © Robert Crumb, 1972. All rights reserved.

favored strong calves, boots, and thighs ending at the waist (Crumb 2016, 166). Women's heads are hidden because turned away, or because pressed into the floor or the wall (Crumb 1998, 112, 133; Crumb 2018, 4). Some of these images depict a concrete, physical violence, but often the turning away takes the form of social dismissiveness, or the textually formal transformations that disregard the personhood of the figure depicted. Crumb uses exercises attributed to Jack Hamm's *Cartooning the Head and Figure* (1967) to explore his preferred body type, and he uses abstract markers of identity (arrows, boxes, labels) to characterize this figure, along with his analogy of the "bean" shape as he approaches an abstract purity of form (Crumb 2018, 12, 59). The many reiterations of women he knows, including his partners, prominently Aline Kominsky-Crumb, and imagined others, agglomerate to the concept of a shared form. This "Platonic form" of erotic arousal is pushed to its most vivid limits in 1972's "Girls Girls Girls" in *XYZ Comics* wherein a mimetically rendered figure of a woman in the upper left panel leads, in a nonlinear set of transformations indicated by diverging arrows, to ever-extreme caricature, enlarging the sexual characteristics and attenuating away the head (lower tier), the clothes and hair (upper tier/far-right panels), and finally the torso (lower right) to leave widely spaced, strong leg shapes, the globes of but-tocks, and a tenuously linked, rudimentary vagina (fig. 13.2).[8] All specificity is abstracted, until only the sexually charged stimulus shapes remain. This exercise in abstraction has perhaps unsurprisingly been taken to express a personal evaluation of women on Crumb's part. The misogyny that appears to be implied here has led to calls to exclude Crumb from canonization, or at least never to forget in discussing his work the need for a critical stance that challenges his own urging to take the drawings at face value.

NON-SIGNIFYING ABSTRACTION

Crumb is often raising questions about meaning, and resisting meaning. "It's only lines on paper," as we have noted, and, in a repeated refrain: "The mind can't know it" (for example, Crumb and Poplaski 2005, 371–72). The non-mimetic explorations in abstraction discussed in the section above begin to press against the limits of meaning, and approach the abstract as non-signifying. However, the avoidance of meaning, and the disruption of meaning enacted in the drawing of non-mimetic form, nonetheless point toward signification, or at least raise the question of possible signification. Crumb dots his work with questions about meaning: "What are they saying in these art magazines? Beats the hell out of me! You read it, I can't!" (Crumb and Poplaski 2005, 300); "Yeah, but is it art?" asks Crumb on the poster for an exhibit of his work (Crumb and Poplaski 2005, 344); "You tell me, I don't know . . ." he answers himself. Mr. Natural, who on the cover of *Mr. Natural* #3 tells us: "Stick with me, folks! I got all the answers!," has already told us on the cover of #2 that it "[d]on't mean sheeit." Even his early characters the Silly Pidgeons ask, "What is the meaning of life?" in a circular fashion to no fruitful reply (Crumb 1998, 65; Crumb 2016, 98).

This can be read as disingenuous, a disavowal of the responsibility for making meaning that pressed on Crumb, especially when elevated to a position of cultural prominence. But, as discussed above, Crumb's interest in the abstraction of music and the pleasures of drawing speak to image-making as a release from meaning-making. I have focused so far on the creative and abstract experiments in Crumb's sketchbooks, but the pages as published frequently return to observation exercises that are more or less tied to the mimesis of present experience. These images mimetically represent but do not take part in a narrative: they are just cars, the city, still life, the woodpile in the corner, the reclining partner, the view. Crumb takes pleasure in mark-making, in the trace of the line, the sculpting of figure, the creation of shadow, shade, and shape in the crosshatching of the pen.

ABSTRACTION AS TEXTUAL

Crumb's line and his crosshatching are a distinctive feature of his work and a remarked-upon pleasure of viewing it. In an interview, Steve Bell (2005) reminds Crumb that "[o]ne of your fans once told you that he enjoyed your crosshatching more than being stoned." Crumb acknowledges his careful work with crosshatching and the debt it owes to eighteenth- and nineteenth-century printmaking, although he learned of these things later in his career. But Bell also points out the allure of the line quality in Crumb's early 1960s work: "[T]he strips are something special, and what I like about them is the looseness of your line." At the level of the line and the technique of rendering, we reach a non-signifying textual abstraction: those qualities of line work that cohere an artist's work as belonging to a certain period, and perhaps to a certain work, and that identify a creative individual (apart from the expressive indexical functions they may also sustain). In *Understanding Comics*, at the end of chapter 5, "Living in Line," Scott McCloud illustrates the way in which line work becomes abstract when viewed at close quarters, even when it forms part of a mimetic image (or wording) at normal scale (McCloud 1993, 118, 137). I end this exploration with this level of abstraction that is present throughout Crumb's work, namely the qualities of his line and, in particular, the development through periods of a sensually charged aspect of his work: crosshatching.

In the earliest sketchbooks presenting Crumb's adult work, the line work is shaky, continuous, and unshaded in large measure, especially the architectural studies and studies of cars in the city around him. Shading in this first period is done with a distinctive vertical line, with most shadow and shade rendered with overlapping upward strokes. Crumb comments on this as a self-consciously developed style in discussion with Todd Hignite: "I went through this phase in the mid-sixties with this vertical shading technique. I don't know what I was trying to prove, come up with some stylistic gimmick or something" (Hignite 2006, 20). The abstract marking qualities are there to provide a signature, to identify the work as Crumb's. This vertical hatching rarely attempts to describe contours, with the exception of hair, which follows the direction of the locks in contrast to the skin. Line that follows and describes contours emerges in the cartoon drawing, not rendered from life but created from imagination; in the observational sketches, lifework changes direction to the diagonal and then to follow the shapes of desired bodies. The vertical hatching style persists for many of these studies, however, gradually giving way to a more sculptural style.[9] By the *Zap Comix* years, line work is multidirectional but more attenuated, confined to scratchy edges "influenced by early cartoon strips like *Mutt and Jeff*, *Krazy Kat*, stuff like that" (Hignite 2006, 20).

Crumb was "intentionally avoiding crosshatching" at this period but using descriptive contour "hatching" to mimetically render bodies, objects, walls, and surfaces and even to describe abstract shapes (Crumb 2016, 410). This hatching work gives concreteness and texture to abstract elements such as texts and word balloons during this period, too, and that modalization of these elements—the making-concrete of the abstract as well as the abstraction and distortion of what is diegetic—becomes a marker of Crumb's work. During the experimentation of this period, he explores the abstracting-away of the figurative into pure, clean line and ink (fig. 13.3).

In *R. Crumb: From the Underground to Genesis*, the editors propose that 1981 marks a change in Crumb's work to "fine lines and hatching with a rapidograph" (Crumb et al. 2017, 22). However, after early experiments and the loose drawing of the late 1960s and early 1970s, a return to crosshatching appears a little sooner than that in the sketchbooks. Combinations of diagonal hatching along with vertical and horizontal appear during the *Sketchbook*, vol. 2 period (1968–1975), first in imaginative architectural drawings, especially in shadows, and then in renderings of faces and bodies by 1970 (Crumb

Fig. 13.3. R. Crumb, "Kozmic Kapers," Copyright © Robert Crumb, 1967.

2017, 195, 217). Multidirectional hatching to describe contours appears from the very first images in *Sketchbook*, vol. 3 (January 1975–December 1982). This style appears in observations from life, in abstracted and cartoonish distortions (for example, an open mouth drawn as a clean, carefully shaded concave circle), and above all in the shaping and rendering of women's legs. Hatching enacts a devotion to shape and an expression of personal value for the object, as well as marking an artist's style.[10]

Crumb reaches a mature hatching style in the work collected in *Sketchbook*, vol. 3. In the wake of his LSD experiences of the 1960s and 1970s, he "immediately got interested in drawing again for its own sake, the technical aspects of drawing, and got interested in crosshatching again, really got into perfecting crosshatching as much as possible" (Hignite 2006, 20). He aspires to the careful quality of the "old guys," in particular Thomas Nast—inspiring, powerful, and "more lively" than other artists of the nineteenth century. He explicitly comments on the return to the radiograph as a tool, corroborating the view of *R. Crumb: From the Underground to Genesis* (Crumb 2018, 269). His experiments with abstraction at this time, though, are as likely to be exploring the resources for representing abstract thought (in the sense of non-concrete) as in the diagrammatic work on the same page or in "Upward Striving," as well as reveling in the lively hatching for its own sake. This is explored in the abstract experiments alluded to from this period in "Whutizzit?," and beautifully in "Ego," with its crosshatched patterns that may be cloud, skin, or just sheer texture and the trace of Crumb's mark on the page.[11]

CONCLUSION

While Crumb is dismissive of modern art, in particular "abstract expressionist super ultra modernistic" work, he has both flirted with abstraction as a form for exploration in itself and consistently used abstract elements in his comics. While non-mimetic abstraction is the form that is most striking to readers, willfully evading the expectation that comics should have ideational content, the non-concrete has always been at the heart of Crumb's work. His gleeful use of emanata, onomatopoeia, and all the abstract lines that mark motion, thought, and speech in comics energizes his work, and these often take on concrete features, engaging in a cline of abstraction that unifies his pages and makes more concrete those features of experiences like listening to music. Further, his generalizations of human experience, and the abstraction of his own desires, have steered him to images that have proven controversial in that they make concrete, personal, and particular that which is generic and social. Finally, the textures of his drawings both carry his distinctive mark as a creator and express his fascination with the forms he depicts, whether abstract or concrete. Turning away from the question "What does it mean?" in the sense of "What is its ideational content?" can lead us to interesting considerations of the interpersonal: the engagement with form, the love expressed in the line work, and the textual distinctiveness that offers pleasures for the reader and viewer of his work.

NOTES

1. For more on this notion of abstract comics, see the introduction to Molotiu 2009.

2. For an example of this view, see Cohn 2009.

3. See Davies 2013 and Davies 2017 for a fuller discussion.

4. For instance, see the experimentation with brushwork alongside represented hair evident in Crumb 2016, 324–25.

5. Examples include Crumb 2017, 74–79, 166–67, among many others.

6. Examples include Crumb 1998, 208; Crumb 2018, 396–97; and Crumb and Poplaski 2005, 371–72, 375–76, 378, 380, 382.

7. These experiments also appear in Crumb 2016, 183–84.

8. Earlier explorations of this can be found in the sketchbooks. See Crumb 2017, 314.

9. For examples of these, see Crumb 2016.

10. The attention to qualities of the surface, the description of shiny leather and muscular bodies straining at clothing, is reminiscent of the erotic art of Touko Laaksonen (Tom of Finland), who publishes erotic comics silently recounting the encounters of "Kake" during this period. Although Laaksonen's work predominantly uses pencil shading to carefully render the contours of bodies, clothing, and leather, in his comics work he tends more to use pen and ink—experimenting at times with hatching techniques like the ones Crumb tends toward, to craft and shape the erotic contours of the fetishized materials. See Tom of Finland 2014.

11. These drawings are included in Crumb 2018.

WORKS CITED

Arnheim, Rudolf. 2004. *Visual Thinking*. Berkeley: University of California Press.

Bell, Steve. 2005. "Robert Crumb." *Guardian*, March 18. https://www.theguardian.com/film/2005/mar/18/robertcrumb.comics.

Cohn, Neil. 2009. "The Visual Linguist: Abstract Comics and Visual Language." Visual Language Lab. http://www.thevisuallinguist.com/2009/08/abstract-comics-and-visual-language.html.

Crumb, R. 1998. *The R. Crumb Coffee Table Art Book: Crumb's Whole Career, from Shack to Chateau*. Edited by Peter Poplaski. London: Bloomsbury.

Crumb, R. 2013. *The Weirdo Years, 1981–'93*. London: Knockabout.

Crumb, R. 2016. *R. Crumb Sketchbook. Vol. 1, June 1964–September 1968*. Edited by Dian Hanson. Cologne: Taschen.

Crumb, R. 2017. *R. Crumb Sketchbook*. Vol. 2, *September 1968–1975*. Edited by Dian Hanson. Cologne: Taschen.

Crumb, R. 2018. *R. Crumb Sketchbook*. Vol. 3, *1975–1982*. Edited by Dian Hanson. Cologne: Taschen.

Crumb, R., Fabrice Hergott, Joann Sfar, Sébastien Gokalp, M. Todd Hignite, Jean-Pierre Mercier, and Jean-Luc Fromental. 2017. *R. Crumb: From the Underground to Genesis*. San Diego: IDW.

Crumb, Robert, and Peter Poplaski. 2005. *The R. Crumb Handbook*. London: MQ Publications.

Davies, Paul Fisher. 2013. "'Animating' the Narrative in Abstract Comics." *Studies in Comics* 4, no. 2: 251–76.

Davies, Paul Fisher. 2017. "Making Meanings with Comics: A Functional Approach to Graphic Narrative." PhD thesis, University of Sussex. http://sro.sussex.ac.uk/69049/.

Gaze, Tim, and Michael Jacobson. 2013. *An Anthology of Asemic Handwriting*. The Hague: Uitgeverij.

Groensteen, Thierry. 2013. *Comics and Narration*. Translated by Ann Miller. Jackson: University Press of Mississippi.

Halliday, M. A. K., and Christian Matthiessen. 2014. *Halliday's Introduction to Functional Grammar*. Abingdon, Oxon, England: Routledge.

Hamm, Jack. 1967. *Cartooning the Head and Figure*. New York: Perigee Books.

Hignite, Todd. 2006. *In the Studio: Visits with Contemporary Cartoonists*. New Haven, CT: Yale University Press.

McCloud, Scott. 1993. *Understanding Comics: The Invisible Art*. New York: Harper Perennial.

Molotiu, Andrei, ed. 2009. *Abstract Comics: The Anthology*. Seattle: Fantagraphics.

Tom of Finland. 2014. *Tom of Finland: The Complete Kake Comics*. Edited by Dian Hanson. Cologne: Taschen.

Walker, Mort. 2000. *The Lexicon of Comicana*. Lincoln, NE: iUniverse.

SELECTED BIBLIOGRAPHY OF WORKS BY R. CRUMB

R. Crumb's work has appeared in a wide range of periodicals, books, and other media such as posters and album covers. Due to the sheer volume of his work, this selected bibliography focuses on readily available and recently in-print book collections of Crumb's comics, sketchbooks, and other art. For a thorough account of his work that includes all periodical publications as well as reprints, see Carl Richter, *The Crumb Compendium: The Definitive R. Crumb Bibliography* (Seattle: Fantagraphics, 2018).

COMICS BY R. CRUMB

The Big Yum Yum Book: The Story of Oggie and the Beanstalk. Berkeley, CA: Snow Lion Graphics, 1995.
The Book of Genesis Illustrated by R. Crumb. New York: W. W. Norton, 2009.
The Book of Mr. Natural. Seattle: Fantagraphics, 2010.
The Complete Crumb Comics. 17 vols. Seattle: Fantagraphics, 1987–2005.
The Life and Death of Fritz the Cat. Seattle: Fantagraphics, 1998.
The "Weirdo" Years: 1981–'93. San Francisco: Last Gasp, 2013.

COMICS BY R. CRUMB AND COLLABORATORS

American Splendor Presents Bob and Harv's Comics, by Harvey Pekar and R. Crumb. New York: Four Walls Eight Windows, 1996.
The Complete Zap Comix. Seattle: Fantagraphics, 2014.
Drawn Together, by Aline Kominsky-Crumb and Robert Crumb. New York: W. W. Norton, 2012.
Kafka, with David Zane Mairowitz. Seattle: Fantagraphics, 2007.

SKETCHBOOKS, LETTERS, AND DIARIES

R. Crumb Sketchbook. 4 vols. Cologne: Taschen, 2016–2018.
R. Crumb's Dream Diary, edited by Ronald Bronstein and Sammy Harkham. Jericho, NY: Elara Press, 2018.
Your Vigor for Life Appalls Me: Robert Crumb Letters, 1958–1977, edited by Ilse Thompson. Seattle: Fantagraphics, 2012.

ART BOOKS AND EXHIBITION CATALOGS

Art and Beauty Magazine: Drawings by R. Crumb. New York: David Zwirner Books, 2016.

Bible of Filth. New York: David Zwirner Books, 2017.

The Complete Record Cover Collection. New York: W. W. Norton, 2011.

The R. Crumb Coffee Table Art Book, with Peter Poplaski. New York: Back Bay, 1998.

R. Crumb: From the Underground to Genesis. San Diego: IDW, 2017.

The R. Crumb Handbook, with Peter Poplaski. London: MQ Publications, 2005.

R. Crumb's Heroes of Blues, Jazz, and Country. New York: Harry N. Abrams, 2006.

R. Crumb's Sex Obsessions. Cologne: Taschen, 2019.

The Sweeter Side of R. Crumb. New York: W. W. Norton, 2000.

INTERVIEWS

Dean, Michael, ed. *The Comics Journal Library*. Vol. 9, *Zap: The Interviews*. Seattle: Fantagraphics, 2015.

George, Milo, ed. *The Comics Journal Library*. Vol. 3, *R. Crumb*. Seattle: Fantagraphics, 2004.

Holm, D. K., ed. *R. Crumb: Conversations*. Jackson: University Press of Mississippi, 2004.

CONTRIBUTORS

JOSÉ ALANIZ is professor in the Department of Slavic Languages and Literatures and the Department of Comparative Literature at the University of Washington, Seattle. He is the author of *Death, Disability, and the Superhero Narrative: The Silver Age and Beyond* and *Komiks: Comic Art is Russia.*

IAN BLECHSCHMIDT received a PhD in communication studies from Northwestern University in 2016, where he studied visual rhetoric, gender, and comics and graphic novels. He lives in Chicago.

PAUL FISHER DAVIES has published in the *Journal of Graphic Novels and Comics*, *Studies in Comics*, and other journals, including academic articles in comics form. He teaches English language at East Sussex College in Lewes, England. His book *Comics as Communication: A Functional Approach* was published in 2019.

ZANNE DOMONEY-LYTTLE is a tutor in biblical studies and an affiliate in theology and religious studies at the University of Glasgow. Her research centers on comic book adaptations of the Bible through the perspectives of literary criticism, comics theory, and gender studies. She is the author of *The Bible and Comics: Women, Power and Representation in Graphic Narratives.*

DAVID HUXLEY is the editor of the *Journal of Graphic Novels and Comics* and was a senior lecturer at Manchester Metropolitan University until 2017. Most recently, he is the author of *Lone Heroes and the Myth of the American West in Comic Books, 1945–1962.*

LYNN MARIE KUTCH is professor of German at Kutztown University of Pennsylvania. Her anthology *Novel Perspectives on German-Language Graphic Novels: History, Pedagogy, Theory* was published in 2016, and she is a cofounder and co-coordinator of the German Studies Association's Comics Studies Network.

JULIAN LAWRENCE is senior lecturer in the comics and graphic novels program at Teesside University. His work as an artist/researcher/teacher investigates the freehand narrative drawing of comics and its impacts on representations of identity. His latest graphic novel, *The Dripping Boat*, was published in 2020.

LILIANA MILKOVA is the Nolen Curator of Education and Academic Affairs at the Yale University Art Gallery. She has held curatorial positions at Oberlin College's Allen Memorial Art Museum, the National Gallery of Art, and the Philadelphia Museum of Art.

STILIANA MILKOVA is associate professor of comparative literature at Oberlin College. Her scholarly work examines the intersection of word and image with a focus on Russian, Italian, and Bulgarian literatures, and she edits the online journal *Reading in Translation*.

KIM A. MUNSON is an artist and art historian focused on works on paper and popular culture. She is the editor of *Comic Art in Museums* and author of *Dual Views: Labor Landmarks of San Francisco* and *On Reflection: The Art of Margaret Harrison*. She recently curated *Women in Comics: Looking Forward and Back* at the Society of Illustrators in New York with Trina Robbins.

JASON S. POLLEY is associate professor of English at Hong Kong Baptist University. He has published widely on contemporary comics, film, and literature. He is coeditor of two essay collections, *Cultural Conflict in Hong Kong* and *Poetry in Pedagogy*.

PAUL SHEEHAN is associate professor in the English Department at Macquarie University, Sydney. He is the author of *Modernism and the Aesthetics of Violence* and the editor of "Post-Archival Beckett: Genre, Process, Value," a special issue of the *Journal of Beckett Studies*.

CLARENCE BURTON SHEFFIELD JR. is professor of art history in the College of Art and Design and a faculty affiliate in the School of Individualized Study at the Rochester Institute of Technology. His scholarship, research, and teaching focus on the modern era, with a special emphasis on Scandinavia.

DANIEL WORDEN is associate professor in the Department of English and the School of Individualized Study at the Rochester Institute of Technology. He is the author of *Neoliberal Nonfictions: The Documentary Aesthetic of Our Age* and *Masculine Style: The American West and Literary Modernism*, and the editor of *The Comics of Joe Sacco: Journalism in a Visual World*.

INDEX

Page numbers in *italics* refer to illustrations.